"*ESG Mindset* is a fantastic, insightful, and smart resource that navigates the complexity and nuances of ESG. Matthew Sekol delivers a practical and refreshing perspective on the roles and responsibilities of stakeholders, addressing issues for originators, funds, and industry professionals on their journey to sustainability."
Matt Bird, President and Editor-in-Chief, ESG News

"Matthew Sekol's approach to ESG is not just innovative but also deeply insightful, challenging conventional wisdom and pushing the boundaries of how we view corporate responsibility and sustainable business."
Gihan Hyde, CEO and Founder, Communique

"Matthew Sekol has articulated the multi-faceted and interconnected considerations of ESG. *ESG Mindset* is for anyone interested in gaining a holistic perspective of the past, present, and future of ESG and a terrific primer for those of us leading the ESG charge at companies."
Veena Jayadeva, Chief Equity and Impact Officer, Conductiv

"Matthew Sekol brings ESG back to its origins: as a tool to assess and advance a company's efforts to navigate a volatile and increasingly uncertain world. *ESG Mindset* is a valuable contribution that offers insight and inspiration on how ESG can inform business operations and strategy to create a just, sustainable, and prosperous future."
Joel Makower, Chairman and Co-founder, GreenBiz Group

"If you find yourself filled with purpose and values and are looking for a way to integrate those into your business and daily work in a lasting way, you've come to the right place. Matthew Sekol will prompt you to ask: what more can we do? What more should I be doing? A must-read primer for ESG for everyone."
Theodora Lau, Founder, Unconventional Ventures and author of *Beyond Good* and *The Metaverse Economy*

"*ESG Mindset* is focused on the changes happening inside every enterprise today. Matthew Sekol's book will help everyone to grasp the mind shift needed to succeed in a complex context, to move faster, and to speak louder."
Graham Sinclair, Host of *ESG and Coffee* Podcast, Instructor at Harvard University, and Adjunct Professor at Villanova University

"*ESG Mindset* is Engaging, Smart, and a Great read. Matthew Sekol makes sense of ESG. He capably explores what ESG means, its history, its challenges, and its potential. And he gives invaluable guidance for companies that want to put ESG into practice."
Paul Washington, Executive Director, The Conference Board ESG Center

"This is an invaluable resource for anyone, or any employee, or any company, to address all of the elements of effective ESG. This book covers it all! A must-read for anyone wanting to make a difference in the world through their work in ESG."
Shannon Houde, ESG Leadership Coach, Walk of Life Consulting, Ltd.

"This book is a bold and engaging attempt to unpack the confusion and provides an objective view of an all-round stock taking on where we go from here with ESG. Well worth a read for practitioners and skeptics alike!"
Helene Li, CEO and Co-Founder, GoImpact Capital Partners

"*ESG Mindset* successfully wrangles the complexities of ESG into an accessible, informative, and engaging narrative useful to folks at all stages of their journey. This is both a great primer for beginners and a refresher for more experienced corporate sustainability professionals about the emerging challenges and opportunities of ESG."
Mike Hower, Founder and Principal Consultant, Hower Impact

"Matt Sekol's brilliant ESG landscape analysis, insights and actionable ideas in this important book provide a much-needed guide for today's leaders as they navigate the real-world challenges of building and running businesses. This book is a must-read for those who strive to drive crucial and impactful returns for their business and society."
Samantha Katz, Co-Founder, IDiF

"Matthew Sekol offers a deep exploration of how companies should approach the fundamental changes required to integrate Environmental, Social, and Governance performance factors. This is the perfect book to help you build your ESG expertise and conquer the biggest business challenges of our times."
Christine Uri, Founder, ESG for In-house Counsel

"Matthew Sekol provides a straightforward way of thinking about how ESG can provide value creation by integrating rather than prioritizing ESG into strategic decision-making."
Amanda DeSantis, Founder, The Intangibles Initiative

"Matthew Sekol underscores the value of ESG as an investment indicator. *ESG Mindset* shows how ESG can be the innovative solution to both rectifying material risk and to seizing an opportunity to create value for investors."
Colleen C Davis, Delaware State Treasurer

"*ESG Mindset* delves into the world of ESG from a business impact perspective, skilfully drawing parallels between a company's long-term vision and its commitment to ESG pillars. Matthew Sekol's insightful exploration sheds light on the corporate value of ESG. A must-read for anyone seeking to comprehend the evolving dynamics of sustainable business practices."
Tahmina Day, Global ESG Solution Lead, Archer Technologies

"Every page of *ESG Mindset* equips you with tools to navigate the evolving landscape of business. It's an invaluable crash course in corporate sustainability supported by thorough research and practical examples. If you're just starting your journey, picking up this book is an absolute must!"
Prerana Tirodkar, Senior Sustainability Analyst, Tango

ESG Mindset

Business Resilience and Sustainable Growth

Matthew Sekol

KoganPage

First published in Great Britain and the United States in 2024 by Kogan Page Limited

2nd Floor, 45 Gee Street	8 W 38th Street, Suite 902	4737/23 Ansari Road
London	New York, NY 10018	Daryaganj
EC1V 3RS	USA	New Delhi 110002
United Kingdom		India

www.koganpage.com

Kogan Page books are printed on paper from sustainable forests.

© Matthew Sekol, 2024

ISBNs

Hardback	978 1 3986 1426 0
Paperback	978 1 3986 1424 6
Ebook	978 1 3986 1425 3

British Library Cataloguing-in-Publication Data

A CIP record for this book is available from the British Library.

Library of Congress Cataloging-in-Publication Data

Names: Sekol, Matthew, author.
Title: ESG mindset : business resilience and sustainable growth / Matthew Sekol.
Description: London ; New York, NY: Kogan Page, [2024] | Includes bibliographical references and index.
Identifiers: LCCN 2024000970 (print) | LCCN 2024000971 (ebook) | ISBN 9781398614246 (paperback) | ISBN 9781398614260 (hardback) | ISBN 9781398614253 (ebook)
Subjects: LCSH: Corporate governance. | Social responsibility of business. | Sustainable development. | Organizational resilience.
Classification: LCC HD2741 .S4457 2024 (print) | LCC HD2741 (ebook) | DDC 658.4–dc23/eng/202401010
LC record available at https://lccn.loc.gov/2024000970
LC ebook record available at https://lccn.loc.gov/2024000971

Typeset by Integra Software Services, Pondicherry
Print production managed by Jellyfish
Printed and bound by CPI Group (UK) Ltd, Croydon CR0 4YY

To my stakeholders

Julie, my present

Nora, Anna, and Liam, the future

And Charlie, who just wanted the good pats

CONTENTS

LIST OF FIGURES AND TABLES

All figures are the original work of the author.

ABOUT THE AUTHOR

Matthew Sekol is an ESG and sustainability advocate at Microsoft, based between New York City, New York, and Philadelphia, Pennsylvania. He came into ESG several years ago through working with some of the world's largest ESG data aggregators and financial services firms.

Today, he guides companies across industries to new value by unpacking their ESG and sustainability challenges along the intersection with technology. In his current role, he also sits on the LP Advisory Committee of Morgan Stanley's Next Level Fund, which invests in diverse-led and -founded start-ups and ventures, providing technology and ESG mentoring while advising on the portfolio. Sekol speaks and writes about ESG topics regularly and has authored and co-authored whitepapers and online articles on ESG, biodiversity, how technology is an ESG risk and more. In 2023, Onalytica named him in its "Who's Who in ESG" list.

FOREWORD

Not long ago, I wrote a piece that summarizes my ongoing perspective on the topic of ESG titled "The ESG Arc Bends Towards Progress." For those in the know, you can see that this title is based on the well-known quote from Dr. Martin Luther King (repeated by many since) about the moral universe and justice. Putting a twist on this important statement, it occurred to me that similarly perhaps it was true that:

"The arc of the ESG universe is long but bends towards progress."

In other words, and as Matthew exquisitely documents in this book, ESG has been around in many shapes and forms for a long time but will continue to evolve—with steps forward and steps back.

Put another way: If the arc of ESG doesn't bend towards progress—even with likely steps back and other setbacks—this planet's businesses are doomed to failure. If we don't:

- Mind the gap in climate and environmental crises at the personal, professional, communal, business, governmental, and international levels today; we will fail

- Care about societal risks like human rights and human slavery, involuntary migration, labor abuse, lack of diversity, inequity, and exclusion; we will not thrive, let alone survive as businesses

- Learn how to govern the "easy" stuff (which by the way isn't easy)—let alone learn how to integrate exponential technologies like Generative AI, synthetic biology, and quantum into governance; how do we expect to have security, safety, ethics in the loop to prevent material accidents, competition or business model destruction, and even existential dread?

So, when Matthew asked me to write this Foreword, I was not only honored to accept but also delighted to underscore the above idea once again and with gusto, as I believe Matthew's ongoing ESG work both prior to writing this book and through this book is a major contribution to how ESG (or whatever it morphs into in the future) contributes to value creation and progress in business.

ESG in context

ESG does have an arc, and it has a very real and concrete context as well. And I do believe that arc bends slowly but surely towards progress despite a proliferation of roadblocks, challenges, and confusion. It's pretty much two steps forward, one back.

While ESG is not the equivalent of "the moral universe," it represents concepts and concerns that go from the hyper-local to the most global and even extra-planetary.

As Matthew makes eloquently and abundantly clear in this book, ESG is not a new or radical concept—neither a passing fad nor a political football. The nomenclature has changed over time, but whether you call it corporate social responsibility, corporate responsibility, sustainability, or ESG, we are talking about common themes, risks, and opportunities that range from tactical to existential in several key categories of intangible risk and opportunity—environmental, social, governance (and I add technological). Indeed, the concepts embedded in what we loosely call ESG today are age-old concepts that have recently come into stark relief for both the right (climate change) and the wrong (political polarization) reasons.

And why has ESG emerged as a focal point of economic, social, and political discourse in recent years? I would argue that there are five converging overarching reasons why the ESG universe will continue to bend towards progress – despite setbacks, curve balls, polarization, and politicization. Let me explain.

Convergence #1—Long-term megatrends are materially reshaping the world

There are long-term, multi-year global megatrends that revolve heavily around environmental, social, governance, technological, and, of course, economic issues. I call them the ESGT Megatrends in my own work, and there are five: tech disruption at the speed of light, geopolitical tectonic shifts, complex interconnected socio-ecological risk, leadership trust in decline, and the rise of new forms of capitalism.

Convergence #2—Human-based systems thinking is the new black

Despite the abundance of Generative AI solutions—the good, bad, and ugly—human-based, AI-assisted, systems thinking is necessary for our hyper-complicated world, which is getting ever more so daily. How does one deal with just one sliver of what is happening at any given time, for example, with the explosion of information, misinformation, disinformation, and mal-information from every corner of the digital and physical world at any given minute?

The only way to do so productively is to engage in systems thinking—whether it is for strategy, enterprise risk management, product development, or governance. While there will always be skirmishes below, there will always be patterns above that we must capture to impulse ourselves forward in a constructive manner. The need for a systems-based resilient organizational strategy has never been greater.

Convergence #3—Demographics and stakeholders rule

In this massively interconnected digitized world, there truly is nowhere to hide, and the emerging generations especially will not allow two steps forward and two steps back—they want progress. They feel empowered, focused, and even angry and have reprioritized what is most important – it isn't making the most money; it's saving the planet from committing hara-kiri. Thus, for the business world to compete successfully, it must accommodate and prioritize the perspectives of new generations of employees and those of other critical stakeholders like consumers, regulators, and suppliers.

Convergence #4—Technological power turbocharged

In case you didn't notice—the explosion of Generative AI solutions is changing the world. And it's just the beginning. ESG and technology are intimately and intricately intertwined. As Matthew points out in a couple of his chapters—ESG uses technology, and ESG has technology risks and opportunities. Businesses that miss this boat will simply sink.

Convergence #5—Love of our unique blue planet

The globe presently faces a series of material, strategic, and even existential matters that require collective, cross-disciplinary, intersectional, and international attention. That includes a powerful hand from business. A hand that will be rewarded in value creation, talent acquisition and retention, and better products and services.

The ESG train is leaving the station—hop on or miss out

Some of the biggest challenges and opportunities of the medium- to long-term future are: (1) getting climate policy right at the most micro (business) and macro (planetary) levels; (2) continuing to raise global society to higher levels of education, equality, health, and so on, including through business initiatives; and (3) ensuring that governance—especially climate and tech governance—at all levels including the corporate boardroom is up to the challenge and adapts and innovates rapidly accordingly.

There are only three real options for business on the ESG—or what I like to call ESGT—story:

1 Identify and mainstream ESG (or whatever you choose to call it) holistically and seriously into your business (or other organizational form) and run with it.

2 Nibble around the edges, doing little or nothing, and let your competitors eat your lunch while the world becomes more polluted, less resilient, more inhumane.

3 Work deliberately against environmental progress, social progress, and better governance in the pursuit of short-term gain that will inevitably become long-term loss.

ESG is a journey not an end state. As a business leader you can either be on the train or hop on at the next station or bury your ostrich head in the sand while the whirlwind gets you and your business.

Another way to put all of this into context is by paraphrasing what my great friend and mentor, Keith T. Darcy, once said about "ethics":

"ESG (ESGT) isn't about perfection, it's about progress!"

Andrea Bonime-Blanc, Founder, CEO, Director, Author

PREFACE

This book will not save the world, at least not directly. So, to future generations, I apologize. The path to impact does run through ESG, but it's a little circuitous. Still, it isn't quite that simple. If you find yourself filled with purpose and values and are looking for a way to integrate those into your business and daily work in a lasting way, you've come to the right place.

Unfortunately, ESG isn't quite purpose or values, but it does represent three interconnected pillars that cover much of what a business needs to worry about and focus on beyond the financials. Rife with pitfalls, puzzles, and potential, ESG is both complex and complicated. It requires adaptable, soft skills that cut across domain-specific expertise to bring new perspectives. Yet, ESG is also extremely difficult and driven to corporates from financial services pressure to inform investing, lending, and insuring. As a result, a company perspective and common definition is lacking, but much needed.

Rather than define it here, let me explain the relevance of ESG to a company with a personal story.

I have a confession to make. I do not like the outdoors. Ever since I was a kid, I've had horrible allergies, which made the ordinarily pleasant seasonal weather in Pennsylvania much less enjoyable. I like watching the fall leaves change color, but only from the view of my office window. While the indoors aren't much better with dust mites and pet allergens, pollen was the absolute worst. During certain times of the year, every surface outside is covered in a thick shade of yellow. The Lehigh Valley, where I grew up and still live, ranks in the top 25 for worst allergy seasons in the US. There are days when I honestly wish that I didn't have a nose.

On the other hand, my wife grew up on a dairy farm and would spend time outside regularly. Her family owned over 80 acres, including a pond stocked seasonally with fish from a local hatchery. I grew up with computers, and she grew up with tractors. Our childhoods were the opposite in many ways, but we met in the middle, figuratively and literally, at Penn State. After college, we moved to Maryland and married. Unfortunately, the company I worked for was caught up in the Enron scandal (Governance issue!), so we decided to move up to the Lehigh Valley and start a family.

A few years into living in our new home, my wife decided to take up gardening, so we installed a raised bed garden at the end of our property. At first, it was a simple 8' by 16' wooden bed with a little walkway in the middle. Next, we installed an overhang for some tomato planters, which included chicken wire running across the back for vines of peas to climb up. The garden grew and grew as my wife developed her green thumb over the years. We tried several raised bed configurations and built a wooden fence with two gates to keep deer out. Later, we ran a water line down, tore down the fence, and repaired the beds. Recently, we strayed away from wooden beds and installed new steel beds that should last at least 20 years. We also started to compost our scraps, reducing our food waste while contributing to new topsoil.

From a sustainable and organic gardening perspective, I think we do pretty well. I do till an area that isn't part of the raised beds because our ground is mostly shale and rocks. This activity is almost an annual requirement. My wife doesn't use pesticides and will manually pick the pests off of flowers and vines. She also encourages pollinators and discourages other insects in sustainable ways, like planting specific flowers.

The inside of our house, where I spend most of the time, is similarly sustainable, but not as much as we could be doing. We replaced old light bulbs with high-efficiency LEDs and have two heat pumps running with an AI thermostat, which we regulate. In addition, we've recently purchased more energy-efficient appliances, but to be honest, with five of us in the house, any appliance's energy savings is a huge challenge. We haven't gone solar yet, but I've started down that journey with research and some conversations with installers. In the meantime, I found a reasonably priced renewable utility as our electricity provider.

From a social justice perspective, I was involved in a program in college to mentor first-generation college students on their transition into Penn State. Like many, I've always tried to 'do what's right' at work. At home, we're active in the local community. We both volunteer at the local church regularly. I've been on our church's Council and Finance Committee for six years, and all five of us volunteer for Sunday School every week. My wife also volunteers on the local nursery school's board. I believe we're instilling a sense of community service in our kids.

All in all, we're doing what I would consider akin to what companies do to meet their Environmental and Social goals. As board members of the family, I think my wife and I (very much her) keep things running smoothly. These activities are all 'good' things that have various benefits. Still, the results here are largely values-driven across sustainability, family, hard work, connections to neighbors, volunteerism, and purpose, to name a few.

None of these fantastic things address risk.

Now, homeowners have ways to address risks. For example, a homeowner can perform routine maintenance on the house and its various appliances. Regarding financial protections, insurance can cover unexpected disasters. But, of course, there are always crises that cannot be mitigated well, even with the best intentions.

This is how I found myself on a ladder during Hurricane Isaias trying to cover the top of our sliding glass door's frame with plastic and duct tape, a futile effort. After having the door for a few years, no previous storm had quite the combination of strong winds and heavy rain to push the siding above the door inwards, driving rainwater into our kitchen. Meanwhile, the water dripped into the basement below, where groundwater was coming up through our French drains. Unfortunately, I had no sump pumps on hand, so it became a reactive exercise in our family of five getting the generator going so that the wet–dry vacuum could run, while others wrung out towels into buckets and carried them up.

It was one of the most exhausting days of my life.

In the end, all of the sustainable and community work we do didn't help us mitigate that risk. The event didn't almost take us down despite our lack of Governance, but it did make us reassess several extreme weather scenarios.

Just like a homeowner may overlook climate, but still do all sorts of wonderful value-based activities, so do companies. While all the sustainable and social justice efforts are phenomenal, if a company doesn't take care of its risks and opportunities, it will find itself reacting to crisis after crisis, and never taking advantage of the changing world around it. In the wake of globalization, these crises are now joining forces, creating even more unproductive pressure and pushing opportunity even further away. Companies must understand and address their ESG issues if they are to last long enough to take on the more meaningful work of doing well by doing good.

Supporting resources for the book can be found at koganpage.com/esg-mindset-resources.

ACKNOWLEDGMENTS

The story of how an English graduate from Penn State came to write a book about ESG is a twisty tale. Along the way, there has been a lot of encouragement, but even more thoughtful conversations that have incrementally dripped into my brain's basement long enough to create a flood.

I could say it started as a teenager when a co-worker at the mall handed me a copy of Kurt Vonnegut's *Cat's Cradle*. In it, I learned about ICE-9, which is a massive Environmental risk, uncontrolled through poor Governance, leading to a Social disaster (and satirical commentary). Similarly, it could have started with Alison Cummings and the inclusive program at Penn State Berks, where I mentored first-generation college students from urban areas. Both had value upon reflection. It could also have been working at PG&E NEGT supporting Blackberries and Outlook Web Access, the early technologies enabling hybrid work. Still, none of these are quite right.

It wasn't until I connected with Simon Frostick, Colin Cassidy, Sháka Rasheed, and my counterparts Sue Griffin and Ruchi Nanda in the capital markets team at Microsoft that ESG came into focus, and I saw all of these other events and more through an ESG mindset. Here's to the originals on the sustainability team: Sana Dubarry, Christoph Pawlowski, Margaret Ann Splawn, Gina Kirby, Matt Hellman, Ramon Bosch, Maria Ferreira, and Michelle Lancaster. I owe them all many thanks for encouraging me to pursue this topic and entertaining my ESG philosophizing whenever the mood struck.

As Covid hit, I tipped over into ESG and cultivated an inspring community. Dr. Andrea Bonime-Blanc, who wrote the foreward, blew my mind when she connected Technology as a fourth pillar of ESG in her book, *Gloom to Boom*. Liz Simmie, co-founder of Honeytree Investment Management similarly flipped a switch in me when she wrote that "Everything is ESG" in an online chat.

Two people deserve a special thank you for grounding me on the idea that an ESG approach for companies takes a specific mindset. Early on, I pitched the title to Alexandria Fisher, who understood it instantly, propelling me forward. Then, in the middle of writing, I was waxing philosophical with Veena Jayadeva at GreenFin, and she mentioned having an ESG mindset without me prompting it. That conversation was validating.

A special thank you to Nick Hoar and Isabelle Cheng from the Kogan Page team who helped get this book over the finish line, and Bronwyn Geyer who got me started.

I owe much to the counsel of Theodora Lau, Founder of Unconventional Ventures and two-time co-author of *Beyond Good* and *The Metaverse Economy* (in addition to about a million other things she does). Theo was there along every step of this journey and answered every question about the writing and publishing process with the utmost patience. This book would not exist without her friendship.

Over the course of writing a book, you learn just how patient your family is. I would bring up news every chance I got, and then my family would have to listen to me relentlessly explain how these issues tied back to ESG. They supported me throughout the non-stop writing and editing while all having extremely busy schedules, including appearances in *Radium Girls*, which, I'm convinced, is an ESG story. I really do see ESG in everything.

And lastly to you, dear reader. Here's hoping this book builds up a new mindset in you and new experiences that make your companies last long enough to try to save the world with what you learn along the way. Good luck!

01

Introduction to ESG

Why should a company care about understanding ESG? Well, depending on who you ask, the answers may range from "It's a distraction," cutting across "It helps deliver a win-win for the company and its stakeholders," and ending the scene with "It drives outperformance of the stock." None of these is entirely or consistently accurate. Companies should care about ESG because it can build resilience and long-term sustainable growth in a changing world. ESG constantly shifts and adapts to the world around it, but companies and their leaders also need to change to take advantage of the perspective it affords.

To figure out why a company should care to understand ESG, we need to define it first and understand what it is, where it came from, and some of the things people believe about it. Ultimately, to figure out the answer as to why, we need to bring some consistency to its meaning in the context of the company's perspective, which is not what it is used to.

ESG means a lot of different things to a lot of different people. After all, Environmental, Social, and Governance categories encompass a seemingly infinite universe of ideas, topics, and pursuits. While the power of the acronym lies in the breadth, depth, and interconnected nature of its pillars, it doesn't necessarily include everything. This differentiation is critical, as everything that comes after will build on this common understanding of the term and requires this context.

Unfortunately, no global standards organization defines and maintains the acronym ESG, although many are working with and around it. As a result, inconsistency rules its nature, and every time a regulator, company, or financial services firm uses the acronym, they tend to explain what it means to them in that unique context. Usually, the explanation fits the communicator's purpose and objective, whatever those may be, which can stretch the definition far.

The UN's Global Compact initiative and players in the financial markets created ESG as a perspective for investing. However, in that initial framing, it appears as though something was lost. An investment opportunity isn't available without a company to invest in or lend to. Yet, companies were not the target of the efforts from the start, only the target of the financial analysis. As a result, ESG remains an ill-defined corporate practice that has morphed to take on multiple interpretations.

Defining ESG within your organization

Again, the more thoughtful of those trying to engage their stakeholders around ESG will include the definition at the beginning of any piece of content because they recognize the challenge across its inconsistent meanings, and this book is no different. Our goal here is to enable a consistent corporate perspective on ESG to help companies build resilient businesses long enough to save the world, if they choose. With that in mind, jumping right into the definition rather than building towards it with its history is best, as its history may be part of the problem.

ESG: The material Environmental, Social, and Governance risks that affect a company and opportunities that drive towards long-term value and sustainable growth.

This definition has several components to review, each with nuance. There are deeper dives on the Environmental, Social, and Governance pillars in Chapters 3, 4, and 5, respectively and we will cover ESG investing as opposed to other investment methodologies in Chapter 8. For now, let's review some high-level ESG examples for each pillar to set the stage.

Environmental: Focused on the planet's effect on the company, including climate and transition risks, sustainable material substitution, and differentiation of products through sustainable credentials and processes.

Social: Working with stakeholders across diversity, equity, and inclusion (DEI) and the intersection with talent management and diverse stakeholder perspectives. Social examples also include critical topics like forced labor issues and cultural stakeholder norms across market segments.

Governance: Occurs at the board and management team level, representing the principles, ethics, and purpose of the company. Governance examples include board experience and accountability, executive pay, and corruption and bribery concerns.

While the definition of materiality differs worldwide, it typically means information or matters that would be decision-useful to a reasonable person, usually an investor. For materiality regarding ESG, the definition is similar, except with an obvious focus on ESG issues that matter to the company, but includes a view over the long-term horizon. Not every issue that falls into the Environmental, Social, or Governance categories is necessarily relevant to the company or has the same degree of relevance. For example, a national pharmacy chain might consider stakeholders' health material instead of the emissions its retail store might generate. The first is a material Social issue because health is relevant to its core business, and the other might be regarded as operational table stakes related to sustainability.

Next, we can build on the idea of materiality to understand how ESG concerns material risks and opportunities. These two concepts focus on how the world can affect the company at the intersection of what is relevant to the company. For example, any company with real estate assets, like office buildings, factories, or stores, should worry about climate risk against its physical assets and take steps to adapt and protect against damage and unplanned downtime, a material business disruption. Not focusing on diversity for an AI-based healthcare company is a material Social risk because several factors could cause unknown biases to surface, striking down what might be a product opportunity to serve the community at scale better. Let's contrast these against a non-material risk. A bank may selflessly choose to conserve water and should indeed have efficient water management in its building as part of a modern operating license in a civil society. However, water management isn't a material risk for a bank as it is for a hotel chain. Without water, a hotel could not service its guests, so it might go beyond its local operations to protect watersheds in the area to mitigate the risk.

ESG isn't only about risk, however. There are material opportunities around ESG that a business can capitalize on. For example, a Chief Human Resources Officer could leverage DEI programs to support pay equity and an inclusive culture, driving the best talent to the company. Talent management and retention are core material Social issues. For a consumer product goods company, moving to sustainable packaging or building sustainable materials into the product can be an opportunity to differentiate against the competition and perhaps get ahead of a sustainable transition.

In these examples, ESG is about Environmental, Social, and Governance issues that affect a company through its risks and opportunities but don't represent the company's impact on the world. However, this statement can get complicated as stakeholders echo this perspective, turning non-material issues into material ones, as in the examples of material opportunities that leverage impact.

Nothing with ESG is simple.

Yet, there are differences between the effect of the world on the company and the impact of the company on the world. Often, the word "impact" is used to describe both directions. Before going further, it is worth differentiating between "effect" and "impact" for most of its use throughout this book, especially in Chapter 11.

Effect: Meaning the world's effect on the company through changing climate and evolving stakeholder issues, including climate change, shifting cultural norms, regulations, war, and so on.

Impact: Refers to a company's impact on the world through its operations and value chain, including pollution, contributions to society, philanthropy, and so on.

The differences between the effect on the company and the impact from the company trip companies and their leaders up because it is where the nuance and uncertainty live, allowing a wide gap for interpretation. People may consider both to be different impacts, to be fair, but the word "effect" differentiates it for our purposes. It is incumbent on a company's management team to understand both effects and impacts and communicate efforts across both inbound and outbound paths effectively as they intersect with value and values. Different stakeholders will care about each for various reasons. This isn't easy in practice, rife with ambiguity, something business leaders may not be comfortable with. Yet, prioritizing and categorizing efforts drives funding and subsequent execution across these efforts and likely will depend on how each intersects with the company, bringing us back to materiality. While both can be pursued, too much of a pivot towards non-material impact issues may show that a company and its leadership don't understand its material ESG issues.

A NOTE ON EMISSIONS

Emissions reporting and management is a hot topic due to the escalating climate crisis. However, solely addressing or whittling down the acronym to emissions alone does not align with ESG because it ignores the interconnected nature of the acronym and materiality.

Climate change supercharges extreme weather events, harming the company's physical assets. If we take this example further, greenhouse gas emissions contribute to climate change, so logically a company must manage its emissions. However, it is unreasonable to expect that the company's reduction in emissions will impact the localized extreme weather that may result, yet this doesn't mean every company shouldn't do its part.

Emissions might affect the company in several ways that have less to do with the company's impact on the world. First, regulators may require ESG-related data disclosures, making it a Governance risk addressed by the company's Compliance team. Second, emissions might impact the local community in high enough concentrations, making it return as a Social risk through health concerns for employees, fines, and reputational damage. Similarly, customers may seek to align their sustainability values with purchasing habits, adding a financial or reputational risk. The longer a company waits to transition, the more expensive it is to change and catch up to competitors, which is a Governance risk wrapped in an Environmental one. Bizarrely, the effect on the company in its emissions reductions may not be related to the Environmental pillar from an ESG perspective but is from an impact perspective.

The next part of the definition of ESG covers long-term value and growth, not transient issues. The intent is to derive long-term value and resilience by addressing ESG risks or creating opportunities. Of course, unexpected, point-in-time ESG crises always affect companies, creating short-term issues that the company must manage. Still, if a company leads with attention to ESG in addition to quality Governance, it can create practical foresight into emerging trends and be better prepared. A sound strategy around these insights can make a company more resilient through those shocks. For example, a company that transitions to more sustainable components in its product will increase customer sentiment along their values and potentially save in long-term transition costs as unsustainable materials become unavailable. This switch ultimately builds value in the pursuit of product improvement. In other words, a company with attention to the long-term management of risks and opportunities would already see and seize this opportunity, regardless of its attention to ESG.

So, do companies need ESG to be successful?

Governance is one area that can take a company down, but regarding ESG? Not necessarily, but that doesn't mean there isn't value in attention to ESG. As it turns out, there is a hidden meaning, perhaps unintentional, in how ESG is constructed as a single acronym, and that maybe its most incredible power. ESG risks and opportunities, which require domain expertise to manage, don't exist only within their siloed pillars. These issues are related and interconnected, involving considerations of effects and impact. For example, an Environmental expert consulting on a company's risk must also consider the impact of the problem and its resolution in the context of the Social and how the company will manage it, which is a Governance concern. In this way, many consider ESG solely a function of risk management or quality Governance, but there's more. If companies relegate ESG to the next iteration of risk management or scrap the acronym entirely, they lose the domain specificity and the interconnected way to think about these issues. This evolution can't happen before companies mainstream ESG and this way of thinking through their organizations.

In defining ESG, the reasons why a company should pursue it are apparent. These issues are core to the company. Yet, per a PwC survey of board directors, 55 percent say that ESG is on the board agenda, but only 45 percent say that they see value in it.[1] This dichotomy reveals a massive disconnect between the broad understanding of the topic and how companies might or might not approach it. If a management team, leader, or business unit can't effectively construct a case for an ESG issue because they don't understand it, they will find themselves on poor ground to defend the strategy, or they may find the approach is more aligned with impact and potentially concessionary with little value. By understanding and internalizing a consistent definition of ESG and its value to corporates, everyone in the business can deliver and protect value and prioritize meaningful impact in parallel.

Types of materiality and considerations of externalities

As attention to ESG has risen in the past few years, the concepts surrounding it have experienced an acceleration of analysis, and nuance has developed. When considering ESG's integration into a company's strategy and operations, materiality and externalities are two key terms to expand on.

While we've covered a broad definition of materiality in the context of a universal ESG meaning over a long-term horizon, a company may find different definitions depending on where it operates and which stakeholders it engages.

Like ESG, materiality was first coined around the financial markets. The US Securities Act of 1933 refers to "material facts" that could influence the purchase of a security.[2] The US Supreme Court has also defined information as material, at least regarding a proxy statement and investing, if there is a chance that omitting the item would be viewed as having altered the entire mix of information presented.[3] The US Securities and Exchange Commission (SEC) defines an issue as material "if there is a substantial likelihood that a reasonable person would consider it important."[4] This type of materiality is commonly referred to as "financial materiality" due to its relation to the markets and shareholders. As we will see with the origin of ESG, these are market concepts overlaid onto the corporate world.

Materiality, while simple in explanation, creates much confusion around ESG because financial materiality is in the eye of the person conducting the analysis, making it subjective. Stakeholders, companies, and investors don't always agree on what is material. This challenge may be unlikely to be resolved as opinions will always differ. One way a company and its management team can bring consistency is to mainstream ESG throughout the organization, which will be covered more in Chapter 7. Companies must collect and analyze data to create an understanding of these issues to know what may be financially material and communicate it effectively. The company should always consider input from stakeholders, but if the board and management team are doing their jobs, they already understand these issues better than others.

Still, other concepts of materiality that have emerged can help a company build on a foundation of ESG and financial materiality to create defensibility when addressing impact. The European Financial Reporting Advisory Group (EFRAG)[5] and the Global Reporting Initiative (GRI)[6] subscribe to the additional idea of double materiality, which adds impact materiality to financial materiality. While financial materiality focuses on information in a shareholder context, impact materiality focuses on the impact of the company on the world, or that outbound impact to stakeholders and the planet.[7] In double materiality, financial and impact materiality are considered together for a complete picture across all stakeholders, including shareholders, extending beyond the return to the company towards the benefits for others and matching the effects of financial materiality with impact, as defined earlier.

The key differentiator with double materiality is the focus on the impact. Unlike financial materiality, which has a cost, even if it is over time, impact materiality is more challenging to account for because it also typically has a concessionary cost and involves a company's externalities. Externalities impact another party as part of the company's operations and can be negative or positive, but often refer to the negative due to growing ESG attention and accountabilities. For example, an energy company will account for complying with Environmental and local jurisdictional regulations. Still, it may not price in considerations like its emissions on the balance sheet or in its internal reporting. While there are ways to account for the emissions with standards like the GHG Protocol (see Chapter 2), which informs the measurements and emissions calculations, it does not account for the unintended consequences of the emissions, which have a negative cost across the Environmental and Social through climate change and health, respectively.

Some companies—about a quarter globally—have figured out how to account for externalities in one specific area by tracking a carbon price internally.[8] Yet, emissions are only one externality to focus on, albeit one that gets much attention. Emerging techniques and research, like the Impact Weighted Accounting Project, create new ways to account for impact across "human, social and natural capital."[9] Until tools like this are a broadly accepted accounting practice, companies not adopting this practice, at least internally for analysis, may have an ESG risk around their impact as these issues might return in the form of regulations, fines, or reputational risk. In other words, companies may not be effectively accounting for their true operating costs, which include both their internal ESG risks and externalities.

The way that measuring impact might return to a company as a risk over a future horizon is another concept called dynamic materiality. Here, an issue may become material over time as conditions change. In theory, double materiality and its focus on impact, often a lever from shifting stakeholder preferences, may account for this change over time. After all, as the climate changes and systemic social justice challenges persist, these issues will eventually become material to a company somehow. So, while double materiality covers the potential future return of a company's impact on the world, there is more to dynamic materiality than the impact example alone.

While issues like a government-imposed carbon tax that stems from stakeholder pressure on politicians might affect the energy company mentioned previously, completing a renewable energy transition, which is a Governance decision, may create new material issues. For example, transmission lines would need to be run from coastal areas with wind, or regional areas with direct sunlight to other locations. The company and its value chain must source materials to construct transmission equipment, process those materials, and install new lines through communities, affecting the Environment and Social risk to the company. While other material issues exist under legacy energy models, this new risk wasn't a consideration before, and now it is, making it dynamic. With how fast the world changes, companies need to refresh their understanding of materiality in case a new issue arises. It won't always take entering a new business market for this to happen, especially as stakeholder sentiment evolves.

These are important concepts for a company to understand as they intersect ESG with other values-based ideas. Stakeholders, covered more in Chapter 4, are critical to any company, and are increasingly demanding change around impact, quickly turning non-material impact issues into material ones through reputational risk. A company that can leverage domain expertise and its intellectual capital to uncover and manage ESG risks and create opportunities will build resilience and defensibility to address issues as only it can.

On the origin of ESG

Understanding ESG means examining how it intersects with value and the markets, as it started as an investment perspective in the early 2000s. Yet, there is a related investment strategy worth discussing first because companies may hear the terms used interchangeably, but they are not quite the same.

Going back hundreds of years, investors realized that they had the power to leverage their capital to invest how they chose. Much of this was based on religious beliefs and stretched across Judaism to teachings in the Qur'an to Methodists and Quakers in the 18th century who condemned investments in the slave trade.[10] Since these strategies led with religion, they were considered values-based investing and often used methods like divestment, or simply not investing in the 'sin,' to control the use of capital.

In the 20th century, this values-based investing, now commonly known as socially responsible investing (SRI), continued but also shifted to gain new supporters. For example, in the 1960s, Catholic and Protestant organizations started driving their investments away from companies not supporting equity in South Africa due to Apartheid, which grew until the end of Apartheid in 1994.[11] Activists leveraged similar strategies with companies around the Vietnam War, bringing broader political attention to an investment's role in social change.[12]

Another trend began to take hold in parallel in the business world, focused on companies and the social value they create and maintain. In 1953, Howard Bowen authored *Social Responsibilities of the Businessman*, largely attributed as kicking off the Corporate Social Responsibility (CSR) era for corporates. The ideas put forth aligned businesses and their actions with society's values.[13] This idea is in contrast to the Friedman doctrine, published in 1970, which kicked off the shareholder primacy era.[14] Interestingly, Friedman's ideas are not far removed from companies engaging in social activities but place shareholders, not the management team, in control of those decisions.

In 1971, the Committee for Economic Development (CED) in the USA wrote about shifting public preferences toward Environmental and Social issues in *Social Responsibilities of Business Corporations*. This publication included what may have been a glimmer of an early ESG perspective for corporates, coining the expression "enlightened self-interest," which effectively recognized "that corporate self-interest is inexorably involved in the well-being of the society of which business is an integral part, and from which it draws the basic requirements needed for it to function at all-capital, labor, customers."[15] Statements like this unravel the fiction that a business can operate in a silo without broader sets of stakeholders or the planet considered, but more importantly, draw the lines between the effect of the world on the company and the impact of the company, and why each matters.

Globalization increased through the 1980s and 1990s, and countries began working together on worldwide, systemic issues. As a result of this increase, companies began having to comply with new international regulatory frameworks and work in cooperation with various governments. Attention, legitimacy, and a more cohesive definition of CSR grew throughout the 1990s, and companies found new global accountabilities and reputational risks.[16] In 1997, countries signed the Kyoto Protocol, which committed the industrialized world and growing economies to limit and reduce greenhouse gas (GHG) emissions through mitigation and reporting efforts.[17]

By 2000, UN Secretary-General Kofi Annan had focused on corporates and their role in changing the world with the UN Global Compact, which listed 10 principles focused on several categories of issues, including Human Rights, Labor, Environment, and Anti-Corruption.[18] This effort added to those early glimmers and the growth of CSR reporting over time with an

ESG perspective that kept the attention on corporates. Shortly after, the UN launched the Millennium Development Goals, a framework to address specific global issues, such as Poverty, Education, Maternal Health, Environmental Sustainability, and more by 2015.[19] In 2015, these goals led to the popular and related Sustainable Development Goals, which are now staples for CSR reports and set for 2030.[20]

In 1992, the United Nations Environment Programme Finance Initiative (UNEP FI) team formed to engage financial institutions on sustainability.[21] By the early 2000s, the group realized a connection between the markets and companies to support broader principles and goals. At this point, SRI was still primarily values-based, relying on exclusionary practices to shift capital away from companies engaged in activities the investor disagreed with, like weapons, tobacco, and defense. A new idea came from the UNEP FI team, who realized an opportunity to focus on materiality and the long term that could drive capital into responsible investments, and they believed that banks would pay attention.[22] From this financial perspective, ESG was born, and everything that came next carried forward this perspective.

In June 2004, the UNEP FI published a briefing with 12 global asset managers that put ESG together for the first time, albeit a bit out of its final order and without reference to the acronym. *The Materiality of Social, Environmental and Corporate Governance Issues to Equity Pricing* published the findings from a study of over 50 stock brokerage firms to identify material Environmental and Social issues across seven industries.[23] The results were an "agreement that environmental, social and corporate governance issues affect long-term shareholder value. In some cases, those effects may be profound."[24] The focus on shareholders here is a critical differentiator from stakeholders, not mentioned in the paper, and will be covered more in Chapter 4. The group had several recommendations for governments, regulators, and companies regarding ESG issues related to the financial markets. For a company's board and management teams, they notably called out two things. First, to include ESG information in their annual reports and financial statements, and second, to work with their employees' pension funds to reflect the links between ESG and financial returns.[25] The first focus here on data remains vital to driving ESG outcomes, as we will see in Chapter 2. Still, the intention was either to inform financial markets of a company's ESG progress or to discuss ESG risks in employees' retirement accounts, not educate the company on this emerging perspective.

That same month, the UN Global Compact, in partnership with the UNEP FI and 20 banks, published *Who Cares Wins*, a paper that called out the ESG acronym and incorporated the related ideas around materiality and long-term value. This paper targeted financial services firms with the subtitle "Connecting Financial Markets to a Changing World." Here, ESG was set apart from SRI, as the paper focused on "issues which have or could have a material impact on investment value. It uses a broader definition of materiality than commonly used—including longer time horizons (10 years and beyond) and intangible aspects impacting company value."[26] The paper also considers ethics in the context of the company's ethical practices, not concerning the investor's values or preferences.

The authors also presciently set ESG apart from other related impact topics. "Throughout this report we have refrained from using terms such as sustainability, corporate citizenship, etc., in order to avoid misunderstandings deriving from different interpretations of these terms. We have preferred to spell out the environmental, social and governance issues which are the topic of this report."[27] This note is vital, but the differentiation appears to have been lost over time. Companies, many of which were already well into their CSR strategies and reporting, continued in the same manner with their values-based reporting and perspective around ESG topics without this consideration.

UNEP FI published another paper in 2005 with Freshfields Bruckhaus Deringer, an international law firm. The report examined the legal perspective of ESG integration into financial services across several jurisdictions. The report states that there are links between ESG and financial performance, concluding that integrating ESG considerations, which can predict performance, into financial analysis is, therefore, likely required all over the world. [28] In other words, ESG is relevant to investment analysis, so much so that it may be a requirement for a responsible financial institution to consider. Whether or not ESG can lead to market stable performance or outperformance is a link that academics and financial institutions have continually studied and argued about ever since. Meanwhile, companies and management teams see these arguments and struggle to see ESG's value as they have not necessarily been the direct focus from the start.

The focus on finance reduces ESG's effectiveness

The idea of leveraging the market's existing pursuit of an investment's long-term growth is a brilliant way to get financial institutions to direct capital responsibly to companies. However, the papers just discussed only enable the thoughtful consideration of ESG from the perspective of investment managers to support this effort, with companies playing a supporting role. This priority flip leaves companies without a context to understand how to mainstream ESG or execute it. Of course, there is an argument that management teams should know what they are doing regarding material, long-term issues, ESG or not. However, that isn't always the case, especially as companies looking to understand these topics often need domain expertise working alongside their intellectual capital in the context of their business.

A recommendation for companies came in 2010 after the UNEP FI set up working groups to examine and align companies better with investors. The group published the results in a report called *Translating ESG into Sustainable Business Value*.[29] But, again, this focused less on enabling a company to understand its ESG risks and opportunities and more on what information financial services firms need to assess and understand the financial materiality of a company's ESG issues and the requirements around communicating this information.

The report notably calls out several gaps between companies and investors on ESG topics, including:

- Investors and companies have not integrated ESG into value.
- Neither party agrees on what is material, but companies understand their material issues best.
- Improved communication, comparable data, and a focus on materiality are needed.
- The markets and corporates have not mainstreamed ESG.

Some of these areas have improved since 2010, but mostly around getting financial institutions the data they need to make an informed decision. For example, comparable data has emerged through ESG rating agencies and standards organizations, leading to new regulations for even better consistency. Improved investor communication manifested as well. From 2018 to 2020, there was a 671 percent uptick in references to ESG on earnings calls,[30] pointing to advances in the acronym's use, at least from corporates to their investors. Yet, many of these issues persist, including integrating ESG into corporate value and ongoing disagreements about what is material or what ESG means. With so much confusion in the market, it is evident that companies have not mainstreamed ESG into their respective businesses.

The initial intent of ESG and its continued evolution towards data that informs the financial markets may be partly responsible for its current confused state. ESG has historically focused on using the flow of capital into companies, comparable data to inform that flow, and the role of the financial markets to drive attention to the pillars in the hopes of addressing these issues at the company level. Yet, ESG's meaning was defined from the top-down from investors to their investments, leaving much to the imagination of boards and management teams, perpetuating various definitions throughout their value chain.

The focus on the comparable language of finance has exacerbated the issue as ESG moved towards disclosures rather than outcomes. What emerged were attempts to rate and rank companies and a mix of material and non-material disclosures and standards for financial institutions assessing investments and subsequently Procurement teams analyzing suppliers. While data is core to understanding a company's approach and attention to ESG, the metrics are not the goal. Data can inform action, but it doesn't necessitate it. Therefore, the outcomes need to be the focus.

Unsurprisingly, companies haven't mainstreamed ESG, outside of perhaps the world's largest companies that can bring in domain expertise and integrate it accordingly. For the remainder, these companies serve as an example, but as they manage ESG effects and impact, there is much inspiration but few lessons to internalize.

Besides the inability to mainstream ESG effectively due to a lack of a consistent corporate definition and attention, there are other challenges. There are no standard enablement processes or strategic approaches, which opens up ESG for individual company interpretation and execution. With CSR in the mix, companies may quickly align both, muddying the nuance between values and value into an amorphous blob of reporting. As a result, the priorities behind and motivations to address material issues become conflated, inviting questions on fiduciary duty, shareholder value, and stakeholder desire with little hope for clear communication around any related effort.

Further, the inability to translate comparable experiences and outcomes across companies reduces agreement and can eliminate the usefulness of the lessons learned. As management teams serve across various boards and employees move across companies, they will find no singular approach to integrating or mainstreaming ESG into their business, even across the same industry.

On the other hand, a benefit is that companies can self-govern their unique ESG efforts if they understand it, which creates a competitive advantage but may also have downsides. For example, a company that embraces a sustainable transition early may find increased costs in updating its suppliers and components before its competitors but gain long-term price stability versus late adopters. This type of tradeoff is typical with ESG, and companies can apply strategies already employed, like analyzing the timing and risk around this type of effort, to find balance. Tradeoffs are almost always unavoidable regarding ESG and provide another example of how the acronym works across pillars to intersect with other business areas and across the value chain. However, even those companies considering ESG well and consistently will not always get things right as ESG issues and stakeholders constantly change. The management team and its investors need to consider the ongoing maintenance of a company's ESG issues and approach.

The creation of ESG around the markets has primarily worked as intended, but not quite. Capital flows into ESG investments, and attention to these issues has grown. Bloomberg predicted that total ESG assets under management would reach $50 trillion, or more than a third of the global market, by 2025.[31] Still, companies must take ownership of the term and execute against ESG outcomes. While financing is essential for driving ESG improvements and innovation, new inflows of capital are not the only means by which a company takes on ESG work, and loans to transition may not be available, nor may the stubborn persistence of the status quo allow a board to make a change. Many corporate activities have focused on measuring and communicating the data around their ESG efforts to financial services firms and not investigating the critical transition work or financing needed, which was the point from the start.

The effects of the evolution of ESG will be seen throughout this book, along with unhelpful conflations of ESG with CSR, SRI, and impact, resulting in the co-opting of its definition to suit different purposes. We'll also work through how ESG can help create a defensible position for impact. If companies claim ownership of ESG and use it to inform their business strategies, they will better understand the differences between material ESG risks and opportunities, values-led impact initiatives, and where the two meet.

What ESG isn't

What ESG means is open for debate because it is so broad, but the acronym often gets whittled down to its simplest forms, even beyond its conflation with CSR and impact. Due to the universal nature of the intangibles behind ESG, it tends to be everything to everyone, serving a range of specific agendas. Deconstructing these other reductions will help create the right frame of mind by helping us understand what ESG is by looking at what it isn't.

With rising ESG regulations born out of the need for comparable data, companies are in a frenzy to disclose, turning the Chief Sustainability Officer into a compliance function. Due to the focus on investors, ESG is often equated with data, but not all data is relevant or material. Data without action is simply disclosure. Data and metrics inform ESG strategies and can work towards outcomes, but the data is not ESG, unless it is related to a material issue.

Regarding data, rating agencies often use ESG and non-financial data to inform a score that an investor might use to make an investment decision. These scores are not the equivalent of ESG either but are helpful in understanding how a researcher or analyst sees a company's ESG performance.

We've covered how ESG differs from values and impact through materiality, but some connections can surface, often at the intersection of the issue with stakeholders. If a key stakeholder group pushes their values on the company through divestment, pressures, or engagement, the management team must examine this perspective and take action or face reputational risks. Yet, fundamentally, ESG differs from values-based initiatives because it is material and in pursuit of long-term value. As a result, much of what appears in CSR reports, such as annual volunteering, charitable giving, or philanthropy, while great pursuits, are often not ESG.

Due to the conflation with values, politicians, especially in the West, have latched onto ESG as a values-based effort to deliver a specific liberal agenda. Even with what we've looked at so far in this introductory chapter, it should be obvious that this is not the case. ESG represents core business issues, and a consideration alongside all the things that boards and management teams have worked on for years. Companies should not prioritize ESG over other activities, but should integrate it as a consideration when making strategic decisions. Still, companies should also focus on ESG with purposeful intent for it to be adequately mainstreamed, helping to capture risks and opportunities that may have fallen outside of the company's traditional management processes.

An ESG mindset may be just the thing

So, back to the original question. Why should a company care about understanding ESG? On the one hand, it is a perspective that financial institutions have on the company and should be well understood so capital can be appropriately allocated and deployed. Understanding that ESG goes beyond ESG scores and disclosures helps a company see that it must manage its risks and opportunities in the pursuit of outcomes. This broader perspective should give back returns to investors over the long term.

On the other hand, it represents an additional perspective from which to think about emerging issues along a broad set of interconnected topics. While the board and management teams should already have a view of the long term, ESG gives them new information that will inform the company's critical decisions as stakeholder pressures mount. However, it is also something that leaders may have ignored or executed poorly as the original intent never drove to the company level with much consistency or enablement.

ESG has been called many things over its short life, including a framework, scores, an investment strategy, the devil, and more. So, why add a mindset to the mix? Over the years, I've talked with many financial institutions and companies and found that many are missing something regarding ESG. To address ESG risks and create new opportunities in the new world of globalization, controversies, intangibles, and polycrises (all of which we'll get to), companies need a new frame of mind to think about their business across every level of the organization.

ESG is admittedly an imperfect and imprecise way to think about the effect of the world on the company while looking at the company's impact. Still, perhaps it is exactly the right tool to address an imperfect and imprecise world.

Notes

1 PwC (2022). Charting the course through a changing governance landscape. PwC, p. 16. www.pwc.com/us/en/services/governance-insights-center/assets/pwc-2022-annual-corporate-directors-survey.pdf (archived at https://perma.cc/Q24A-868S).

2 The 73rd Congress of the United States (2022). Securities Act of 1933. 42. www.govinfo.gov/content/pkg/COMPS-1884/pdf/COMPS-1884.pdf (archived at https://perma.cc/FPF3-VEKB).

3 U.S. Supreme Court (1976). TSC Industries, Inc. v. Northway, Inc., 426 U.S. 438 (1976). Justia Law. https://supreme.justia.com/cases/federal/us/426/438/ (archived at https://perma.cc/KK63-3HF2).

4 U.S. Securities and Exchange Commission (1999). SEC staff accounting bulletin no. 99: Materiality. SEC. www.sec.gov/interps/account/sab99.htm (archived at https://perma.cc/P4GP-2TDG).

5 European Financial Regulatory Advisory Group (2022). [Draft] ESRG 1 Double materiality conceptual guidelines for standard-setting Working paper. EFRAG, p. 4. www.efrag.org/Assets/Download?assetUrl=/sites/ webpublishing/SiteAssets/Appendix%202.6%20-%20WP%20on%20 draft%20ESRG%201.pdf (archived at https://perma.cc/7JYY-K7K3).

6 Global Reporting Initiative (2022). The materiality madness: Why definitions matter. Global Reporting Initiative, p. 2. www.globalreporting.org/media/ r2oojx53/gri-perspective-the-materiality-madness.pdf (archived at https:// perma.cc/5LBH-8UEJ).

7 Global Reporting Initiative (2022). The materiality madness: Why definitions matter. Global Reporting Initiative, p. 2. www.globalreporting.org/media/ r2oojx53/gri-perspective-the-materiality-madness.pdf (archived at https:// perma.cc/M5VX-DDVU).

8 Fan, J., Rehm, W., and Siccardo, G. (2021). The state of internal carbon pricing. McKinsey. www.mckinsey.com/capabilities/strategy-and-corporate- finance/our-insights/the-state-of-internal-carbon-pricing (archived at https:// perma.cc/9DLT-JBNT).

9 Impact-Weighted Accounts (n.d.). Impact-Weighted Accounts. Harvard Business School. www.hbs.edu/impact-weighted-accounts/Pages/default.aspx (archived at https://perma.cc/MEH7-67CN).

10 CFI Team (2020). Socially responsible investment (SRI). Corporate Finance Institute. corporatefinanceinstitute.com/resources/esg/socially-responsible- investment-sri/ (archived at https://perma.cc/74TE-EY3H).

11 Gethard, G. (2019). Protest divestment and the end of apartheid. Investopedia. www.investopedia.com/articles/economics/08/protest-divestment-south-africa. asp (archived at https://perma.cc/MHQ3-FP7U).

12 Hale, J. and Ginty, B. (2020). ESG investing comes of age. Morningstar. www.morningstar.com/features/esg-investing-history (archived at https://perma. cc/S67Y-XLZ5).

13 United Nations Economic and Social Commission for Asia and the Pacific (2013). *From Corporate Social Responsibility to Corporate Sustainability.* UN iLibrary, p. 10. www.un-ilibrary.org/content/books/9789210564779c005 (archived at https://perma.cc/BT2Q-HFSQ).

14 Friedman, M. (1970). The social responsibility of business is to increase its profits. *The New York Times*. September 13. https://www.nytimes.com/1970/09/13/archives/a-friedman-doctrine-the-social-responsibility-of-business-is-to.html (archived at https://perma.cc/4ZLW-MQJ7).

15 Committee for Economic Development (1971). *Social Responsibilities of Business Corporations*. Committee for Economic Development, pp. 26–27. www.ced.org/pdf/Social_Responsibilities_of_Business_Corporations.pdf (archived at https://perma.cc/QDP5-FEH2).

16 Agudelo, M.A.L., Jóhannsdóttir, L., and Davídsdóttir, B. (2019). A literature review of the history and evolution of corporate social responsibility. *International Journal of Corporate Social Responsibility*, 4(1), pp. 1–23. https://doi.org/10.1186/s40991-018-0039-y. (archived at https://perma.cc/P96D-Y3K9)

17 United Nations (2019). What is the Kyoto Protocol? UNFCCC. unfccc.int/kyoto_protocol (archived at https://perma.cc/M75X-XRUT).

18 United Nations Global Compact (n.d.). United Nations Global Compact. https://unglobalcompact.org/what-is-gc/mission/principles (archived at https://perma.cc/MRX3-7AFL).

19 United Nations (2015a). Millennium Development Goals. United Nations. www.un.org/millenniumgoals/bkgd.shtml (archived at https://perma.cc/KF9M-ZJDW).

20 United Nations (2015b). Transitioning from the Millennium Development Goals to the Sustainable Development Goals. United Nations Sustainable Development. www.un.org/sustainabledevelopment/blog/2015/09/transitioning-from-the-millennium-development-goals-to-the-sustainable-development-goals/ (archived at https://perma.cc/4AXZ-Y2S4).

21 United Nations Environment Programme Finance Initiative (2019). About. United Nations Environment Programme Finance Initiative. www.unepfi.org/about/ (archived at https://perma.cc/D3AF-B8CA).

22 Clements-Hunt, P. (2021). The United Nations free-thinkers who coined the term "ESG" and changed the world. LinkedIn. www.linkedin.com/pulse/united-nations-free-thinkers-who-coined-term-esg-paul-clements-hunt/ (archived at https://perma.cc/BVK5-CQRB).

23 UNEP Finance Initiative (2004). *The Materiality of Social, Environmental and Corporate Governance Issues to Equity Pricing*. United Nations Environment Programme, p. 2. www.unepfi.org/fileadmin/publications/amwg/ceo_briefing_materiality_equity_pricing_2004.pdf (archived at https://perma.cc/7KGJ-T83V).

24 UNEP Finance Initiative (2004). *The Materiality of Social, Environmental and Corporate Governance Issues to Equity Pricing*. United Nations Environment Programme, p. 3. www.unepfi.org/fileadmin/publications/amwg/ceo_briefing_materiality_equity_pricing_2004.pdf (archived at https://perma.cc/MKB3-25T3).

25 UNEP Finance Initiative (2004). *The Materiality of Social, Environmental and Corporate Governance Issues to Equity Pricing.* United Nations Environment Programme, p. 3. www.unepfi.org/fileadmin/publications/amwg/ceo_briefing_ materiality_equity_pricing_2004.pdf (archived at https://perma.cc/3ACA-KGJ9).

26 United Nations (2004). *Who Cares Wins.* p. 2. www.unepfi.org/fileadmin/ events/2004/stocks/who_cares_wins_global_compact_2004.pdf (archived at https://perma.cc/G8RT-FZSY).

27 United Nations (2004). *Who Cares Wins.* pp. 1–2. www.unepfi.org/fileadmin/ events/2004/stocks/who_cares_wins_global_compact_2004.pdf (archived at https://perma.cc/MB5E-YL7A).

28 UNEP Finance Initiative (2005). *A legal framework for the integration of environmental, social, and governance issues into institutional investment.* United Nations Environment Programme, p. 13. www.unepfi.org/fileadmin/ documents/freshfields_legal_resp_20051123.pdf (archived at https://perma. cc/47ST-ZN2A).

29 World Business Council for Sustainable Development (WBCSD) and UNEP Finance Initiative (2010). *Translating ESG into sustainable business value: Key insights for companies and investors.* www.unepfi.org/fileadmin/documents/ translatingESG.pdf (archived at https://perma.cc/YC4P-68YM).

30 Tomlinson, B., Whelan, T., and Eckerle, K. (2021). How to bring ESG into the quarterly earnings call. *MIT Sloan Management Review.* sloanreview.mit.edu/ article/how-to-bring-esg-into-the-quarterly-earnings-call/ (archived at https:// perma.cc/26NH-DLZ6).

31 Bloomberg (2021). ESG assets may hit $53 trillion by 2025, a third of global AUM. Bloomberg Professional Services, February 23. www.bloomberg.com/ professional/blog/esg-assets-may-hit-53-trillion-by-2025-a-third-of-global-aum/ (archived at https://perma.cc/AA9B-SKSA).

02

ESG Data: Standards, Rating Agencies, and Value

There's a common axiom for ESG, often spoken by those working at financial institutions, standards organizations, and ESG rating agencies.

ESG is data.

As we saw in the first chapter, ESG isn't simply data. Yet, it should be no surprise that there is an extremely close connection and that companies and stakeholders can derive ESG insights from data. Since the allocation of capital from the financial markets is where ESG began, stretching back into simple data that informed socially responsible investing (SRI) strategies, conducting ESG investment analysis requires comparable data in the same manner that financial analysts examine quantitative data and use material content from corporate filings to determine value. From these data points, investors can compare companies and evaluate the risks or opportunities for investing.

Still, financial numbers across a comparable accounting format are less nuanced than the breadth and depth of available ESG information. Most financial data is quantitative, meaning a company can measure and report measurable numbers for the related monies aligned to common standards built on long-established accounting principles. ESG data varies as far as the differences in companies and resides in a mix of quantitative and qualitative data, the latter being more descriptive narratives, open to interpretation. In some cases, looking at ESG data is like comparing two novels. Each company is like a unique author telling a different story in their own writing style, sometimes even in a foreign language with colloquialisms. Layer on the combination of people participating in writing the tale who may only understand a fraction of the plot, and you have a recipe for information that someone can reason over but is not comparable, even across the same industry or, in the case of this metaphor, genre.

Despite this implication, the term ESG has become inextricably tied to comparable Environmental, Social, and Governance data, as any investor can use this information to conduct their unique analyses, making the data valuable across investment types. The breaking down of the acronym is intentional here, as this data encompasses a universe of material and non-material reported metrics along each pillar. Most people call this information ESG data, but its application may vary. An SRI investor or activist investor might examine Environmental and Social metrics over time to see which companies positively impact the world. In contrast, an ESG investor would look at the same metrics to try to uncover how well the company manages a particular material risk or opportunity. In this way, the same data informs different stakeholder decisions. If you consider the observation from the previous chapter that investors and companies cannot agree on what is material, the pressure to report everything is massive, resulting in the volume of reported data spiraling out of control, trading quantity for quality.

As attention to ESG has grown, stakeholders beyond investors are examining this same reported data for additional purposes. For example, a consumer compares ESG data in advertising or on the product's label to determine which product to buy, or a prospective employee might use this information to determine which company aligns with their values or which is handling their ESG issues and is therefore a stable bet. Storytelling and marketing have evolved, as effectively communicating a particular ESG message can drive alignment with these stakeholders, resulting in additional opportunities for the company.

The result is volumes of company-reported ESG data to help capture capital and opportunity, leading to regulators stepping in to control its quality. ESG data has evolved through financial assessments to stakeholder use to its current state of regulatory pressure, with no data audience any less critical than the other. ESG is data because the data is what informs the decisions being made within and around the company, which have a material impact across stakeholders. Unfortunately, like the stories companies tell, every stakeholder is looking for something different out of the story, and the company may not understand what data will matter to which stakeholder for what reason, leaving the outcomes a mystery. Whether the company reports data around material or non-material activities, published data leads to a risk in that anything could be a material issue through stakeholder interpretation, just as omitting anything could cause stakeholders to make a different decision about the company.

Even with the high volume of data, a common complaint is that the reported data is too much for financial services firms, not comparable enough, and further complicated by interpretations from ESG rating agencies. Yet, this ever-increasing obsession with data is a constant pressure that strains companies because the same challenges in the market analysis apply to assessments across their value chains. Companies also struggle with variations and evolutions in stakeholder motivations, including those focused on impact, leading to reported data proliferation. In early 2023, the *New York Times* reported on candid executive conversations at the World Economic Forum at Davos and lamentations that there is an overemphasis on measurement, with some stating, "The debate over what metrics to use to measure ESG achievements, such as reducing carbon emissions, has become a distraction."[1]

This insatiable need from stakeholders for data, paired with the compliance pressure of new regulatory requirements, has driven a flurry of corporate activity and new hires of experts who can deal with standards or have domain expertise. Some companies were early adopters, aligning their strong sense of purpose to projects around broad areas such as sustainability and diversity. With the rise of new regulations for reporting, many companies now consider their ESG data collection and reporting as an exercise in transparency and compliance, moving the responsibility into a compliance or controller-like position to wrangle its complexity.[2]

Unfortunately, the universal nature of ESG has allowed it to become a catch-all for every matter conceivable, and wrangling that complexity and nuance is no easy task. Many companies now sit at ESG's natural evolution from its creation as a financial services mechanism—collecting and reporting the company's ESG data. Yet, ESG data has a valuable purpose in that it can surface some of the company's unknown risks and opportunities, building resilience through informing high-quality actions. This analysis and subsequent actions represent steps companies cannot miss as they also pursue impact efforts out to the world. As one might expect, organizing the company around efforts born from ESG data is a Governance task, but collecting the data is no simple task.

The new ESG data supply chain

To effectively communicate its efforts to stakeholders and provide evidence of its actions through a story, a company must collect, analyze, and report its ESG data. This effort can prove a massive challenge as a company has analog records or digital equivalents of much of its operations locked away in various platforms and systems. From an ESG risk and opportunity perspective, and regarding impact, a company must also consider its entire value chain in its data exploration. Across relationships, contracts, and even the use of its products and services, a company represents everything it brings in and whatever goes out into the world, all with associated data points. With an insatiable need for stakeholders to review ESG data and new regulations, the company must now account for everything, creating a sprawling ESG data supply chain.

Self-reported data

Companies are sitting on a treasure trove of operational data across their internal technology systems and possibly printed storage areas. This information is invaluable to the company's management team, stakeholders, and investors who want to reason over the data and make more informed decisions. Unfortunately, companies did not build these digital or analog systems for reporting ESG data but to support specific critical corporate functions, nor should all internal data be readily shared due to competition. These systems and their data are an overall metaphor for ESG, as the company wasn't created to support ESG efforts, nor should it exist solely in their service. In other words, the acronym doesn't supplant what companies are doing, but the company can gain additional value from a perspective that considers it.

Many of these internal systems contain quantitative metrics that require additional context to uncover materiality and impact. For example, a payroll system tracks every employee's salary. This data alone reveals a company's benefits offered to its key internal stakeholder group, employees. Still, it may lack the diversity, equity, and inclusion (DEI) context from Human Resources systems to determine a material Social issue like pay equity, which can impact talent retention. In another example, a company with a large real estate footprint might monitor its energy usage or utility bills but perhaps lacks sensors that monitor proactively for various building equipment failures, which could result in more efficient energy management. The pay equity issue is one that external stakeholders would care about, especially prospective employees. Yet, the building management issue, while potentially material, depending on the company's reliance on real estate, is needed for internal quality controls; however, its value may surface in the improvement of reported energy usage, related carbon emissions numbers, or even cost savings.

One of the early steps in a company's ESG journey is to inventory its data estate. This exercise, which the IT department should lead in partnership with business units for that important context, informs where and what kind of data exists across different business systems. Without this baseline understanding and inventory—an IT Governance exercise—companies will struggle to understand their data outside the strict context of the system that data resides in.

From here, business units must thoughtfully explore new connections between internal data systems, taking direction from management teams on priorities and leveraging their intellectual capital of what matters to the company. Next, management teams and employees can sort out competitive information and intellectual property—which should remain internal for analysis—and what can and should be self-reported externally to stakeholders for review. Yet, this is only part of the data needed for quality analysis.

Material external datasets

Even if a company has evaluated, modernized, and connected its internal systems around related ESG data in preparation for reporting, stakeholders expect it won't stop there. First, actions that lead to outcomes are needed, as stakeholders expect progress, whether for ESG risks and opportunities or impact. Beyond that point, stakeholders understand an entire data ecosystem needs consideration, and some, like financial institutions, use additional data to supplement what the company reports to uncover material risk and evaluate borrowers and investments for opportunities. Companies should use similar external data to supplement their analysis alongside connected internal datasets to form a holistic picture of the company's context and operations in an ever-increasingly complex and interconnected world.

Every company is subject to the effects of the physical and digital world and interacts with various stakeholders. These domains have datasets that may help inform the company about evolving trends and the direct forces that can affect the company. Financial institutions will leverage these additional datasets to help bring context to analysis, and companies should, too. By weaving in external datasets with the company's internal data, the company can uncover new insights and additional ESG context.

Each pillar of ESG has valuable external datasets for the company to use, but they require a thoughtful approach to uncover the useful ones. For example, the company may overlook external systemic datasets that could expose Environmental risks. Returning to the real estate example, maintaining the physical locations of buildings in an internal facilities management system is not enough to model climate risk. To do that, a company must obtain external climate data and models, and information on local biodiversity changes, land mapping, flood zones, and more.

The Social pillar also has valuable external datasets, like census and population data, social media and related sentiment, and more. Building on the prior example of pay equity, externally sourced data can help a company understand where its efforts sit with its peers, which could yield a competitive talent advantage. Regional demographic information can help inform the strategy to accelerate pay equity programs in certain areas to help acquire diverse talent where it exists.

From a Governance perspective, the company is likely already following regulatory trends. Still, it could layer on industry players' ESG reports to understand how others view industry-related ESG issues. There is a caution here, however, as not every company defines its ESG strategy the same way. As long as the company is researching with that understanding, it should be able to make an effective competitive analysis on how its peers are handling material ESG issues.

Data about the board and management team's material experience may have Governance implications. Across the company, newsfeeds can be an especially powerful dataset to integrate into the company's data and is likely one that management teams and business units are already monitoring. For example, a Research and Development division should watch for scientific papers and news for developments around materials used in the company's products. An Operations team would be wise to monitor the news for extreme weather and changing conditions around its facilities and adapt accordingly.

These external datasets can come from various providers, including commercial climate data providers, governments, non-governmental organizations (NGOs), non-profits, competitors, and consortiums, or publicly available datasets. While IT is needed to forge the data connections, uncovering the logical relationships between internal and external data requires domain expertise in partnership with the company's internal experts to unpack, analyze, and report against.

Value chain data: Upstream suppliers

No company operates in a silo; every company depends on suppliers. Each affects the company in one way or another, and the company impacts them in turn. Since suppliers are also companies, they also have supply chains. These intricate relationships and their activities would not exist without each link in the chain, resulting in additional shared accountabilities. Along with this comes related data that each connected company needs to collect, analyze, and account for in its ESG analysis.

With the need for this value chain data, new connections form that extend beyond the contractual relationships. As of 2022, four of five surveyed Procurement teams have started bringing ESG into their strategic objectives.[3] Companies are leveraging their supply chain to meet their ESG commitments and looking to align on purpose. In this case, an issue that was a non-material concern to a supplier suddenly becomes a material issue due to a request, as the data could become an additional consideration in continuing the relationship. The result is that any data point in the value chain could prove material, which makes ESG a constantly moving target, at least in its current state. As with most things ESG-related, there is also an innate connection with a company's impact that reinforces this connection.

Building on years of effort, in October 2004, the World Business Council for Sustainable Development (WBCSD) published a paper on a corporate standard for emissions measurement called *The GHG Protocol: A corporate reporting and accounting standard*, which has become widely adopted as the set of standards and tools by the same name.[4] This paper recognized the need for connecting value chain emissions to its related activities, moving beyond just a company accounting for its direct activities. The flow of Environmental information and accountability parallels the business dependencies on the value chain. This idea has evolved into three scopes of emissions:

- Scope 1: Emissions created directly as a result of a company's operations
- Scope 2: Indirect emissions from activities or sources that the company has purchased
- Scope 3: Value chain emissions from sources not owned or operated by the company.

The requirement to account for Scope 3 emissions links a company and its value chain in the same way ESG does but for different reasons and outcomes. ESG focuses on material links, but the GHG Protocol may also have non-material impacts. For an agriculture company, understanding its value chain's emissions could be an impact exercise to influence an ecosystem to decarbonize. From an ESG perspective, agriculture, forestry, and land use account for around 18.4 percent of global emissions.[5] As governments and regulators scrutinize emissions in the face of climate change and prioritize a transition, adopting sustainable practices early and working with suppliers doing the same could lower transition risks.

While emissions are a connection between companies and their value chain along the Environmental pillar and necessary operations, material or not, this isn't the only link, just one cast in a standard. For example, a fashion company relies on its dye suppliers having access to a renewable water source, an unrelated emissions issue. Many material ESG links like this exist along every pillar and between them across the value chain. For example, forced labor issues at a supplier, related to the Social pillar, can damage the downstream company's brand and indicate other poor business practices, like substandard, inefficient materials, or lack of safety controls. The lack of attention to an issue like this is a Governance matter that hopefully data, like audits, interviews, and social media, would surface.

This connection has led to new reporting-based relationships that infinitely reach into a company's supply chain, attempting to extract data from every player. To adapt and mitigate its value chain-related risk and opportunities, a company must go beyond data collection to analyze the data and act.

The reason this becomes complex sits in its name, the value chain. At what point in the chain does a company need to stop accounting for its effects and impacts? For example, a company that produces a laptop has a vast supply chain stretching from raw material sourcing to refining and processing, component manufacturing, shipping, product assembly, delivery to its retail chain, and delivery to the customer for use. Each one of these steps involves a range of value chain players whose operations would not happen if not for the company and final customer. Obtaining material or impact information from every player upstream to the activities related to mining rare Earth minerals is arduous. Even then, it doesn't end. What was the manufacturing process and value chain that surrounded the equipment used at the mine? And on and on it goes.

The company needs to set boundaries around data exploration and accountability, perhaps following the GHG Protocol's original recommendations of Scope 3, "Companies may want to focus on accounting for and reporting those activities that are relevant to their business and goals, and for which they have reliable information."[6] This callout is good advice for most data collection activities related to the value chain, even beyond emissions, because it forces a company to recognize the material connections, creating an ESG mindset. The company should start with what matters and then move into other areas.

The global semiconductor company Nvidia calls out two suppliers involved in its wafer manufacturing in its 2023 Corporate Social Responsibility (CSR) report and names even more subcontractors and contract manufacturers.[7] It also lists how it uses various tools, such as the Responsible Business Alliance (RBA) Code of Conduct, to monitor supply chains around several areas, including Labor, Health and Safety, Environmental, Ethics, and Management Systems.[8] The RBA covers the electronics industry and "full compliance with the laws, rules, and regulations of the countries in which it operates. The Code also encourages Participants to go beyond legal compliance, drawing upon internationally recognized standards, to advance social and environmental responsibility and business ethics."[9] Read that statement carefully to find all three pillars of ESG.

Metrics like these can be improved through the procurement-supplier relationships. After all, a company does have some control and influence over a supplier's activities and resulting data through the threat of divestment and the possibilities of engagement, similar to financial institutions with investments. For example, research and development around the company's products can reduce transition risks and drive impact through sustainable choices while partnering to monitor suppliers for Social issues upstream. The company can also control and manage the efficiency of the product's downstream use, repairability, and final disposition or recycling through the design, marketing, and circularity programs. While the relationships connect the value chain, the data moves them.

Value chain data: Downstream and back in

Data surrounds the entire value chain upstream and downstream. Suppliers only cover the upstream direction but are a material component of operations and can impact the company's various ESG goals through connected data flows. Yet, stakeholders downstream, including those inside the value chain data flow, also play a material role across the company's operations and have related datasets.

Employees are stakeholders that can influence reported metrics through their activities, needs, and the company's culture. For example, a management team can uncover productivity data through collaboration tools, and the company can report, as part of Scope 3 under the GHG Protocol, its employees' business travel and commuting in carbon accounting. Customers are also a critical stakeholder group, whether business clients or consumers, and create signals that can surface in various data formats, like social media sentiment, news feeds, and more. We will review these two specific stakeholder groups more in Chapter 4 from the Social perspective. For the purposes here, it's essential to recognize that data surrounds each group.

Depending on the reporting company's transparency and willingness to share the information collected, ESG data will appear in its material financial filings, sustainability and CSR reports, and perhaps on its website. Out of the publishing, the data supply chain continues to grow as even more stakeholder groups are waiting to review the company's reported ESG data, even affecting the company's reporting strategies.

STANDARDS AND REGULATORS

Collecting, accounting, and reporting ESG data to stakeholders is complex enough. How a company does these things and what it chooses to disclose is largely a matter of opinion and can vary from company to company, even in the same industry. Standards organizations and regulators affect the manner and data the company discloses but may not capture every material issue the company should consider.

Surrounding the data is an "alphabet soup" of reporting standards and frameworks that attempt to guide companies towards standard reporting along consistent data points. Many attempt to create comparability in datasets across companies but are adopted by companies at varying levels with the acronyms and their relevant data sprinkled in tables published in CSR reports. Even the UN's colorful Sustainable Development Goals (SDGs), which are not standards, often appear in CSR reports to give stakeholders a common framework for the reported metrics.

Due to the range of standards and their voluntary nature, stakeholders may find it impossible to find comparable data across companies as each company may subscribe to different ones, even in the same industry. Luckily, standards and frameworks have consolidated and built integration points over time. In 2020, five common standards organizations, CDP, CDSB, GRI, IIRC, and SASB, created a joint vision for working together.[10] Later that year, the IIRC and SASB merged under an organization called the Value Reporting Foundation (VRF).[11] In 2021, the International Financial Reporting Standards (IFRS) Foundation, which sets global accounting standards, announced CDSB and VRF would consolidate further under a new organization, the International Sustainability Standards Board (ISSB).[12] In 2023, the ISSB took on oversight of the Task Force on Climate-related Disclosures (TCFD).[13] From an ESG perspective, it is less important to understand the history here than to recognize the volume of movements and amount of acronyms to track, which companies must be mindful of as they report.

This consolidation will make it easier for companies to report by reducing variability and providing clear integration points, but progress remains ongoing, and participation stays voluntary. Still, with stakeholder pressure and the potential for capital to flow based on the data, there are quite a few standards organizations and frameworks to keep track of (Table 2.1), meaning that universal comparability hasn't been reached and may be a way off.

TABLE 2.1 ESG-related standards and frameworks

Standard/Framework	Scope	Description	ESG uses
Global Reporting Initiative (GRI)	Broad metric coverage across Environmental, Social, and Economic	Voluntary standards that outline standard metrics that should be reported. Data broken down by Universal, Sector, and Topic.[1]	Benchmarking. Metrics may be related to ESG, but the company must provide the materiality context.
Sustainability Accounting Standards Board (SASB)	Sustainability-related metrics	Industry-specific disclosures, now under ISSB.	Helps to identify material issues and related metrics.
UN Sustainable Development Goals (SDGs)	Global goals-based	Environmental and Social goals for the world to meet by 2030.	Sometimes used to align metrics to impact and context.
CDP	Climate, water, forests	Collects metrics and information from companies and drives accountability for impact around the three areas.[2]	Procurement teams and Financial institutions use CDP's data for analysis on progress.

(continued)

TABLE 2.1 (Continued)

Standard/Framework	Scope	Description	ESG uses
Task Force on Climate-related Disclosures (TCFD)	Climate, transition risks	Collects metrics and information from companies related to their climate and transition risks.	Meant as a reporting framework for companies to inform the movement of capital by pricing in risks related to climate change.[3]
Taskforce on Nature-related Disclosures (TNFD)	Biodiversity and nature-based impacts, risks, and opportunities	Consistent framework with TCFD.	Meant to surface the importance of nature to the global economy and provide a related reporting framework.[4]
GHG Protocol	Greenhouse gas emissions	Guidance for public and private companies to report their emissions.[5]	Carbon accounting.
Science-Based Targets Initiative (SBTi)	Environmental	When companies set their Environmental goals, they should consider the science to ensure they are met on time. SBTi can help validate plans.	Reviews science-based Environmental goals and plans to help companies and financial institutions understand what is needed to transition.[6]

1 GRI (2022). How to use the GRI Standards. GRI. www.globalreporting.org/how-to-use-the-gri-standards/.
2 CDP (2022). About us CDP. www.cdp.net/en/info/about-us.
3 TCFD (2022). About. TCFD. www.fsb-tcfd.org/about/.
4 Greenhouse Gas Protocol (2016). About us. Greenhouse Gas Protocol. https://ghgprotocol.org/about-us.
5 Science Based Targets (2023). Science Based Targets. https://sciencebasedtargets.org/.
6 Grant Thorton (2023). CSRD reporting: What you need to know. Grant Thornton. www.grantthornton.com/insights/articles/esg/2023/csrd-reporting-what-you-need-to-know.

Those listed in Table 2.1 are just some common standards and frameworks, mainly focused on the Environmental pillar, that guide companies along ESG or impact reporting. Since they are voluntary, companies can choose which to follow, meaning comparability remains an issue. As a result, new regulations have emerged, some of which align with the concepts presented in the standards and frameworks to ease the reporting burden while holding companies accountable for delivering data of the quality expected by financial institutions. There may be regulations to comply with regionally, but three extensive ESG reporting regulations are putting pressure on companies and their global value chains since modern business can stretch far due to globalization (Table 2.2).

As with any regulation, there are costs in implementing and ensuring the data and processes back the disclosure accurately. After reviewing the SEC's proposed climate rule draft, over half of the companies surveyed by Workiva and PwC thought the compliance exercise would cost them over $750,000 in the first year alone.[14] Still, if the management team views ESG disclosures as solely a cost and a compliance exercise, a couple of Governance risks will emerge. First, the company will miss the opportunity to uncover the value the financial markets attempt to discover. Second, compliance with regulations is not a substitute for ESG analysis, which is where the value lies. Third, disclosures and regulations do not encompass every data point or connected datasets the company must consider to uncover value.

The company that analyzes its required disclosures and takes ESG data beyond compliance may be better prepared to develop a comprehensive strategy around ESG risks and new opportunities. When it comes time to seek capital to fund transition projects or new ventures, the right mix of data will help the company make its case to lenders, secure the capital, and act. When stakeholders question the company's motivation around these projects, the understanding and consistency from the data will be the defense, not the standards or the regulatory reports.

ESG DATA AGGREGATORS AND RATING AGENCIES

If nothing else is clear so far, it should be that many of the standards and regulations are in the service of the needs of financial institutions for the movement of capital. Yet, the number of companies and their value chains across the global markets are too great for any investment firm to analyze. As companies publish their ESG information to stakeholders, other companies will aggregate and analyze that data at scale. These ESG data providers

TABLE 2.2 ESG-related regulations

Regulatory body	Regulation	Jurisdiction	Status
EU Commission	Corporate Sustainability Reporting Directive (CSRD)	Coming in various stages for companies headquartered in the EU from fiscal year 2024 through to 2028, and includes companies operating in the EU by 2028.[1]	Signed November 2022. Covers broad ESG metrics and considers financial and impact materiality, or double materiality.[2]
US Securities and Exchange Commission (SEC)	Climate Rule Draft	US publicly traded companies	As of 2022, the draft proposal focuses largely on emissions, as aligned with the GHG Protocol. Climate risk with a material impact is also considered.[3]
Standards organization	**Standards**	**Jurisdiction**	**Status**
International Financial Reporting Standards (IFRS)	International Sustainability Standards Board (ISSB) informs regulatory agencies	Jurisdictions may adopt this standard as a regulation and many jurisdictions leverage the IFRS's accounting standards for financial reporting. Since this consolidates standards in use, ISSB recommends companies review and integrate proactively.[4]	ISSB S1 focuses on sustainability. ISSB S2 focuses on climate-related physical and transition risks. Financial materiality is a consideration in these standards.[5]

1 European Financial Regulatory Advisory Group (2023). First set of draft ESRS. European Financial Regulatory Advisory Group. www.efrag.org/lab6.

2 U.S. Securities and Exchange Commission (2022). SEC proposes rules to enhance and standardize climate-related disclosures for investors. SEC. www.sec.gov/news/press-release/2022-46.

3 IFRS (n.d.). ISSB: Frequently Asked Questions. IFRS. www.ifrs.org/groups/international-sustainability-standards-board/issb-frequently-asked-questions/.

4 IFRS (n.d.). ISSB: Frequently Asked Questions. IFRS. www.ifrs.org/groups/international-sustainability-standards-board/issb-frequently-asked-questions/.

5 IFRS (n.d.). ISSB: Frequently Asked Questions. IFRS. www.ifrs.org/groups/international-sustainability-standards-board/issb-frequently-asked-questions/.

collect the data from various sources, compile it, score companies based on proprietary rating models, create related indexes, and sell the information to financial institutions. As such, ESG data providers are another one of a company's stakeholders, but ones that may be overlooked or misunderstood, as covered more in Chapter 9.

It isn't only public companies that may be subject to ratings; private companies may be as well. These ESG data providers and rating agencies include companies like MSCI, S&P Global, Refinitiv, Sustainalytics, and Preqin. There is little consistency across the ratings, with different agencies having unique research capabilities, perspectives on materiality, and preferred datasets. Some will focus on ESG materiality, some on impact, and others will publish information for both. Often, interpretation, even with a description of scoring methodologies, lies in the eye of the stakeholder. For example, in 2021, McKinsey suggested that Procurement teams could also leverage ESG rating companies to help with supplier analysis.[15]

Carrying forward the analogy of ESG reporting as a novel, ESG rating agencies are similar to a group of book reviewers. Each may uncover something different from the analysis and report their findings accordingly. In some cases, financial institutions will incorporate aggregated ESG information and external datasets to support internally created scoring.

Within a rating agency's scores lies a certain level of comparability, but not nearly as much between rating agencies. As a result, it can be difficult for a company or firm to understand the exact factors that shape a score because each rating agency takes a unique approach built on its intellectual property. The irony is that ESG scores across rating agencies aren't necessarily comparable despite the attempts to drive a comparable perspective on the data.

Companies need to pay attention to their various scores as they could influence the favorable movement of capital, but it is a fool's errand to attempt to game the scores. While companies often don't agree with the scores, or regulations for that matter, the goal is to build a resilient business and drive long-term success or impact, not to support the scores.

In many cases, these additional downstream stakeholders will review ESG scores, supplement them with other datasets, and publish the results in various formats, including other proprietary analyses and even custom ESG scores, further refining reported data. As a result, even the data the company publishes may be changed and fed back into the data value chain in another format, delivering new perspectives across the company and its ecosystem.

Measuring and managing

Across the data value chain of the company, there are many pressures to collect data and report, but a company shouldn't pursue data for data's sake, nor should it chase ESG scores. Stakeholders want to see data for their analysis, meaning a company must measure its activities and report accordingly. A company will typically report ESG data at a point in time annually, cobbled together from the previous year's worth of data as collected over several months. Unless the company has built robust data collection strategies from its systems of record, by the time the data is published, it could be 18 months old. The published result is measured and reported data, but likely stale and outdated.

Annually, CSR reports, like end-of-year financial statements, help communicate to external stakeholders since a company can't publish data in real time. In 2021, American Express published an interim ESG report between annual reports with status updates and a particular focus on DEI progress,[16] so breaking the annual reporting cycle in favor of more frequency isn't unheard of but not the norm. An interim report does have its benefits, as it may keep control of the ESG narrative at the company rather than through sources outside of its control. Still, stakeholders will continually monitor the company through the court of public opinion and news in between and then across CSR reports to try to glean progress. The measurement is the company's proof of its story, despite the surrounding noise.

And so, there is another popular ESG axiom to examine:

You can't manage what you can't measure.

There is an assumption in this axiom, which is that the data alone indicates progress. This assumption isn't always valid, however. For example, a company may lead DEI efforts with metrics on its workforce's composition. Yet, this doesn't inform whether or not the company has fostered a healthy and inclusive culture that values diverse thought, or what the outcomes associated might translate to. A data point like workforce composition informs a stakeholder about the company's makeup and changes over time. In this case, the metrics may miss the point entirely.[17]

In this way, ESG data standards, regulations, and the resulting pressure may give a company the impression that reporting data is the goal, which is forgivable considering the evolution of ESG from the perspective of comparable data for financial institutions. Indeed, stakeholders want to review this information, and compliance is critical, but a company cannot overlook the context of the data when reporting. Carrying the example forward, informing stakeholders about workforce composition without the context of issues like cultural strength, pay equity, benefits, and employee support is of little value. To return to the book analogy, this is like a story where the number of pages is listed in an online store, but there is no other information.

This issue is even more prevalent with the world's attention on carbon emissions. If a company reports a 5 percent drop in carbon emissions but sold off a division that carried those emissions, has it managed or achieved anything? The data alone is meaningless without tying the context of the activities surrounding the data movement.

The word 'managing' here is shorthand for taking action through projects and transitions informed by the data, not managing the data. In other words, your company can't manage outcomes when you aren't measuring what is happening. Changes in the data represent an opportunity for the company to insert important context and tell its story. Since ESG data has applications across materiality and impact, the interpretations of progress will vary, and stakeholders will fill in the gaps if the context is absent. Some stakeholders, like financial institutions, may want to analyze whether the company addresses its risks and opportunities over time. In contrast, others want to ensure the company and its value chain support their public commitments and look to the data to hold them accountable for progress on impact.

Rather than focus on measuring and managing the data alone, companies should manage the ESG processes within the business and its value chain to drive outcomes and progress. This effort may not help investors uncover comparable data, but it will help the company improve and innovate over the long term, providing ongoing context to stakeholders over time. The company will also be better prepared as new crises and trends emerge and build resilience towards the future, which would serve all stakeholders.

ESG data can deliver value

ESG data has many uses when communicated externally with the appropriate context, but one data axiom explains its power concerning stakeholders.

ESG data is the proof of your story.

Indeed, this is true. For example, if a company commits to reducing emissions by a certain percentage through a particular year, the story of its progress, or how it manages the issue, will be backed by the data it reports. While the company can reap value in this communication to stakeholders, the power of the data is somewhat limited as data reported for disclosures

FIGURE 2.1   The path of leveraging ESG data for disclosures only

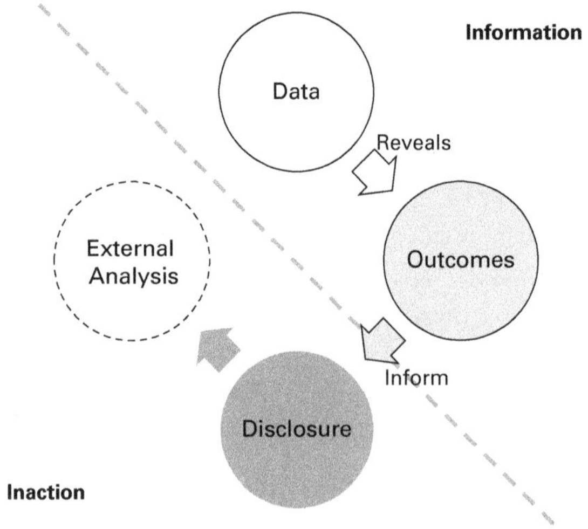

and external analysis quickly ends its useful life. The World Economic Forum (WEF) put it this way in a 2021 article, "Reporting, ultimately, should be a by-product of an ESG program where real-time data is integrated into decision making on a continuous, ongoing basis."[18] Figure 2.1 is a visual representation of the linear path of data reporting.

As data is collected and analyzed, it can reveal outcomes to pursue. For example, measuring emissions and understanding what business units generate them can result in a potential outcome; in many cases, a reduction goal. The company will pursue those outcomes and use the data to inform its disclosures and outcomes, then report. At this point, two things may happen. A stakeholder group may interpret the data and make a decision. If that happens, the data has reached the end of its useful life. The other path is where a stakeholder combines the reported data with other datasets, analyzes the results, and transforms the data for other uses. Someone may make decisions on the transformed data at this point, but the data is now out of the company's control, and the result is the same as the useful life of the data ends.

It is worth noting that if a company follows the disclosure process alone, the outcomes it chooses to follow may be based on standards and frameworks and not material issues. This situation may lead the company to report irrelevant data, which external stakeholders will use regardless to make decisions. Being mindful of the data reported and the company's motivations to disclose or not are important considerations.

Everyone loves a story, and for companies looking to tell their stories around ESG, data that improves through outcomes is a compelling narrative because there is an assumption of activities underneath. Along the path of disclosures, companies may struggle to spin up meaningful activities that lead to improvements and innovations around ESG issues as they attempt to lead ESG efforts with increasingly accurate measurements, not strategy. By leveraging data to inform strategy, however, data jumps off the disclosure path, becomes cyclical, and feeds progress in a cycle. With this approach, ESG data takes on new power and meaning, driving a resilient and sustainable business model.

This option extends the useful life of ESG data for the company's purposes. As before, ESG data is collected and reveals outcomes to pursue. The management team uses the data and its potential outcomes to inform strategy. The strategy is executed by business units and individual contributors, which creates activities that generate new data for review. The company can uncover new outcomes to pursue, or possibly adjust the strategy as new data comes in. In this cycle, reporting isn't cast out; it's removed from the diagram to focus on renewing company value. Data can and should still be collected and reported to stakeholders, as illustrated in Figure 2.1.

Consider scaling this concept by adding external and value chain data. As these datasets come into the company, the company can layer on new

FIGURE 2.2 The cycle of leveraging ESG data to inform strategy and activities

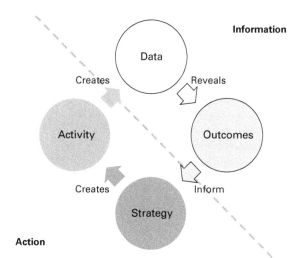

analysis, as external stakeholder groups will. These datasets also change over time and integrate into the cycle as they refresh, revealing new outcomes and allowing for adjustments to the strategy, as in Figure 2.2.

Indeed, ESG is data in many ways, but there are too many false equivalencies to state it simply. A company might think the 'data' in that short axiom refers to the company's disclosures or ESG scores because of unproductive pressures. ESG data is material information for stakeholders, which, if omitted, would have caused them to make a different decision, regardless of its materiality or impact context.

To effectively get the most value out of ESG data, companies must give it the same level of attention as financial information. Its collection should be prioritized, not solely in the pursuit of disclosures and compliance, but because analysis of its outcomes, how it can inform strategies, and its inspiration of meaningful activities drive long-term value for the company. In this cycle, ESG data becomes a valuable and renewable resource that can drive capital, stakeholder sentiment, and business strategy. As a company claims ESG for its purpose in this manner, a more suitable axiom might be:

ESG data can deliver renewable value.

Notes

1   Sorkin, A.R., Mattu, R., Warner, B., Kessler, S., Merced, M.J. de la, Hirsch, L., and Livni, E. (2023). Why some executives wish E.S.G. "just goes away". *The New York Times*. January 19. www.nytimes.com/2023/01/19/business/dealbook/esg-business-davos.html (archived at https://perma.cc/9GB2-83SC).

2   Runyon, N. (2023). Increase in regulatory reporting across jurisdictions drives demand for ESG controller role. Thomson Reuters Institute. www.thomsonreuters.com/en-us/posts/esg/controller-role/ (archived at https://perma.cc/Z77N-UCGA).

3   Nouguès, X., Rochet, T., Scharlach, A., Swette, K., Grunwalk-Henrich, T., and Devant, L.-H. (2022). Procurement's journey to sustainability: First signs of systemic change? Oliver Wyman, p. 4. www.oliverwyman.com/content/dam/oliver-wyman/v2/publications/2022/sept/Oliver_Wyman_Procurement%27s_Journey_To_Sustainabilty_final.pdf (archived at https://perma.cc/6ZL7-W6ZK).

4   World Business Council for Sustainable Development (WBCSD) (2004). *The GHG Protocol: A corporate reporting and accounting standard (revised edition)*. World Business Council for Sustainable Development. www.wbcsd.org/Programs/Climate-and-Energy/Climate/Resources/A-corporate-reporting-and-accounting-standard-revised-edition (archived at https://perma.cc/8TRX-89EW).

5 Ritchie, H., Roser, M., and Rosado, P. (2020). Emissions by sector. Our World in Data. ourworldindata.org/emissions-by-sector#agriculture-forestry-and-land-use-18-4 (archived at https://perma.cc/YXU5-59E5).

6 World Business Council for Sustainable Development (WBCSD) and World Resources Institute (2004). *The Greenhouse Gas Protocol*. World Business Council for Sustainable Development, p. 31. www.wbcsd.org/contentwbc/download/2670/33469/1 (archived at https://perma.cc/WCV2-PRSL).

7 Nvidia (2023). *Nvidia Corporate Responsibility Report Fiscal Year 2023*. Nvidia, p. 27. images.Nvidia.com/aem-dam/Solutions/documents/FY2023-Nvidia-Corporate-Responsibility-Report-1.pdf (archived at https://perma.cc/5ZUX-QMG6).

8 Nvidia (2023). *Nvidia Corporate Responsibility Report Fiscal Year 2023*. Nvidia, p. 29. images.Nvidia.com/aem-dam/Solutions/documents/FY2023-Nvidia-Corporate-Responsibility-Report-1.pdf (archived at https://perma.cc/5ZUX-QMG6).

9 Responsible Business Alliance (2004). Responsible Business Alliance Code of Conduct v7.0. Responsible Business Alliance, p. 1. www.responsiblebusiness.org/media/docs/RBACodeofConduct7.0_English.pdf (archived at https://perma.cc/7EQR-EY87).

10 Impact Management Project, World Economic Forum and Deloitte (2020). *Statement of Intent to Work Together Towards Comprehensive Corporate Reporting: Summary of alignment discussions among leading sustainability and integrated reporting organisations CDP, CDSB, GRI, IIRC and SASB*. SASB Standards. sasb.org/wp-content/uploads/2023/01/Statement-of-Intent-to-Work-Together-Towards-Comprehensive-Corporate-Reporting.pdf (archived at https://perma.cc/DC5E-TSX2).

11 Medress, A. (2020). Answering your questions about the Value Reporting Foundation. SASB Standards. sasb.org/blog/answering-your-questions-about-the-value-reporting-foundation/ (archived at https://perma.cc/594E-5XJA).

12 IFRS (2021). IFRS Foundation announces International Sustainability Standards Board, consolidation with CDSB and VRF, and publication of prototype disclosure requirements. IFRS. www.ifrs.org/news-and-events/news/2021/11/ifrs-foundation-announces-issb-consolidation-with-cdsb-vrf-publication-of-prototypes/ (archived at https://perma.cc/BQ8D-M38D).

13 IFRS (2023). IFRS Foundation welcomes culmination of TCFD work and transfer of TCFD monitoring responsibilities to ISSB from 2024. IFRS. www.ifrs.org/news-and-events/news/2023/07/foundation-welcomes-tcfd-responsibilities-from-2024/ (archived at https://perma.cc/4END-828U).

14 Vanderford, R. (2023). SEC's climate-disclosure rule isn't here, but it may as well be, many businesses say. *The Wall Street Journal*, April 25. www.wsj.com/articles/ secs-climate-disclosure-rule-isnt-here-but-it-may-as-well-be-many-businesses-say-854789bd?mod=Searchresults_pos1&page=1 (archived at https://perma.cc/ Q3KD-MQ5Q).

15 Cherel-Bonnemaison, C., Erlandsson, G., Ibach, B., and Spiller, P. (2021). Achieving sustainable procurement. McKinsey. www.mckinsey.com/ capabilities/operations/our-insights/buying-into-a-more-sustainable-value-chain (archived at https://perma.cc/M235-P3TL).

16 American Express (2021). American Express releases *2021 Interim ESG Update Diversity Equity and Inclusion Progress Report*. American Express. https://about.americanexpress.com/newsroom/press-releases/news-details/2021/ American-Express-Releases-2021-Interim-ESG-Update-Diversity-Equity-and-Inclusion-Progress-Report-05-24-2021/default.aspx (archived at https://perma. cc/773R-LRFC)

17 Edmans, A., Flemmer, C., and Glossner, S. (2023). The value of diversity, equity, and inclusion. CEPR. cepr.org/voxeu/columns/value-diversity-equity-and-inclusion (archived at https://perma.cc/QGZ9-X4WB).

18 DiGuiseppe, M. (2021). The No. 1 ESG challenge organizations face: Data. World Economic Forum. www.weforum.org/agenda/2021/10/no-1-esg-challenge-data-environmental-social-governance-reporting/ (archived at https:// perma.cc/Q5JW-RUQG).

03

Saving Your Company and Saving the Planet

When it comes to ESG, many reduce it down to simply the first pillar, the Environment. Of course, coming first has advantages as it garners tremendous attention. Still, that attention is as complicated as the breadth of stakeholder pressures forcing companies to address a myriad of issues and report volumes of data for what is material today and what might be material in the future.

Many companies have reported on their Environmental impact via CSR reports against various standards for years. In fact, by 2022, 96 percent of the S&P 500 and 81 percent of the Russell 1000 were publishing sustainability reports.[1] Still, much of the focus in recent years has been moving towards reporting accurate carbon emissions due to intense global regulations and cries from stakeholders for quality information, and with good reason. Between 1970 and 2004, global greenhouse gas (GHG) emissions rose 70 percent, trapping more heat around our planet and increasing global warming.[2] Emissions contributing to this problem occur throughout a company's activities and value chain, from raw material sourcing to manufacturing, processing, and delivery to the customer. In addition, if the company's product or solution needs electricity and the final user discards it, there are emissions throughout its life to its disposition.

One could argue that the Environment is the most critical ESG matter companies could pay attention to, which is why it is first. All of us are affected by climate change. This very pressing issue has the potential to disrupt, not only through short-term extreme weather events but over the long term, across unpredictable systemic planetary changes. But conversely, it also dictates nearly every aspect of modern business operations, whether recognized or not. For example, climate change's effects are far-reaching across stakeholders' physical health and safety, the ability to transport goods and services safely and quickly—a critical factor in productive agriculture—and so much more. Moreover, as the Environment changes, companies must be ready to adapt to growing challenges.

Still, not all stakeholders understand or care that companies must adapt to material risks to drive the needed change. Activists, including activist shareholders, are pressuring companies to improve their sustainability standing against the overwhelming evidence of climate change.[3] Many want companies to deal with the transition to green energy and lower operational and value chain carbon emissions. This desire represents the right thing to do for companies and can fall under the category of "doing well by doing good," but it isn't necessarily ESG as it may not be material and drive long-term value.

Achieving a win-win isn't always possible, especially with the complexities within the Environmental pillar and across ESG. External Environmental improvements can be challenging to manage as change is a delicate balancing act between non-material improvements and material risks and opportunities. While company leaders must carefully weigh these Environmental issues, they cannot ignore the transition and climate risks that will impact them in the short and long term.

Climate change, sustainability, and ESG

Addressing climate change, moving operations towards sustainable options, and ESG have all become conflated over the past few years. So, let's be clear on their meanings.

- Climate change is often used as a catch-all term for various systemic planetary changes, but refers to the long-term changes in temperature or weather patterns, locally or globally.

- Sustainability means the responsible management of natural resources to maintain Environmental equity, as often used regarding business operations.

- ESG refers to the material Environmental, Social, and Governance risks that affect a company and opportunities that drive towards long-term value and sustainable growth.

If we revisit 2004's *Who Cares Wins* UN paper, the authors note how they omitted words like "sustainability" and "corporate citizenship" in the discussion of ESG to avoid misunderstanding.[4] Even 20 years ago, they saw the potential for confusion as CSR reports proliferated. Yet, the confusion between all these terms happens today, and it is easy to see why. These terms are closely related, and many issues center around their interconnected nature. In addition, a fine line exists between saving the world and your company. That line is fuzzy and can be picked up and moved around, depending on who you are talking to, their perspective, and their priorities. Only through context and clear communication can intent be discerned, and even then, things don't always fit into one bucket, nor do they need to. What we call things is less important than our intent, approach, and outcomes.

Let's consider what is becoming a typical example. Activists often bring shareholder proposals before banks, asking them to stop funding fossil fuels.[5] In deconstructing this example, we can see how it could align with all three terms.

First, every company on the planet intersects with climate change through its operations or value chain. There is some Environmental impact, whether energy usage, component manufacturing, technology use, logistics, business travel, or something else. There are specific sectors, like energy and fossil fuels, where the impact is difficult to abate. When the thing you burn to drive your value proposition creates emissions, the model immediately runs afoul of climate change. Emissions trap heat, heat warms the planet, and the climate changes as a result. By shifting funding away from fossil fuel companies, activists hope to influence banks to redirect capital away from new and existing fossil fuel projects and influence a transition to cleaner energy sources. The ultimate goal is to transition away from fossil fuels and eliminate their emissions entirely to mitigate climate change.

Second, companies are attempting to drive sustainability through operational changes for a similar reason. Since fossil fuels impact much of a company's Scope 1 and 2 emissions, some companies are trying to transition to renewables, like wind and solar, for energy usage in their commercial facilities and factories. Companies negotiate long-term contracts with utilities to source renewable energy through green power purchase agreements (PPAs) and renewable energy credits (REC) in this effort. Green PPAs allow companies to purchase long-term contracts for certified renewable energy at a predictable rate. In addition, companies may decide to purchase RECs, which certify that an energy company produced renewable energy and added it to the grid somewhere. Companies can use these options in addition to outright switching to renewable energy sources to shift to sustainability. As renewable energy becomes available on the grid, companies are also turning to electrification at their facilities in the hopes of greener energy to drive even more sustainability improvements. The more the company can electrify while purchasing renewable energy, the less fuel it will need to burn directly or in its value chain, lowering its emissions. Of course, companies are also modernizing their operations to drive more efficiency, resulting in emissions reductions. They may look to the banks to finance these projects, which activist investors would likely be in favor of.

Third, the fossil fuel business model must transition and diversify its portfolio, pursue other low emissions options, and explore carbon capture as the world attempts to lower emissions due to the first issue, climate change, and as companies pressure energy suppliers to shift to renewables to improve sustainability. Investors focused on long-term risk management will assess how energy companies are or are not planning for this shift and how they align with activist pressure, depending on the investment goal, saving the planet or the company. This stakeholder risk management and the opportunity around transitioning business models is ESG, even though it appears to align more with sustainability.

As you can see, we've come full circle across the three terms as they flow in and out of each other, centered on a basic example. Still, two more specific risks are worth exploring to build on the ESG perspective: transition and climate risks.

Transition risk

As companies delay progress towards transitioning to low-carbon operations, the emissions impact on climate change increases over time. Thus, a potential future state exists where companies are disrupted quickly under even more urgent pressures to transition, and they will have to react. For companies, this represents a risk they must manage. Transition risks regarding the Environment represent several specific types. The Task Force on

Climate-related Financial Disclosures (TCFD) released four types of transition risks that companies should consider:[6]

- Policy and legal risks: Several new regulatory pressures have emerged over the past few years as governments look to address the changing Environment. New litigation pressures are also emerging around the Environment, targeting industries that are significant emissions contributors.

- Technology risks: Adopting new low-carbon or efficient technologies represents a risk. There typically would be transition costs, including capital expenses, implementation, research and development, and training costs associated with the new technology. However, it's worth noting that inaction can also be a risk.

- Market risks: Investors and Procurement teams may prioritize suppliers with better Environmental data. Similarly, consumers have increasingly paid closer attention to the Environmental credentials of brands and products.[7]

- Reputational risks: A company's mismanagement of Environmental issues and the other risks can lead to reputational issues.

The company must examine all transition risks as many will intersect with stakeholders in various ways, may result in fines and fees, and can impact revenue and the brand. Some overlooked starting points are to plan how the company will transition to a low-carbon economy and address the company's most material Environmental risks.

Per McKinsey, the funding needed to support the global decarbonization transition is $225 trillion through 2050, or approximately $9.2 trillion annually.[8] If a company were interested in its transition risks and building on its collected operational data, it would focus on disclosures as a compliance exercise and ask itself what part of that cost it needs to take on across itself and its value chain. From there, it needs to further consider its Environmental impact in other material areas and the costs to mitigate those risks. For example, a logistics company might need to report emissions across its operations to stay compliant with emerging transportation policies. Still, transitioning to a fleet with renewable energy might entice its B2B clients to use them over a competitor. The former here is a Governance risk that comes through in data and disclosures, while the latter is an Environmental opportunity to differentiate.

And so, there's quite a bit of consideration and nuance to considering these risks. Companies must not let the compliance exercises, typically a leading focus, hinder progress around transition risk and must consider the broader pillars to make informed decisions. So, let's investigate these risks more closely.

Policy and legal risks

Governments are creating new incentives and prioritizing the systemic shift to renewables, adding transferable pressure from corporates to energy companies.[9] Global regulators and standards bodies released three major climate draft proposals in 2021, including the EU Commission's Corporate Sustainability Reporting Directive (CSRD), the SEC's climate rule proposal, and the International Sustainability Standards Board's (ISSB) creation. As a reminder from the last chapter, CSRD focuses on broad ESG metrics, the SEC's climate ruling and the ISSB proposal focus more on the Environment and reporting sustainability metrics around emissions and climate risk on the balance sheet.

However, new Environmental disclosures are not the beginning or the end of what companies need to report and manage. For example, companies must also manage Environmental, Health, and Safety (EHS) regulations. These long-standing regulations are typically more familiar and integrated into existing operations. Workers, an important stakeholder group, are at risk if not adequately protected, and fines may result. In addition, governments have enacted other policies around operational management and processes. For example, several countries have banned plastic bags due to their contribution to global waste.[10]

Separately, there has also been a rise in litigation against energy companies concerning their impact on climate change globally. For example, a small town in Peru is suing Germany's RWE for its contribution to climate change affecting local glacial flooding.[11] The premise is that if a company contributes a certain percentage to climate change, the contributing company should pay that percentage of damage out from a localized climate disaster to the affected community. There has been a broader rise in litigation around climate change, with a Missouri judge siding with young activists.[12] In this case, the judge agreed that a policy that didn't require the impacts of climate change to be considered for fossil fuel permits was unconstitutional.

The Compliance team and General Counsel should be aware of new and existing regulations and emerging litigation, as these are material Governance risks and opportunities related to the Environment.

Technology risks

Driving the transition through technological advancements or new internal and value chain processes is no small undertaking and many businesses are built on stable and proven models where any minor disruption could cause significant problems. For example, transitioning an energy contract to renewables represents low operational risk around new sustainable energy technologies that are external to the company, but transforming the core materials or business processes to drive efficiencies around sustainability intersects with a material ESG risk.

USE CASE: THE LEGO GROUP AND SUSTAINABLE PLASTICS

The LEGO Group has a compelling example of managing technology-based transition risk. In 2015, The LEGO Group recognized that 75 percent of its emissions came from suppliers and that the plastic used to make its iconic bricks was oil-based, connecting the product to fossil fuels.[13] In that same report, LEGO committed to sustainable materials and packaging by 2030.

The LEGO Group has progressed by leveraging new plastics technologies through rigorous research and development. In 2018, it announced a new sustainably sourced polyethylene plastic based on sugar cane, which accounts for about 1–2 percent of elements.[14] In 2021, LEGO announced progress on a prototype brick made from recycled PET (rPET) plastics from water bottles, acknowledging the need to keep it as strong and durable as its previous bricks.[15] Unfortunately, rPET plastics have proven to be difficult, causing the company to pivot to other strategies like other investments, integrating circular principles, and extending the lifecycle of play.[16]

This close attention to detail is vital for new sustainable bricks, which need to interlock with traditional PET plastic bricks from earlier years.

Market risks

For companies that directly cater to consumer stakeholders, such as retail and consumer product goods, sustainability credentials have widely been touted as a competitive differentiator to capture market segments and stakeholder preferences. For example, in 2022, the IRI and NYU Stern Center for Sustainable Business released a study stating that 77 percent of consumers consider sustainability when purchasing.[17] This sentiment is a market risk if ignored but remains an ESG opportunity to capture. Yet, there is work to do to capture the opportunity. Per a BCG study, the vast majority of consumers were concerned about the Environment, confused about their role in supporting it, and disillusioned by what companies do about it.[18]

This consumer sentiment isn't stopping companies from trying new things, however. Target, a retail chain, provides an example of how a company might address these challenges and create market opportunity. Target has launched an effort focused on waste, a sustainability credential that plagues consumer product goods. Through Target Zero online and in stores with signage, consumers can find curated products with a low waste footprint if that aligns with their preferences.[19]

Reputational risks

Reputational risk isn't a direct risk to manage per se. However, as we've seen in the examples discussed here, a company needs to consider its attention to transitional shifts in regulatory pressures, technological advancement, and stakeholder preference around the Environment. In other words, even though TCFD identifies reputational risks, transition risks intersect across ESG. Managing these risks also happens through quality Governance principles.

Fossil fuel companies, construction, and airlines have high transition risks since their core business model contributes significantly to climate change and is difficult to pivot around. In addition, there may be resulting reputational risks due to their contributions to the overall climate crisis. For these companies, a range of attentions to transition risk can help manage their reputations. For example, politicians, celebrities, and CEOs have come under fire recently for the Environmental cost of private jets.[20] More sustainable travel would result in less reputational damage.

Of course, something as foundational as these four transition risks around complying with regulation, innovating with new technologies, and improving business models around stakeholders requires the entire company's attention from roles like General Counsel, Operations, Research and Development, Sales, Marketing, and more. A Chief Sustainability Officer can bring expertise to these risks, but sweeping changes should not be up to that one role, as it lacks the unique knowledge of other business areas.

Climate risk

Climate risk can be a challenging topic for companies to address. Even if the world's companies cut emissions tomorrow, we would still be dealing with the effects of climate change for a while as carbon, methane, and other GHGs take time to break down.[21] As a result, billions of dollars have been poured into carbon removal technologies, but they remain very nascent and not often on a commercial scale.[22] As reductions progress and new technologies emerge, companies must attend to climate risk to build long-term resilience. For example, suppose a company doesn't assess its climate risk as a material issue and only focuses on emissions due to policy risks. In that case, it may experience severe internal or value chain disruptions, be subject to high commercial insurance rates, and either constantly react to extreme weather events or not survive long enough to drive the necessary sustainability improvements.

If we look back to TCFD again, there is guidance on how companies should think about climate risk across two areas: acute and chronic.[23] Both represent ESG risks that companies must consider in long-term planning in a broader risk management strategy.

As we've covered, sustainability initiatives contribute to long-term emissions reductions and perhaps other Environmental systems like water, ocean waste, and biodiversity as part of transition risk. However, focusing on climate risk means the company understands its transient and long-term challenges around climate change and constructs adaptation plans accordingly.

Acute climate risk

Acute climate risk represents the transient extreme weather events resulting from climate change, which have accelerated in intensity and duration over the past few decades. For example, in 2022, the planet experienced

42 billion-dollar weather events, including heat waves, droughts, flooding, hurricanes, monsoons, and wildfires. These catastrophes and disasters caused $360 billion in damages, and led to thousands of deaths.[24]

The severe climate crisis that we are in cannot be overstated. Over the past decade, we've seen growing threats of extreme weather catastrophes in the Global North, drawing attention to what the Global South has long known about our changing world. We've wrought havoc on sensitive planetary systems, and the effects are mounting. For companies, these extreme weather events represent property and liability risks at the surface level. But, at a deeper level, each event can increase a company's cost of resources and insurance and disrupt a company's operations, logistics, and supplies across the value chain. The results can be far-reaching, from financial impacts, delayed deliveries, new value chain pressure, reputational damage, and open windows for competitors to exploit. With how connected the business world is, it is not surprising that acute climate risks impact 70 percent of business sectors globally.[25]

Like many ESG issues, the weather gets more attention when it causes problems instead of when it is stable and provides value. The damage it can cause can vary depending on the location and geography where the company and its value chain operate. As extreme weather risk grows, what had been once-in-a-lifetime events are now more frequent and highly unpredictable.

USE CASE: THAILAND FLOODING AND HARD DRIVES

Flooding and monsoons regularly occur in Thailand, but climate change has aggravated the effects.[26] In 2011, a confluence of issues in Thailand, including urbanization near rivers, severe weather events, and flood mismanagement, led to one of the worst and costliest global floods ever.[27] This event continued for months, impacting several hard drive companies and their manufacturing ability. Ripple effects spread throughout the computer industry as hard drives were unavailable for PCs.[28] Western Digital manufactured 60 percent of its hard drives in Thailand then, but the flooding closed 14,000 factories across the industry and put 660,000 people out of work, a significant Social issue.[29]

Western Digital recovered quickly, rolling out the first hard drive after the event in 46 days, but getting to that point required divers to recover equipment underwater and a hefty Investment.[30] Since then, the company has adapted to the local Environmental risk by building 3-meter-high walls and moving essential equipment to higher floors.[31]

Chronic climate risk

While acute climate risk focuses on catastrophes and disasters, chronic climate risk represents the cumulative effects of long-term climate changes on the Environment. For example, a multi-year drought or sustained rising sea levels can change local conditions to new normals. This type of risk can force a company to invest significantly in costly adaptation efforts to remain in an area or may cause a company and its suppliers to have no choice but to move. Either way, there are impacts on employee stakeholders at the intersection of the Social here as these decisions can impact employment and community revenue.

The criticality of these long-term effects can range considerably. There might be localized systemic adjustments through to global systemic changes. For example, a local region might experience an invasive plant or insect species due to increased sustained heat, wreaking havoc on local ecosystems and agriculture. There can be a significant cost to agriculture as pests already cause around 40 percent of global crop production losses.[32]

Turning to global systemic pressures, scientists have been using the term 'tipping points' for the past 20 years to refer to certain thresholds that might impact these long-term effects on a global scale, including those that could create cascading impacts across the planet.[33] The tipping points are of particular trouble as they are interconnected. For example, thawing permafrost contains twice as much carbon as in the atmosphere.[34] As it melts, it will release carbon into the atmosphere and cause global temperatures to rise further.

Companies face a significant challenge regarding assessing chronic climate risks via current assessment methodologies. In a paper published in Nature,[35] the authors argue three points about these limitations:

1 The Scope of the work does not consider systemic risks. There might even be compounding risks, such as the permafrost example, which can be difficult to uncover or predict.

2 The Data does not use bottom-up, local information. Instead, many models use a global view with satellite imagery without localized sensors to obtain granular data.

3 There is little Transparency in the models and assessment methodologies. In addition, the commoditization of climate risk models can hinder collective understanding.

Companies, boards, and executives do not need to become climate risk experts but should ask thoughtful questions about the materiality of climate risk and seek external expertise. Several teams, including Operations, Real Estate, Facilities, and Procurement, should understand climate risk to create and execute adaptation plans.

Should the "E" be split out?

Between this nuance, complexity, and the urgent climate crisis, some believe that the Environment should be split out from the ESG acronym. Indeed, there is a decent case that activists and Environmental scientists make for companies and governments to focus on this one pillar and transition to a low-carbon economy with speed. This issue is also top of mind globally in most major markets. Per a Pew Research poll from 2022 across 19 countries in North America, Europe, and the Asia-Pacific region, about 75 percent of respondents believe climate change is a major threat.[36] Still, splitting out the Environment doesn't make sense when examining the relationship of this issue to the other pillars. Even at the most superficial level, there is a selfish Social objective with climate change and sustainability. We need to save the planet to save ourselves.

For example, if we build on the Social perspective around the fossil fuel transition, there are limitations to how quickly emerging markets can transition to clean energy. The energy needs of emerging countries may be growing faster than they can deploy renewables, even with adequate funding from banks and government incentives. As a result, the transition may be out of reach even if the costs are cheaper for alternate energy sources over the long run.[37] So, is it fair to ask fossil fuel companies and governments to pause emerging market development based on emissions? That energy might power a school, hospital, or economic engine, driving social services and wealth into the community. Impacted governments understand this challenge and the balance that they must strike. Along these lines, at COP26, the delegates changed the final language of the Glasgow Climate Pact from the "phase-out" of coal to the "phase-down", with coal-dependent India leading the opposition and support from China.[38]

If we ask those in emerging markets, who are often the most impacted by climate change, to slow development and add new risks, have we saved anything or anyone? While continued reliance on fossil fuels is a blow to global emissions contribution and sustainability efforts, it is still a win for those people because localized progress, especially around Social programs and services, can continue. But, of course, there is an argument that none of us will win in the end as a result.

There is another intersection between the Environment and Social for companies and governments to consider with emerging markets. The expression "loss and damage" refers to the human-based effects of climate change. Marginalized communities in developing countries often lack the resources to adapt to extreme weather risks and recover effectively.[39] Addressing this challenge includes financial compensation to those most impacted by climate change, mainly in the developing world. At COP15 in 2009, delegates committed to $100 billion for loss and damage, but this fund has not delivered the total amount, primarily due to a lack of investment from the USA, Canada, Australia, and the UK.[40] In the new wave of extreme climate risk, delegates made progress in 2023 at COP28 and created a new loss-and-damage fund to address this challenge.

Developed countries must ask the same nuanced questions and consider multiple angles around the timing of the adoption of renewable energy at the intersection of the Social and risk. For example, Germany and other EU countries, dependent on oil from Russia, are accelerating their renewable transition due to the war in Ukraine.[41] This move comes at a potentially difficult time for Germany as the country has also turned off the last of its nuclear plants.[42] While acceleration to renewables looks promising, governments must balance natural resources against citizens' energy requirements.

In addition to Social intersections, there are also connections to Governance. Over the past 50 years, the global energy demand has grown 3.8 times, and renewables have doubled, yet fossil fuels are still 75 percent of global energy usage.[43] Moreover, renewable energy use is increasing, but far too slowly. New sustainability and ESG pressures may change that, however. Companies are making decisions about electricity purchasing, building management systems, and logistics around stakeholder pressure to transition to lower emissions. This modernization represents a Governance opportunity for many building and real estate managers.

How fossil fuel companies, refineries, and pipeline companies react to these same pressures is also a Governance issue for them. For example, Exxon wants to continue its fossil fuel development, work on renewables, and drive towards carbon capture as a leading strategy due to the predicted

$4 trillion opportunity.[44] Chevron is also looking at carbon removals, reductions, and investing in renewables.[45] Energy companies can gain a competitive advantage by recognizing stakeholder pressures and planning around transition risks with a strategic approach through quality Governance.

In 2023, both Exxon and Chevron announced major new acquisitions of fossil fuel companies.[46] From a sustainability perspective, this flies in the face of a responsible transition, but it might be a quality Governance decision if the companies believe that fossil fuels are a long-term business play. The International Energy Agency (IEA), an organization focused on energy security and the clean energy transition, believes that there is sufficient momentum behind clean energy now and that fossil fuel usage may peak before 2030.[47] However, it also recognizes that the investment in fossil fuels must remain to help ease the transition.[48]

Whether an energy company or not, a company's plans around the Environment come from Governance principles, executive leadership, and collective company-wide execution in concert with external stakeholders like customers and governments. These plans are strategic bets on how best these companies can address the long-term changes around the business and related ESG issues. In the future, when investors and regulators look back at these strategies, stakeholders will assess the quality of Governance in the context of the results.

Looking at any singular ESG issue in the context of its impact across the other pillars helps drive a more informed approach. As a result, the Environment cannot be split out from the Social and the Governance as it brings additional context, nuance, and strategic planning that may go overlooked otherwise.

Disclosures and necessary but problematic

One area where a singular focus on the Environment manifests is in disclosures. Details about ESG come through in typically non-reported financial data across activities in digital systems not built to support this type of reporting and certainly not built for this analysis. Nevertheless, the mix of climate change, sustainability, and ESG and their relation to emissions specifically has flooded into corporate attention and spawned a new generation of sustainability accountants. This attention to emissions and its accounting stems from pressure from investors for comparable data and Procurement teams seeking information against the varied disclosures and standards, but ultimately in pursuit of understanding the company's impact.

Investors want this data to support decision-making if their investment thesis focuses on climate change and sustainability. Banks also seek to prioritize lending to transitional projects that drive sustainability objectives to meet their internal commitments to these challenges. Therefore, quality and comparable information between investments and borrowers are required to make informed decisions, which helps manage the firm's Scope 3, Category 15 emissions. This part of the GHG Protocol focuses on financed emissions. Per Bain Capital, financed emissions can make up to 95 percent of a bank's overall emissions.[49] Therefore, if a financial services firm makes a sustainability commitment around emissions reductions, it may have to manage this metric accordingly.

Procurement teams have also integrated sustainability into RFPs and supplier policies to manage the company's Scope 3 emissions against sustainability commitments. Many teams lead with emissions reduction through a mix of engagement and reporting models, like those discussed in the previous chapter. Scope 3 emissions in the value chain usually account for over 70 percent of a company's total emissions.[50]

Across the financial services and procurement use cases, understanding the value chain's emissions is mostly an exercise in managing the company's sustainability footprint through its relationship with other companies. While every company needs to do its part to manage its impact on climate change, this emissions data exercise isn't always ESG-related. Emissions and other reported sustainability metrics are not materially equal for every company and are not always material. Well, not precisely anyway, which is where an ESG mindset comes in.

When looking at one particular metric, such as emissions, the material effect on the company and impact on the world will vary, depending on the industry and the company's operations. For example, as we've seen, fossil fuel companies' emissions impact on the climate is significant, and stakeholders are well aware of it. This effect makes emissions a material matter for the company to manage against overwhelming stakeholder pressure and profoundly profitable business models.[51] On the other hand, emissions are less material for a marketing company that hosts promotional or streaming content in the cloud. Still, for the marketing company, concerns like efficient storage of digital assets and low-energy digital signage and their emissions might help manage reputational risk and avoid splashy news stories about the industry's efforts. This example could be material if the marketing company supports a client's green campaign. Here, the attestation of green credentials for their clients would also be a material Environmental issue because a misstep could impact the marketing company's ability to secure future business.

As financial services firms and other companies collect and report their emissions data, even with consistency, is the data genuinely comparable? Well, not exactly, as other metrics might be needed to uncover material risk. While the fossil fuel company might have a higher overall Environmental risk, a marketing company might have to navigate the complexities of emissions reporting on a campaign basis rather than the company's total emissions contribution. While focused on emissions, these two reporting concepts would not be similar or comparable.

Looking at the emissions reduction outside the context of the Social can add risk. For example, consider if a company contributes to a local region's economy in its supply chain. Suppose the country is in an emerging market without renewable energy. In that case, the emissions may be high. A Procurement team solely focused on the Environment might pivot to a supplier in a region with lower emissions to meet the company's sustainability commitments. If the company pulls out of that region, it could plunge the area into poverty, political uncertainty, or worse. The issue becomes even more complex if we move beyond emissions to material sustainable improvements along the TCFD's technology risk, such as component or raw material changes. At some point, value chain decisions will impact some person or group.

Diving into the data further, stakeholders looking for emissions data must also have access to more data than a single point in time. If sustainability is the goal, which appears to be the case with most emissions reporting, tracking emissions over time is critical. While companies build their disclosure processes, modernize data collection, and drive towards more accuracy year over year, not all companies are looking to sustainable operations and value chain management. According to a *Wall Street Journal* article, companies expect to spend $750,000 in the first year of the US SEC's climate disclosure rule, mainly focused on accurate Scope 3 emissions reporting.[52] Yet the cost of obtaining that accuracy doesn't include projects or engagement models that drive down emissions. To show progress on emissions, a company needs to manage operational reductions, transition to greener energy sources, and manage its suppliers.

Again, disclosures and getting comparable data shouldn't be the ultimate goals. Instead, stakeholders want to see emissions reductions and sustainability in practice to reduce the impact on climate change. Moving into material considerations is where the company can move beyond datasets and into a new mindset.

Material Environmental issues

While we've covered material transition and climate risks and examined the need for disclosures, each company has additional material Environmental issues to address that connect back to its core business operations. These issues might be unique to the company or represent systemic industry or common value chain issues best solved in partnership with competitors. In the same way that sustainability, climate change, and ESG relate, these issues may also cross into these topics, intersect across transition or climate risk, and intersect with Social and Governance. Also, remember that just as a company generates emissions across its operations and value chain, many Environmental issues intersect with the business in several ways.

Covering your company's Environmental issues through the lens of materiality can be a powerful way to show how you understand the world's effect on the company and, in some cases, its impact on the world.

USE CASE: PEPSICO AND WATER

PepsiCo is one of the world's largest providers of beverages and convenient foods, with consumers enjoying its products over one billion times daily.[53] Many consumers associate the Pepsi brand with soft drinks, but Pepsi also covers several food brands that leverage agriculture in their production.

One of PepsiCo's listed material issues is water, which is easy to understand when considering it as a beverage company.[54] Water plays a significant role in the manufacture of drinks. For example, the ratio of water to carbonated soft drinks was reported to be 1.9:1 in 2020, staying under 2:1 over three years.[55] In other words, it takes lots of water to make a carbonated soft drink, which makes water a resource that must be well managed, especially as climate change is leading to extreme weather events like droughts and flooding. PepsiCo is also a founding consortium member in the Beverage Industry Environmental Roundtable (BIER), where this information is from, alongside others like the Coca-Cola Company, AB InBev, Oceanspray, Diageo, and others.[56] This group brings together the industry in the spirit of collaboration around the sector's Environmental issues.

Consortiums like this can play an essential role in solving systemic industry challenges. For example, in partnership with PepsiCo and other members, BIER released a benchmarking study which included water, energy, and emissions along several drink categories so that the industry can effectively collaborate, drive accountability, and develop improvement strategies.[57] After all, going after systemic issues like this alone can be challenging.

PepsiCo and other BIER members have shown an understanding of several material intersections with water across products and in their public reporting and statements. For example, PepsiCo lists the importance of water to the business around three broad areas: operations and manufacturing, agriculture, and the communities in which it operates.[58] These focus areas illustrate an understanding of water's effect on the company and also represent the company's impact on water. In addition, PepsiCo has organized around several priorities concerning this material issue, including driving water efficiency, replenishment, community access to safe water, and policy advocacy.[59]

Across each of these efforts are echoes of how we started off this chapter. A company's relationship with the Environment is complex across climate change, sustainability, and ESG. These issues sometimes exist in their unique categories but often connect in nuanced and unexpected ways that surface only through thoughtful analysis. Not only do Environmental issues span across these material and non-material categories, but each connects with Social and Governance as well. After all, the company impacts the Environment, which affects people. Managing these issues must be a management team priority, with the problem and its outcomes tasked to everyone in the company.

Notes

1 Peterson, E., Arrojado, J., Power, L., Thirugnana Sambantham, K.R., Hoa Lam, G., and West, N. (n.d.). Examining 2021 trends of companies on the S&P 500® + Russell 1000®. Governance & Accountability Institute, p. 4. www.ga-institute. com/fileadmin/ga_institute/images/FlashReports/2022/G_A-2022-Sustainability_ Trends_Report.pdf (archived at https://perma.cc/HP7W-JEYS).

2 National Geographic (2022). Greenhouse Effect. National Geographic Society. education.nationalgeographic.org/resource/greenhouse-effect/ (archived at https://perma.cc/P3QM-ACB3).

3 Copley, M. (2023). Businesses face more and more pressure from investors to act on climate change. NPR. www.npr.org/2023/04/09/1168446621/businesses-face-more-and-more-pressure-from-investors-to-act-on-climate-change (archived at https://perma.cc/GHL9-CNAP).

4 United Nations (2004). *Who Cares Wins.* pp. 1–2. www.unepfi.org/fileadmin/events/2004/stocks/who_cares_wins_global_compact_2004.pdf (archived at https://perma.cc/82C3-6XBG).

5 Foster, L. (2023). Big banks hold the purse strings for fossil fuels. They're not giving them up. Barron's. www.barrons.com/articles/bank-of-america-citigroup-goldman-sachs-wells-fargo-oil-esg-5594fce3 (archived at https://perma.cc/A3TJ-Y8J6).

6 TCFD (2017). Recommendations of the Task Force on Climate-related Financial Disclosures in *Recommendations of the Task Force on Climate-related Financial Disclosures Final Report.* pp. 5–6. assets.bbhub.io/company/sites/60/2021/10/FINAL-2017-TCFD-Report.pdf (archived at https://perma.cc/TY5P-CBM4).

7 Cheung, J., Fillare, C., Gonzalez-Wertz, C., Nowak, C., Orrell, G., and Peterson, S. (2022). Balancing sustainability and profitability: How businesses can protect people, planet, and the bottom line. www.ibm.com/downloads/cas/5NGR8ZW2 (archived at https://perma.cc/6QP2-MUJC).

8 Krishnan, M., Samandari, H., Woetzel, J., Smit, S., Pinner, D., Nauclér, T., Tai, H., Farr, A., Wu, W., and Imperato, D. (2022). A net-zero economy: The impact of decarbonization. McKinsey. www.mckinsey.com/capabilities/sustainability/our-insights/the-economic-transformation-what-would-change-in-the-net-zero-transition (archived at https://perma.cc/4TUX-U3R2).

9 Carrington, D. (2021). World leaders announce plan to make green tech cheaper than alternatives. *The Guardian.* www.theguardian.com/environment/2021/nov/02/world-leaders-announce-plan-to-make-green-tech-cheaper-than-alternatives (archived at https://perma.cc/4FMR-GFNQ).

10 Masterson, V. (2020). As Canada bans bags and more, this is what's happening with single-use plastics today. World Economic Forum. www.weforum.org/agenda/2020/10/canada-bans-single-use-plastics/ (archived at https://perma.cc/E66M-3L27).

11 Elfar, A. (2022). Landmark climate change lawsuit moves forward as German judges arrive in Peru. *State of the Planet.* news.climate.columbia.edu/2022/08/04/landmark-climate-change-lawsuit-moves-forward-as-german-judges-arrive-in-peru/ (archived at https://perma.cc/B3R5-ERFM).

12 Hanson, A.B. and Brown, M. (2023). Young environmental activists prevail in first-of-its-kind climate change trial in Montana. AP News. apnews.com/article/ climate-change-youth-montana-trial-c7fdc1d8759f55f60346b31c73397db0 (archived at https://perma.cc/F4CN-A57X).

13 The LEGO Group (2015). *The LEGO Group Responsibility Report 2015.* lego.com, p. 15. www.lego.com/cdn/cs/aboutus/assets/blt8630ef4d3066bc76/ Responsibility-Report-2015.pdf (archived at https://perma.cc/GRK6-LKD8).

14 The LEGO Group (2018). First sustainable LEGO® bricks will be launched in 2018. lego.com. www.lego.com/en-us/aboutus/news/2019/october/lego-plants-made-from-plants (archived at https://perma.cc/M8JM-78ND).

15 The LEGO Group (2021). The LEGO Group reveals first prototype LEGO® brick made from recycled plastic. lego.com. www.lego.com/en-us/aboutus/ news/2021/june/prototype-lego-brick-recycled-plastic (archived at https:// perma.cc/XF29-2XYJ).

16 Vasil, A. (2023). Lego says it hit a recycled plastic stumbling block. Do its claims stack up? Corporate Knights. www.corporateknights.com/category-circular-economy/lego-recycled-plastic-stumbling-block/ (archived at https:// perma.cc/Y8KH-YBLH).

17 IRI and NYU Stern (2021). *Sustainability and the Consumer.* IRI Publications. Iriworldwide.com, p. 3. www.iriworldwide.com/IRI/media/Library/IRI-NYU-Sustainability-2022-PDF.pdf (archived at https://perma.cc/S255-Q8AM).

18 Sanghi, K., Bharadwaj, A., Taylor, L., Turquier, L., and Zaveri, I. (2022). Consumers are the key to taking green mainstream. BCG Global. www.bcg. com/publications/2022/consumers-are-the-key-to-taking-sustainable-products-mainstream (archived at https://perma.cc/L63Y-T3YZ).

19 Target Brands, Inc. (2022). Target announces Target Zero: A new, curated collection of products aiming to replace single-use packaging. corporate.target. com. corporate.target.com/press/release/2022/03/target-announces-target-zero-a-new-curated-collect (archived at https://perma.cc/632K-8X86).

20 Saner, E. (2023). Flying shame: The scandalous rise of private jets. *The Guardian*, January 26. www.theguardian.com/environment/2023/jan/26/ flying-shame-the-scandalous-rise-of-private-jets (archived at https://perma. cc/5HPN-G7TF).

21 Hersher, R. (2021). Carbon emissions could plummet. The atmosphere will lag behind. NPR.org, April 21. www.npr.org/2021/04/14/981333730/carbon-emissions-could-plummet-the-atmosphere-will-lag-behind (archived at https:// perma.cc/AA9U-MN7H).

22 Ramkumar, A. and Ballard, E. (2022). Carbon-removal industry draws billions to fight climate change. *The Wall Street Journal*, June 8. www.wsj.com/articles/ carbon-removal-industry-draws-billions-to-fight-climate-change-11654640329 (archived at https://perma.cc/JVV2-DF4A).

23 TCFD (2017). Recommendations of the Task Force on Climate-related Financial Disclosures in *Recommendations of the Task Force on Climate-related Financial Disclosures Final Report*. pp. 6. assets.bbhub.io/company/sites/60/2021/10/FINAL-2017-TCFD-Report.pdf (archived at https://perma.cc/TY5P-CBM4).

24 Masters, J. (2023). Dozens of billion-dollar weather disasters hit Earth in 2022. Yale Climate Connections. yaleclimateconnections.org/2023/01/dozens-of-billion-dollar-weather-disasters-hit-earth-in-2022/ (archived at https://perma.cc/G8EW-VFL7).

25 Brusset, X. and Bertrand, J. (2018a). Hedging weather risk and coordinating supply chains. *Journal of Operations Management*, 64, p. 9. https://doi.org/10.1016/j.jom.2018.10.002 (archived at https://perma.cc/BS9X-FC9G).

26 Sousounis, Dr. P. (2012). The 2011 Thai floods: Changing the perception of risk in Thailand. Verisk. www.air-worldwide.com/Publications/AIR-Currents/2012/The-2011-Thai-Floods--Changing-the-Perception-of-Risk-in-Thailand/ (archived at https://perma.cc/BP9Y-QJVN).

27 Bevere, L. and Dhore, K. (2021). The world's costliest flood: The 2011 Thailand flood, 10 years on. Swiss Re Institute. www.swissre.com/institute/research/sigma-research/Economic-Insights/the-costliest-flood-thailand-flood.html (archived at https://perma.cc/9ANP-NPUR).

28 Randewich, N. (2011). Thai floods, hard drive shortage threaten PC sales. Reuters, October 21. www.reuters.com/article/us-thailand-floods-tech-idUSTRE79K76Z20111021 (archived at https://perma.cc/9D8N-CDHP).

29 Dignan, L. (2011). Thailand floods to lead to hard drive shortages for months. ZDNet. www.zdnet.com/article/thailand-floods-to-lead-to-hard-drive-shortages-for-months/ (archived at https://perma.cc/F4TF-Q3JV).

30 Romero, J.J. (2012). The lessons of Thailand's flood. *IEEE Spectrum*. spectrum.ieee.org/the-lessons-of-thailands-flood (archived at https://perma.cc/8Y45-H2XA).

31 Romero, J.J. (2012). The lessons of Thailand's flood. *IEEE Spectrum*. spectrum.ieee.org/the-lessons-of-thailands-flood (archived at https://perma.cc/8Y45-H2XA).

32 United Nations (2021a). Invasive pest spread another fallout from climate change, UN-backed study finds. UN News. news.un.org/en/story/2021/06/1093202 (archived at https://perma.cc/ZW2G-TDS8).

33 Lenton, T.M., Held, H., Kriegler, E., Schellnhuber, H.J., Hall, J.W., Lucht, W., and Rahmstorf, S. (2008). Tipping elements in the Earth's climate system. Proceedings of the National Academy of Sciences, 105(6), pp. 1786–1793. https://doi.org/10.1073/pnas.0705414105 (archived at https://perma.cc/B3RJ-S3P4).

34 Cho, R. (2021). How close are we to climate tipping points? *State of the Planet*. news.climate.columbia.edu/2021/11/11/how-close-are-we-to-climate-tipping-points/ (archived at https://perma.cc/NU8H-S6XH).

35 Arribas, A., Fairgrieve, R., Dhu, T., Bell, J., Cornforth, R., Gooley, G., Hilson, C.J., Luers, A., Shepherd, T.G., Street, R., and Wood, N. (2022). Climate risk assessment needs urgent improvement. *Nature*, 13(1). https://doi.org/10.1038/s41467-022-31979-w (archived at https://perma.cc/G4XQ-FCCD).

36 Poushter, J., Fagan, M., and Gubbala, S. (2022). Climate change remains top global threat across 19-country survey. Pew Research Center's Global Attitudes Project. www.pewresearch.org/global/2022/08/31/climate-change-remains-top-global-threat-across-19-country-survey/ (archived at https://perma.cc/DQD6-FGFK).

37 Tsafos, N. (2021). The battle for coal at COP26. Center for Strategic & International Studies. www.csis.org/analysis/battle-coal-cop26 (archived at https://perma.cc/2CB9-FRTE).

38 Mackey, B. and Hales, R. (2021). The ultimate guide to why the COP26 summit ended in failure and disappointment (despite a few bright spots). The Conversation. theconversation.com/the-ultimate-guide-to-why-the-cop26-summit-ended-in-failure-and-disappointment-despite-a-few-bright-spots-171723 (archived at https://perma.cc/3CDX-UF4P).

39 United Nations (2021b). When disaster strikes, developing countries still too vulnerable. UN News. news.un.org/en/story/2021/10/1102912 (archived at https://perma.cc/2MYC-J5ZJ).

40 Carrington, D. (2022). Revealed: US and UK fall billions short of "fair share" of climate funding. *The Guardian*. www.theguardian.com/global-development/2022/nov/07/us-uk-fall-billions-short-climate-funding-cop27 (archived at https://perma.cc/7LGT-C85L).

41 Weise, Z. and Mathiesen, K. (2022). How Putin made the Green Deal great again. Politico. www.politico.eu/article/putin-made-europe-green-deal-great-again/ (archived at https://perma.cc/R2Q5-E54J).

42 Jordans, F. (2023). Over and out: Germany switches off its last nuclear plants. AP News. apnews.com/article/germany-nuclear-power-plants-shut-energy-376dfaa223f88fedff138b9a63a6f0da (archived at https://perma.cc/2AJP-77F5).

43 Ritchie, H., Roser, M., and Rosado, P. (2010). Energy mix. Our World in Data. ourworldindata.org/energy-mix (archived at https://perma.cc/YVK9-9J8P).

44 Valle, S. (2022). Exxon sees carbon capture market at $4 trillion by 2050. Reuters, April 21. www.reuters.com/business/sustainable-business/exxon-sees-carbon-capture-market-4-trillion-by-2050-2022-04-19/ (archived at https://perma.cc/U39Y-MF5M).

45 Chevron (2022). Chevron Executing Plans to Deliver Higher Returns and Lower Carbon. chevron.com. www.chevron.com/newsroom/2022/q1/chevron-executing-plans-to-deliver-higher-returns-and-lower-carbon (archived at https://perma.cc/5H3N-3V86).

46 Clifford, C. (2023). Why Exxon and Chevron are doubling down on fossil fuel energy with big acquisitions. CNBC. www.cnbc.com/2023/10/25/why-exxon-chevron-are-doubling-down-on-fossil-fuel-energy.html (archived at https://perma.cc/3AJD-9AWX).

47 International Energy Agency (2023). *World Energy Outlook 2023*. International Energy Association, p. 26. iea.blob.core.windows.net/assets/2b0ded44-6a47-495b-96d9-2fac0ac735a8/WorldEnergyOutlook2023.pdf (archived at https://perma.cc/7SH5-XYNQ).

48 International Energy Agency (2023). *World Energy Outlook 2023*. International Energy Association, p. 27. iea.blob.core.windows.net/assets/2b0ded44-6a47-495b-96d9-2fac0ac735a8/WorldEnergyOutlook2023.pdf (archived at https://perma.cc/7SH5-XYNQ).

49 Goossens, C., Graf, C., Nandy, A., Kochan, M., D'Acunto, R., and Boualla, A. (2022). Banks' great carbon challenge. Bain & Company. www.bain.com/insights/banks-great-carbon-challenge (archived at https://perma.cc/2WF2-BQJA).

50 Global Compact Network UK (n.d.). Scope 3 Emissions. UN Global Compact. www.unglobalcompact.org.uk/scope-3-emissions/ (archived at https://perma.cc/255K-FL6S).

51 Milman, O. (2023). "Monster profits" for energy giants reveal a self-destructive fossil fuel resurgence. *The Guardian*, February 9. www.theguardian.com/environment/2023/feb/09/profits-energy-fossil-fuel-resurgence-climate-crisis-shell-exxon-bp-chevron-totalenergies (archived at https://perma.cc/HZ6K-BPT9).

52 Vanderford, R. (2023). SEC's Climate-disclosure rule isn't here, but it may as well be, many businesses say. *The Wall Street Journal*, April 25. www.wsj.com/articles/secs-climate-disclosure-rule-isnt-here-but-it-may-as-well-be-many-businesses-say-854789bd (archived at https://perma.cc/9QDV-36WL).

53 PepsiCo (2023). About PepsiCo. www.pepsico.com/who-we-are/about-pepsico (archived at https://perma.cc/JWC2-6Y5Y).

54 PepsiCo (2021). Reporting informed by GRI Standards. pp. 1, 6. www.pepsico.com/docs/default-source/sustainability-and-esg-topics/pepsico_2021_gri_index.pdf?sfvrsn=23b641d1_9 (archived at https://perma.cc/3GM4-BHVJ).

55 Beverage Industry Environmental Roundtable (2022a). *Beverage Industry Continues to Drive Improvement in Water, Energy, and Emissions Efficiency.* p. 2. www.bieroundtable.com/wp-content/uploads/2021-BIER-Executive-Summary-Report.pdf (archived at https://perma.cc/TW82-V63K).

56 Beverage Industry Environmental Roundtable (2019). About: Sustainability collaborations in the global beverage industry. Beverage Industry Environmental Roundtable. www.bieroundtable.com/about/ (archived at https://perma.cc/M5LL-6R3M).

57 Beverage Industry Environmental Roundtable (2022b). *Beverage Industry Continues to Drive Improvement in Water, Energy, and Emissions Efficiency.* p. 18. www.bieroundtable.com/wp-content/uploads/2021-BIER-Executive-Summary-Report.pdf (archived at https://perma.cc/TW82-V63K).

58 PepsiCo (n.d.). Water. Pepsico. www.pepsico.com/our-impact/esg-topics-a-z/water (archived at https://perma.cc/86WE-77DC).

59 PepsiCo (n.d.). Water. Pepsico. www.pepsico.com/our-impact/esg-topics-a-z/water (archived at https://perma.cc/86WE-77DC).

04

The Social Effect: Tipping Points and Stakeholders

If you've ever heard a corporate leader state that their people are their greatest asset, it is said to inspire purpose and culture. In many ways, this statement is true. Human capital, or the value of an employee's work and knowledge, must be nurtured and protected to create value. Besides the operational benefits like talent acquisition, retention, and productivity, it feels welcoming for employees, customers, and the communities where the company operates to hear such proclamations. The company can capitalize on these material opportunities when backed with purposeful action.

But, in reality, people are also fraught with risk and are a company's most significant liability. For example, employees know all your deepest secrets and intellectual property, customers are fickle, and suppliers are out of your control. As a result, people represent a minefield that the board, executives, Human Resources, Sales, Procurement, General Counsel, and managers must navigate while deftly empowering these people to pursue growth successfully with the company's interests in mind.

Sitting right in the middle of the acronym, Social is the influential linchpin of ESG, perfectly representing the nuance and complexity of risks and opportunities. The Social draws connections between Environmental and Governance issues because people and their wants and needs are at the core, and its range is as diverse as the people it represents. People who affect or are impacted by your business and its outcomes are known as *stakeholders*. Looking at stakeholders through an ESG mindset means uncovering their motivations, needs, and wants and then working with them in the context of your business. This analysis, usually driven through Governance principles and tools, drives the material connection that gives stakeholder programs agency.

Of course, this is no easy task, as businesses of all sizes have stakeholders who intersect with their operations in various ways. Moreover, stakeholders' needs and wants can change over time or as crises arise. If a company doesn't continuously listen and adapt to its stakeholders, it can miss opportunities and constantly react to emerging risks. Unfortunately, this empathetic understanding is something modern business has embraced poorly with inconsistent values. In addition, the close alignment with values has led many to see the Social as nothing but a distraction, but there is value to capture. Still, for decades, some companies have missed this connection.

Friedman to Fink

In the early 1980s, companies and the markets began to subscribe to ideas in the Friedman doctrine: *"The Social Responsibility of Business is to Increase Its Profits"*, authored by Milton Friedman, a US economist, in 1970.[1] This perspective states that a company's primary social value is maximizing profits, which puts shareholders in the primary focus, not necessarily stakeholders.[2] However, one could argue this is a close pairing that companies cannot avoid. Yet, if companies set their mindset on profits above all, they will likely ignore ESG issues. This inattention places the company at significant risk while missing opportunities. In effect, Friedman created a new Governance principle that pivoted attention away from a broad range of stakeholders solely to one group: shareholders. By 1997, companies so widely accepted this idea that the Business Roundtable, a collection of America's CEOs, put this view into its Principles of Corporate Governance. While Governance principles changed, people still were the center of the impact, albeit through the public benefits a well-run company can provide, which makes the Friedman doctrine intersectional with the Social pillar.

With only a slight nudge, this mindset of pursuing profits above all pushes stakeholders aside, which could impact long-term shareholder value anyway. When that happens, material risks emerge. For example, a culture built on the pressure to perform in pursuit of endless profits might maximize the economic cost of human capital through unfair wages and expectations, creating a toxic culture. Moreover, these activities would lead to an unsustainable workforce, resulting in attrition and ongoing hiring costs for talent acquisition, not to mention lost time for the company to onboard new employees, and potential social media blowback. In its assessment of Social risks and pressures, a company can augment the focus on ESG, built on the foundational understanding of the material Environmental issues covered in the previous chapter.

When talking with ESG practitioners about the resurgence in attention to ESG, they often point to BlackRock CEO Larry Fink and his annual letters to CEOs as the catalyst. Starting in 2015, Fink began to write about ESG concepts, moving into the alignment of purpose and profitability, including calling out stakeholders directly in his 2019 letter.[3] This callout happened the same year the Business Roundtable also pivoted its Principles of Corporate Governance towards a broader stakeholder view, away from shareholder primacy. That year, the Business Roundtable listed several stakeholder groups: customers, employees, suppliers, communities, and shareholders in its Principles.[4]

It seems that companies began to listen to these changes. Two short years later, Fink's 2021 CEO letter called out an interesting observation related to the evolution of the Social pillar. He pointed to the stark lines that had emerged between the Social within siloed topics like racial injustice, equity, and community engagement.[5] As ESG gained more attention, the Social pillar, led by a resurgence in social justice crises, moved boards and executives to create specific values-based activities, limiting the view of the Social to particular types of programs. Further, Fink noted how companies classified issues as either Environmental or Social when the classification didn't matter. Instead, what matters is how companies address the problem and the value created. While this points back to stakeholder impact, companies cannot ignore the systemic Social issues that plague modern business and our world. There are intersections, but finding them can be difficult.

As we go through this chapter, it is vital to remember Fink's observation. While companies need to understand Social values to correct systemic injustices, this laudable work may cause companies to overlook material risks and opportunities, pull back efforts against transient pressures, and ultimately put the company in perpetual reactive positions. Through this recognition of stakeholders, we find what Social is really about. Social is conveniently located in the middle of the acronym because, as it turns out, people are at the center of everything, including your company and value creation. Therefore, looking at your business through the lens of your stakeholders is critical for delivering long-term value.

Crises: The Social tipping points

We must go back to 2020 for context to understand the unique drivers toward Social that occurred in the short window between the 2019 stakeholder focus and Fink's callout of siloed efforts in 2021. The growing effects of extreme weather and Covid-19 worldwide and the murder of George Floyd, followed by civil unrest in the USA, were seen in 2020. As a result, stakeholders moved front and center of the business. While governments struggled with supply chain stability, Covid policy, and protests, companies reacted to stressed employees who faced mental and physical health risks, customers who shifted their engagement models, and suppliers who struggled to keep up. These challenges represented material matters for companies as all these groups are critical stakeholders. As a result, some leaders saw risks and opportunities and felt compelled to act. It is worth noting that the appearance of a crisis doesn't suddenly make companies and their management teams experts on these topics.

Still, with the priority focus on shareholders and profit looming over business for the past few decades, companies needed a new license to operate, permissions to shift, and a push. To compare this shift with an Environmental analogy, scientists often talk about tipping points for the climate that create cascading effects across the planet. The Business Roundtable update, Larry Fink's letters, and the prominent social issues of 2020 were similar tipping points for Social across the corporate landscape.

During this period, there was a mix of philanthropic and long-overdue changes around Social issues from companies to stakeholders. While these altruistic efforts may intersect with ESG and be material as social norms change, the execution, which is ongoing and continually shifting, doesn't always consider the stakeholders or the materiality and may not be durable enough to create long-term value. Yet, the shift towards the Social with attention to long-term value is underway and often referred to as stakeholder capitalism.[6] Moreover, the tumultuous crises of 2020 illustrate how companies can drive value creation by putting stakeholders and the material issues at the center instead of the tipping points.

Employees: The changing nature of work

While taking care of employees is a noble pursuit, it is also something companies should already be doing, as ethical reasons exist for treating employees fairly. However, from a material perspective, companies need to drive talent attraction and retention for a competitive advantage, and foster trust to get the best out of their employees. Proactively addressing employee issues in this way would connect materially across the Social and Governance pillars.

When it comes to looking at employees as stakeholders, there are several material stakeholder issues that boards and executives should consider that are relatively universal:

- Employee experience, including productivity, burnout, and collaboration
- Access to quality healthcare and benefits
- Pay equity
- Environmental, health, and safety (EHS)
- Education and reskilling
- Career growth and access to opportunity.

Still, 2020 brought a global pandemic. As Covid ravaged the world and uncertainty loomed, businesses struggled to maintain universal table stakes, such as safe operations. Hybrid and remote work, which started previously with digital technology such as VPNs, mobile access, and cloud technologies, was suddenly accelerated. If companies of all sizes didn't already have their systems digitized and with remote access capabilities, they quickly moved in that direction.[7] As a result of new digital capabilities, commutes ceased for many, commercial office buildings sat empty, and new flexible work styles emerged.

No singular new work style emerged because employees, like any stakeholder group, are different. Remote work opened up new opportunities for some, while others felt the move put them at risk. Those who welcomed the flexibility of working from home realized it could open up new career opportunities because proximity to an office building or headquarters no longer mattered. At first, an eliminated commute seemed to deliver a better work/life balance, especially during a stressful time for employees and their families, but employees ended up working 10 percent more.[8] Still, other employees found the isolation crushing, having enjoyed the in-person connection with their peers and leaders. These employees found value in working at the office, uncovering new ideas through chance encounters, traveling to meet peers and clients, and receiving mentoring through in-person exposure.

As a result of this complexity, leaders struggled to please everyone as Covid waned. Over three years, employees adopted personalized working styles. Some management teams demanded employees return to the office, seeing no other clear path to maintain culture, collaboration, and control. Still, other companies thoughtfully adapted to these new working methods by viewing employees as more than just a single stakeholder type, recognizing a productivity boost while increasing employee satisfaction.[9]

USE CASE: THE J.M. SMUCKER COMPANY AND HYBRID WORK

The J.M. Smucker Company is a consumer packaged goods company focused on food. In its 2021 and 2022 Corporate Impact Reports, you will not find references to Covid's impact on the company or its hybrid work approach. However, there are related callouts in the Employee section in both reports that relate. The company calls out supporting the physical well-being of employees and their families, and then it describes how tools and resources are available to help employees take responsibility and share in the cost for their well-being.[10]

After these reports were published, Smucker began a new hybrid work policy that aligns with these two principles. The company expects corporate employees in the office as little as six days per month, allowing employees to live anywhere if they come to the office for 22 core weeks and pay their way to get to the company's headquarters.[11] So far, employees are enjoying the flexibility, and the office is 70–80 percent full during those core weeks.[12]

While the office has been a staple of work culture for a long time, it no longer suits everyone in today's knowledge-worker economy, leading to a decentralization of power that favors the employee.[13] In other words, many other options exist for employees if the company can't figure out what works best. As with the J.M. Smucker Company case, rather than rush to return to the office, employers should continue efforts to understand their employees better across their needs. Recruiting and retaining top talent may mean allowing the flexibility to work from anywhere and adopting new management styles. Companies may also need to account for mentoring in person or remotely to help retain talent and enable employees to grow. Finally, leaders must tread carefully with input from their employees, as sweeping statements and policies without stakeholder consideration will be called out across social media and carried forward in trending topics and media outlets. Still, as with most ESG issues, there are impacts beyond the employee stakeholder to consider.

From the positive perspective, there is a sustainability opportunity with hybrid work as fewer commutes and less air travel means less pollution, which benefits the planet and people. On the other hand, there may be a looming financial crisis in resolving new ways of working as many wonder what's to become of cities and the commercial real estate market.[14] Moreover, when employees spend time at the office, they also spend money on services and products in locations around the office. If they don't come in, that money stays in their pockets and their communities, further creating economic stress on cities and the people there. These issues affect how companies govern the Social challenge of hybrid work.

Employees: Diversity, equity, and inclusion

Globally, companies are not immune to the embedded challenges of systemic diversity, equity, and inclusion (DEI) issues. For example, this risk may manifest visibly through a uniform board with similar viewpoints or in talent loss due to pay equity issues. However, as Social tipping points fell, companies had the opportunity and license to act. To carry these examples forward, a year after George Floyd's murder, boards became more diverse.[15] The Russell 3000 saw improvements from boards with no racial/ethnic diversity dropping from 38 percent in 2020 to 10 percent in 2022.[16] Unfortunately, gender pay equity is proceeding glacially, with only an $0.08 improvement in the 25 years leading up to 2021.[17]

And so, in 2020, a 2015 McKinsey report resurfaced, specifically focused on a diverse board and employee base, helping to guide companies towards driving long-term value through the company's DEI efforts.[18] This renewed attention on research, the new license to operate, and the alignment of doing good and doing well quickly grew DEI efforts in size, scope, and budget, similar to the investment in technology for hybrid work.

What does DEI mean?

- *Diversity* refers to who is represented.

- *Equity* gives all people fair treatment.

- *Inclusion* is the degree to which the company strives to include and empower people.

While DEI programs existed before the 2020 Social tipping points, leaders of these efforts talk about a clear boundary around their programs and George Floyd's murder specifically, in recognition that many companies changed or accelerated their employee efforts after.[19] In the following weeks and months, companies spoke out publicly with commitments, made philanthropic donations, and backed their statements with action and organized programs. Some of these efforts were customer-focused, and Procurement teams implemented new supplier diversity policies. By the summer of 2020, some companies gave their employees the day off to reflect on Juneteenth, a holiday celebrating the end of slavery in the USA. Others were making material and non-material changes to their operations around racial and pay equity issues, such as looking at diverse leadership programs or addressing long-standing DEI issues they should have already addressed.[20]

Like sustainability and responsible Environmental management, DEI issues are table stakes and material for a company. For example, the McKinsey report just mentioned lists several universal opportunities that arise when a workforce is racially and gender diverse, including talent attraction, customer engagement, employee satisfaction, and improved decision-making.[21] While it was a welcome change to see programs increase in 2020, building DEI programs out of a crisis and not material goals may miss business integrations and benefits. In doing so, these programs may not feel authentic, and the success of programs will vary. For example, in a WebMD study from 2023, 9 out of 10 survey respondents said their company had a DEI(&Belonging) program, yet 62 percent didn't find the company to be committed to the program.[22] These numbers are unsurprising since companies have created these programs in reaction to a crisis, not around the stakeholders or material issues. Unfortunately, this reactive approach appears to trip companies up a bit.

Rather than approaching DEI through feedback, listening, materiality, and even mission, the crisis dictated the response, and leaders bolted these programs on. As a result, they've placed the situation at the center, not the people. When the world moves on from a crisis, so do the leaders and the budgets.

While focusing on systemic change can drive DEI in some areas and is critical to pursue from an ethical perspective, considering the stakeholder's wants and needs will further it with durability. For example, leading with purpose and values doesn't help these programs survive an economic downturn. Unfortunately, during 2023, as the markets tumbled and layoffs were rampant, many companies cut DEI programs and slid backward into shareholder primacy.[23] Some hastily created programs executed without consideration of the material intersection led companies to find little business value in the DEI values. When the stock slips, shareholders must be appeased, which manifests in program cuts.

Stopping an underperforming and ineffective DEI program is one thing, but cutting a functionally material DEI program is quite the other and can have long-term repercussions. The least of which is that companies that promised change break trust with diverse employees, leading to higher attrition rates for DEI roles.[24]

If companies place people, the program's impacts, and its outcomes at the center of DEI efforts instead of the situation or impulse to act, it can have a lasting effect. The development and execution of a DEI program must involve your stakeholders and a continual connection to their needs.[25] It means having the courage to shut down programs that aren't working and the self-awareness to recognize when programs are working and should grow. A more thoughtful process that puts stakeholders at the center would include efforts to:

- Create leadership listening forums for employees to give feedback and inform leaders about issues that impact them most.

- Educate employees and leaders on empathetic execution and the material benefits, not just the immediate crisis.

- Build cultural awareness through first-party experiences, geographically or otherwise.

- Follow or conduct research to quell assumptions.

- Find diverse leaders, but also engage non-diverse allies in leadership.

- Hold management teams accountable for the impact.

- Assign budget to those executing.

EMPLOYEE RESOURCE GROUPS

Many companies leverage Employee Resource Groups (ERGs) to gather people from diverse backgrounds while giving them a safe space to discuss sensitive issues. Unfortunately, companies often stop at simply founding the group and making a connection between people, but it can go much further. Using the process tips just listed:

– The ERG should have a clear goal and impact with consideration for the organization's unique context.

- In partnership with the ERG, Marketing should update internal and social media content with specific learnings and successes the ERG achieves, purpose-driven or material.
- The ERG should also have a company leader as its sponsor to champion the group internally while being led by a small group of employees who have a budget assigned.
- The sponsor should actively participate in feedback loops and employee listening events to understand the group's needs and uncover and direct material issues that surface.
- The Human Resources team should create an incentive or recognition structure around the group's outcomes.

An ERG is just one example of a tool companies can create to drive the material results and mission they want to achieve. While DEI is table stakes for modern business and goes well beyond metrics and data to impact and outcomes, thoughtful execution in this area can materially affect the business if approached with an ESG mindset.

Still, the Social pillar is one of the most difficult to get right because one aspect concerns making stakeholders feel valued. While employees are in a company's direct influence, if companies stop with just this one stakeholder group, they may mitigate some risks while only capturing some Social opportunities.

Customers: Ever-changing needs and new opportunities

These same Social tipping points also impacted customers, another important stakeholder group. Customers represent a different minefield for companies to navigate. While a company can build programs to connect and engage employees, customers are fickle and outside of the company's direct influence, having an effect from the outside.

As with employees, DEI is table stakes for customers but can also unlock material opportunities. Employees are the front line and must match your customers' diverse makeup to serve them best and build products that intersect with their unique needs. Some global brands have communities of like-minded customers loyal to the brand, but it is not the norm that companies will always get it right consistently because customers' values vary. One person's values are another person's vice. Balancing messaging for loyal customers while attempting to increase market share with new groups or with changes around the Social is tricky and fraught with risk.

Companies have many processes and tools to listen to market signals, build compelling messaging, and sell to customers. Still, for a company to meaningfully uncover its customers' needs requires deep insights that may not always surface, even in the data. As a result, companies must balance the Social with Governance as they innovate around their customer-facing products and services. In the meantime, management teams, business development managers, and product owners must be on the lookout for disruption and crises.

Brand changes and social justice

Never before have brands reached so many customers at once while aligning with their customers' values and needs, whether sustainability, DEI, accessibility, or something else. Brands can also interact directly with their customers and non-customers through their applications, websites, and social and traditional media. These systems create signals around brand interactions, which companies can use to inform product direction, uncover changing preferences, and more. However, this requires constant observation and careful adjustments.

As with employee engagement and systemic change, companies should already be doing these activities. Companies had the agency to make material changes as systemic pressures built, and consumer attention was drawn to these Social crises. But, as before, risks can arise from the new opportunities to interact when leading change with a crisis.

Due to existing and new pressures after 2020, some companies examined their long-standing controversial brand imagery and naming and decided to update. Aunt Jemima, a Pepsi-owned syrup brand, was an early brand to create a newsworthy change. Unfortunately, Aunt Jemima's old name and image were associated with a racial stereotype for many consumers. So, to reflect its values against the emerging crises, Pepsi announced a name change to the Pearl Milling Company, the original mill the Aunt Jemima name came from, in recognition of consumer opinion.[26] In addition, the logo changed to a flour mill.

In the same consumer product group is Mrs. Butterworth, a syrup brand owned by Conagra Foods, known for its grandmotherly-shaped bottle. Some consumers find the visage to be similarly offensive with racial stereotype overtones. At the same time as Pepsi's announcement, Conagra announced that it was also reviewing changes to its branding, but it appears now to have decided not to make a change.[27]

And so, we have two syrup brands, one changing and one not. Addressing the racist roots of a brand when it is blatantly apparent in the name and logo should not take a crisis, but this has multiple facets. A brand name, logo, or recipe change represents a material risk to the business, but perhaps it is even more challenging to get right when a crisis forces attention to the issue. In the case of Aunt Jemima, some consumers still have a problem with the new name's legacy, while others feel no connection to the brand after the change.[28] Ultimately, these decisions, their long-term value, and their material benefits remain open questions as the sales impact has not been determined.[29] Still, there is no doubt that these crises have changed the landscape of customer-brand relationships around the Social pillar.[30]

Customers and non-customers: Social media amplification

A company can drive attention to its brand in its products, services, and the support provided after purchase. However, there is hardly anything as powerful as the reach afforded to companies via their social media presence. Social media allows brands to interact with their stakeholders more humanly, provide quick support, increase customer satisfaction, and collect information about customers and preferences. Therefore, it represents a material opportunity to engage with a stakeholder group.

However, while companies can reach customers via social media to capture new opportunities, they don't have complete control. Social media is a complex web where customers and non-customers can interact with each other, the brand, and its competitors, which presents risks.

For example, suppose a customer has a problem and takes to social media. In that case, the company may connect via a digitized stakeholder engagement model and resolve the issue. However, social media is rife with people looking to stir up trouble, and customers are constantly changing. As a result, your company may be unable to reach a satisfactory conclusion for the customer and their issue. If this happens, it could remain an issue between your company and that single customer. Still, it can be much more troublesome if the post goes viral, materially impacting reputation and sales or possibly resulting in regulatory engagement.

USE CASE: THE APPLE CARD AND GOLDMAN SACHS

In 2019, Apple and Goldman Sachs launched the Apple Card, a credit card tied to the Apple device ecosystem. A few months later, a developer named David Heinemeier Hansson posted on Twitter about a concern. The claim was that even with a higher credit score, his wife received a lower line of credit than he did. Steve Wozniak, the co-founder of Apple, also reported a similar experience.[31] From there, the claim quickly grew into speculation on social media that the algorithm behind the credit scoring had a gender bias. This rumor wasn't that far of a leap since gender and racial discrimination in lending and credit scoring have the attention of regulators already.[32] These social media posts prompted the New York State Department of Financial Services (DFS) to investigate.[33] By March 2021, the report concluded no fair-lending violations but stated that customer service and a perceived lack of transparency likely contributed to the sudden lack of trust.[34]

As with everything ESG, these issues tend to bring up more questions. Even with Apple and Goldman Sachs cleared, the DFS called out a broader need to update credit regulation and transparency across the industry in its report.[35] This issue even opened up questions by TechCrunch six months later about whether or not financial services and AI developers more broadly need to be regulated around structural bias.[36]

Ultimately, the perception of gender bias on a social media platform resulted in many questions from various stakeholders, including regulators. This use case serves as a reminder of stakeholders' power to create disruption, even with a perceived notion of an ethical issue, and how easily trust can break.

Supply chain: Risk and forced labor issues

Choosing which suppliers to work with is a critical material task. Many companies began publishing and committing to a diverse supplier statement around the tipping points of 2020. In this situation, the Procurement team commits to considering a supplier's DEI credentials as part of its overall value proposition as another factor in the selection process. The goal is often supporting diverse-led and owned businesses to correct ongoing Social injustice. However, it does not mean, or shouldn't, that diversity or support-ing DEI values is the only factor in the decision, as that can introduce risk.

Companies may also find more value, as a 2021 Bain & Company report found material benefits with suppliers who valued DEI, including lower attrition rates and a 0.7% saving for those in the top quartile of diverse supplier spending.[37]

On the other hand, having a diverse group of suppliers, as opposed to diversity in your suppliers, is a material ESG issue, more aligned with quality Governance and risk management practices. In other words, the company can reduce its risk by broadening the range of suppliers in its value chain while considering their sustainability and DEI values alongside other factors in decision-making.

Companies are not limited to these two Social intersections with suppliers. After all, your supplier's employees upstream are a material risk to your business because of your company's dependency. After Covid, supply chains became stressed, and in some cases, the exploitation of workers increased.[38] These employees are second-tier stakeholders for your company in that you don't have direct control but may be able to influence your supplier on their treatment. This particular issue can be one of the most challenging a company can face because extreme Social problems at a supplier are also outside the company's visibility.

A company's risk can sit in upstream suppliers or those feeding materials and data into the company:

- Upstream: supply, where your company is the customer taking in goods
- Downstream: demand post-processing, where customers are purchasing your goods.

Procurement teams can leverage some tools to uncover these issues if people report them, but no panacea is available. For example, a company may look at its suppliers' ESG scores (if available), proprietary supplier scores and data, and publicly available information from sites like Glassdoor and social media to uncover supplier issues. These external datasets may surface issues like worker treatment, benefits and pay equity, and even quality of life. These are similar tools to the ones used to discover your employees' challenges from the outside in. Yet, as you go further into the supply chain, you may find people without access to digital tools or ways to surface these issues anonymously. In addition, government officials in foreign countries where your suppliers operate may also not be monitoring for these Social risks.

Further up the supply chain, you may find issues like forced labor. Forced labor exploits workers and extracts their value under a penalty, with force or threat against them. Unfortunately, disclosures and data won't help here because an unscrupulous supplier using forced labor is unlikely to report it. Instead, the company must investigate and conduct supplier audits. Suppose the media discovers a supplier issue before the company and its Governance processes do. In that case, it can result in reputational damage, fines, boycotts, lost production time from supplier shutdowns, increased costs to switch suppliers, and more.

Mapping your supply chain is the first step. Leveraging datasets from external suppliers, similar to ESG scoring and its data collection, may help uncover suppliers to investigate, audit, or engage. In addition, blockchain and forensic tools can help trace materials back to their origin.[39] Because of the processing of goods that happens upstream, new technologies, like DNA tracking, are also emerging to trace back the components of goods to their sources.[40] From here, the data surfaced needs to be tied back to areas where forced labor issues are known to occur, which may miss regions where it is happening because, unfortunately, forced labor can happen anywhere. As a result, Procurement teams may need new engagement models with countries, NGOs, auditors, and suppliers as part of a disciplined Governance practice to uncover these issues and adjust or influence before the risk emerges.

Lastly, regarding auditors, companies must ensure that practices to find forced labor issues are well documented and should recognize that this is an issue that unscrupulous suppliers will attempt to hide.[41]

Social is in the middle for a reason

The Friedman doctrine established profits and shareholders to deliver a company's Social purpose. Along the way, business perspectives shifted towards considering other stakeholders along the Social tipping points of 2020 and managing those risks and opportunities. As we've seen, the material considerations around stakeholders continually lead back to the company's impact on people and people's effect on the business. While listening to and caring for stakeholders might seem philanthropic or counter to profits, considering the effect of stakeholders on the company is a material ESG issue. Somewhere along the way, the opportunities that can be created from thoughtful Social programs have been lost as DEI programs wind down during economic stress. In other words, what seems like a values-based exercise doesn't supplant core business value but can protect and drive it.

USE CASE: PARAMOUNT AND CONTENT FOR CHANGE

Paramount is a global media company covering production studios, networks, streaming services, live events, merchandise, and more. It manages some of the world's largest and most recognizable media brands. As of spring 2022, it explicitly calls out its response to the racial reckoning and Covid pandemic on the About Us page on its website.[42]

Like many companies at the time, Paramount made commitments around the Social tipping points, but what's interesting is how it took a material approach to the issue. This approach makes sense as its 2020 materiality assessment listed Diverse & Inclusive Content as the top issue for stakeholders and the company.[43] In addition to managing DEI metrics and implementing ERGs,[44] it took stakeholder engagement further into the core of what it does—storytelling—augmenting an existing program started by one of its media properties, Black Entertainment Television (BET), called Content for Change.[45]

A group called Paramount Insights, which conducts audience research, turned its eyes to DEI challenges and surveyed 15,000 people in 15 countries in a program called Reflecting Me.[46] It uncovered many insightful points, including:

- 79 percent of audiences agree that there needs to be more diversity in TV and movies.
- 52 percent feel that there is more accuracy required for the representation of certain groups.
- 59 percent reported that poor representation on screen made them feel unimportant, ignored, or disappointed.

Rather than discussing a supply or value chain, Paramount describes about how it operates in a content creation ecosystem.[47] In its explanation for About Content for Change, it alludes to three stakeholder approaches:

- Content (employees and customers)
- Creative Supply Chain (employees and suppliers)
- Culture (employees and communities).

In order to address systemic issues, Paramount has taken a systemic approach in a way only it can address it, through unique content. For example, per its 2022 ESG report, it leveraged Content for Change to tackle mental health storylines through shows like *Catfish*, *Floribama Shore*, *Siesta Key*, *Cartel Crew*, *Teen Mom OG*, and *Love and Hip Hop Atlanta*.[48] It is also attempting to build new partnerships in the industry through this program.[49]

The Social sits in the middle of ESG, not only because it can tie together Environmental and Governance issues but also because people are in the middle. Often, companies may feel stuck looking uphill at the mountain of systemic Social issues, resulting in impossibly ambitious programs. By keeping materiality and stakeholders in mind, the management team can build durable programs that tackle complex Social issues through what they understand best: their own business.

Notes

1 Friedman, M. (1970). The social responsibility of business is to increase its profits. *The New York Times*, September 13. www.nytimes.com/1970/09/13/archives/a-friedman-doctrine-the-social-responsibility-of-business-is-to.html (archived at https://perma.cc/2PUG-CTRN).

2 Smith, H.J. (2003). The shareholders vs. stakeholders debate. *MIT Sloan Management Review*. sloanreview.mit.edu/article/the-shareholders-vs-stakeholders-debate/ (archived at https://perma.cc/9FY9-CYYD).

3 Fink, L. (2019). Larry Fink's 2019 Letter to CEOs. BlackRock. www.blackrock.com/corporate/investor-relations/2019-larry-fink-ceo-letter (archived at https://perma.cc/SP59-32N8).

4 Business Roundtable (2019). Business Roundtable redefines the purpose of a corporation to promote "An economy that serves all Americans". Business Roundtable. www.businessroundtable.org/business-roundtable-redefines-the-purpose-of-a-corporation-to-promote-an-economy-that-serves-all-americans (archived at https://perma.cc/4DZZ-Q3EM).

5 Fink, L. (2021). Larry Fink's 2021 Letter to CEOs. BlackRock. www.blackrock.com/corporate/investor-relations/2021-larry-fink-ceo-letter (archived at https://perma.cc/N9KD-MMU7).

6 Schwab, K. and Vanham, P. (2021). What is stakeholder capitalism? It's history and relevance. World Economic Forum. www.weforum.org/agenda/2021/01/klaus-schwab-on-what-is-stakeholder-capitalism-history-relevance/ (archived at https://perma.cc/5BRF-DX8Q).

7 Jaumotte, F., Pizzinelli, C., Oikonomou, M., and Tavares, M.M. (2023). How the pandemic accelerated digital transformation in advanced economies. World Economic Forum. www.weforum.org/agenda/2023/03/how-pandemic-accelerated-digital-transformation-in-advanced-economies/ (archived at https://perma.cc/5JTA-ALKF).

8 Murillo, A.L. (2021). It's confirmed: The workweek is indeed longer now that you're WFH. Money. money.com/work-from-home-longer-hours (archived at https://perma.cc/Y4R3-LQX9).

9 Gratton, L. (2021). How to Do Hybrid Right. *Harvard Business Review*. hbr.org/2021/05/how-to-do-hybrid-right (archived at https://perma.cc/8QLQ-MGAK).

10 The J.M. Smucker Co. (2021). *The J.M. Smucker Co. Corporate Impact Report*. p.10. s3.us-east-2.amazonaws.com/jms-s3-com-jms-p-pmc6/assets/news-stories/corporate-publications/2021-corporate-impact-report.pdf (archived at https://perma.cc/BWQ2-Z75D).

11 Cutter, C. (2023). This company created a return-to-office plan that employees actually like. *The Wall Street Journal*, August 27. www.wsj.com/lifestyle/workplace/smuckers-return-to-office-plan-working-a933678 (archived at https://perma.cc/K33N-Y2MA).

12 Cutter, C. (2023). This company created a return-to-office plan that employees actually like. *The Wall Street Journal*, August 27. www.wsj.com/lifestyle/workplace/smuckers-return-to-office-plan-working-a933678 (archived at https://perma.cc/K33N-Y2MA).

13 Tsipursky, D.G. (2023). Why employers forcing a Return to office is leading to more worker power and unionization. Forbes. www.forbes.com/sites/glebtsipursky/2023/03/29/why-employers-forcing-a-return-to-office-is-leading-to-more-worker-power-and-unionization/?sh=3a47efdd43cb (archived at https://perma.cc/8DSY-RNJS).

14 Derby, M.S. (2023). New York Fed board member warns of commercial real-estate risks. Reuters, March 24. www.reuters.com/markets/real-estate-leader-ny-fed-board-warns-commercial-real-estate-risks-2023-03-24/ (archived at https://perma.cc/3X5D-BBMD).

15 Guynn, J. and Fraser, J. (2022). Corporate boards used to be mostly white and male. That's changed since George Floyd's murder. *USA Today*, May 31. www.usatoday.com/story/money/2022/05/31/corporate-board-diversity-george-floyd/9948384002/ (archived at https://perma.cc/5A55-54MP).

16 Michael, F. and Mishra, S. (2022). Racial and ethnic diversity on U.S. corporate boards—Progress since 2020. The Harvard Law School Forum on Corporate Governance. corpgov.law.harvard.edu/2022/07/21/racial-and-ethnic-diversity-on-u-s-corporate-boards-progress-since-2020 (archived at https://perma.cc/QKA2-BF48).

17 Donner, F. and Goldberg, E. (2021). In 25 years, the pay gap has shrunk by just 8 cents. *The New York Times*, March 24. www.nytimes.com/2021/03/24/us/equal-pay-day-explainer.html (archived at https://perma.cc/64X8-8RVA).

18 Hunt, V., Layton, D., and Prince, S. (2015). Why diversity matters. McKinsey. pp. 1–3. www.mckinsey.com/~/media/mckinsey/business%20functions/people%20and%20organizational%20performance/our%20insights/why%20diversity%20matters/why%20diversity%20matters.pdf (archived at https://perma.cc/WC9U-8N9Z).

19 Colletta, J. (2021). DEI after George Floyd. Human Resource Executive. hrexecutive.com/number-of-the-day-dei-after-george-floyd/ (archived at https://perma.cc/UE5Q-Z82F).

20 Friedman, G. (2020). Here's what companies are promising to do to fight racism. *The New York Times*, August 23. www.nytimes.com/article/companies-racism-george-floyd-protests.html (archived at https://perma.cc/47MW-L7PH).

21 Hunt, V., Layton, D., and Prince, S. (2015). Why diversity matters. McKinsey. p. 3. www.mckinsey.com/~/media/mckinsey/business%20functions/people%20and%20organizational%20performance/our%20insights/why%20diversity%20matters/why%20diversity%20matters.pdf (archived at https://perma.cc/WC9U-8N9Z).

22 WebMD Health Services (n.d.). *WebMD Health Services' 2023 DEIB Research Project*. WebMD Health Services, pp. 10, 17. www.webmdhealthservices.com/campaign/webmd-health-services-2023-deib-research-project/ (archived at https://perma.cc/C4JR-Y4LQ).

23 Rogers, T.N. (2023). Cuts to investment in diversity threaten gains. *Financial Times*, March 9. www.ft.com/content/d61ce264-a7ca-4352-bfb7-fef60078bc34 (archived at https://perma.cc/LB8B-U5RR).

24 Bunn, C. (2023). Diversity officers hired in 2020 are losing their jobs, and the ones who remain are mostly white. NBC News. www.nbcnews.com/news/nbcblk/diversity-roles-disappear-three-years-george-floyd-protests-inspired-rcna72026 (archived at https://perma.cc/EA7Z-63C6).

25 Zheng, L. (2022). The failure of the DEI-Industrial Complex. *Harvard Business Review*, December 1. hbr.org/2022/12/the-failure-of-the-dei-industrial-complex (archived at https://perma.cc/AF6R-9EN9).

26 The Quaker Oats Company (2022). Why is Aunt Jemima removing the image from the packaging and changing its name? PepsiCo. contact.pepsico.com/pearlmillingcompany/article/why-is-aunt-jemima-removing-the-image-from-the-packaging-and-cha (archived at https://perma.cc/C7YJ-S56Q).

27 Conagra Brands (2020). Conagra Brands announces Mrs. Butterworth's brand review. Conagra Brands. www.conagrabrands.com/news-room/news-conagra-brands-announces-mrs-butterworths-brand-review-prn-122733 (archived at https://perma.cc/QE6X-EH5R).

28 Schwartz, R. (2021). The real reason people are unhappy with Aunt Jemima's new name. Mashed. www.mashed.com/331520/the-real-reason-people-are-unhappy-with-aunt-jemimas-new-name/ (archived at https://perma.cc/44GD-JVM3).

29 Schultz, E.J. (2021). Aunt Jemima's name change gains wide awareness but questionable impact on sales, according to new poll. Ad Age. adage.com/article/cmo-strategy/aunt-jemimas-name-change-gains-wide-awareness-questionable-impact-sales-according-new-poll/2315056 (archived at https://perma.cc/D7EL-Q8QU).

30 Kubota, S. (2020). Here's how American brands are changing after facing racial reckoning. *Today*. www.today.com/tmrw/list-brands-have-had-change-public-opinion-black-stereotypes-shifts-t184726 (archived at https://perma.cc/2UGA-2TN5).

31 Vigdor, N. (2019). Apple Card investigated after gender discrimination complaints. *The New York Times*, November 10. www.nytimes.com/2019/11/10/business/Apple-credit-card-investigation.html (archived at https://perma.cc/ZW8R-THBX).

32 Halperin, E. and Salas, L. (2022). Cracking down on discrimination in the financial sector. Consumer Financial Protection Bureau. www.consumerfinance.gov/about-us/blog/cracking-down-on-discrimination-in-the-financial-sector/ (archived at https://perma.cc/WD35-TPDJ).

33 Vigdor, N. (2019). Apple Card investigated after gender discrimination complaints. *The New York Times*, November 10. www.nytimes.com/2019/11/10/business/Apple-credit-card-investigation.html (archived at https://perma.cc/ZW8R-THBX).

34 New York State Department of Financial Services (2021). Press Release, March 23: DFS issues findings on the Apple Card and its underwriter Goldman Sachs Bank. Department of Financial Services. www.dfs.ny.gov/reports_and_publications/press_releases/pr202103231 (archived at https://perma.cc/3CEB-5DPB).

35 New York State Department of Financial Services (2021). Press Release, March 23: DFS Issues Findings on the Apple Card and Its Underwriter Goldman Sachs Bank. Department of Financial Services. www.dfs.ny.gov/reports_and_publications/press_releases/pr202103231 (archived at https://perma.cc/3CEB-5DPB).

36 O'Sullivan, L. (2021). How the law got it wrong with Apple Card. TechCrunch. techcrunch.com/2021/08/14/how-the-law-got-it-wrong-with-apple-card/ (archived at https://perma.cc/D9NM-ZD7N).

37 Batra, R., Housh, J., and Schannon, D. (2021). Supplier diversity: How to overcome four key obstacles. Bain & Company. www.bain.com/insights/supplier-diversity-how-to-overcome-four-key-obstacles/ (archived at https://perma.cc/USM2-Y29F).

38 Murray, S. (2023). So you think you know your supply chain? *Financial Times*, March 24. www.ft.com/content/687c2a10-403b-4a93-85c0-3ede41af5d09 (archived at https://perma.cc/P2F6-QH9Q).

39 Santos, A.M. and Rock, L.A. (2023). US Customs and Borders emphasize supply chain transparency. *The National Law Review*. www.natlawreview. com/article/sorry-technology-can-t-replace-your-supply-chain-due-diligence-yet (archived at https://perma.cc/FFD8-T43D).

40 BSR (n.d.). Costly consequences for forced labor. BSR. www.bsr.org/en/ emerging-issues/costly-consequences-for-forced-labor (archived at https:// perma.cc/EWQ4-NYFF).

41 Human Rights Watch (2022). Social audits no cure for retail supply chain labor abuse. Human Rights Watch. www.hrw.org/news/2022/11/15/social-audits-no-cure-retail-supply-chain-labor-abuse (archived at https://perma. cc/25KB-Y68J).

42 Paramount (n.d.a). About. Paramount. www.paramount.com/about (archived at https://perma.cc/GLT3-V3QV).

43 ViacomCBS (2020). Materiality assessment. p.4. www.paramount.com/files/ documents/ViacomCBS_Materiality_Assessment_August2020.pdf (archived at https://perma.cc/EL6D-29CD).

44 Paramount (n.d.b). Diversity equity & inclusion: Introduction. Paramount. www.paramount.com/inclusion-2021/introduction (archived at https://perma. cc/KD2M-ZAA8).

45 Sun, R. (2021). ViacomCBS expands BET's Content for Change into companywide initiative. *The Hollywood Reporter*. www.hollywoodreporter. com/tv/tv-news/viacomcbs-content-for-change-1235025590/ (archived at https://perma.cc/2T5J-WUNG).

46 Paramount (2022). Improving on-screen diversity and authenticity is important to global audiences. Paramount Insights. insights.paramount.com/post/ improving-on-screen-diversity-and-authenticity-is-important-to-global-audiences/ (archived at https://perma.cc/7LKJ-G3QE).

47 Paramount (n.d.c). Homepage. Content for Change. Content for Change. contentforchange.paramount.com/ (archived at https://perma.cc/TLP5-TEGT).

48 Paramount (2023). *Paramount Global ESG Report 2021–2022*. p. 22.

49 Paramount (n.d.d). Get Involved. Content for Change. Paramount. contentforchange.paramount.com/getinvolved (archived at https://perma. cc/7C6L-7QE6).

05

Governance: ESG Leadership and the Board

For as long as companies have existed, people at the top have been in a position of power. This power has responsibilities to create, uphold, and manage the principles, rules, and processes for running the company and driving long-term value. Corporate Governance covers these core business functions and should include activities that shepherd attention to the company's material Environmental and Social risks and opportunities. As expected, these responsibilities sit with the board and the management team. From the top, these people shape the company in ways most stakeholders don't directly see, but their influence is undeniable.

While Governance is last in the acronym, many believe it should be first because it determines the guidelines for how the company deals with its entire operations, the effect of the world on the company, and its impact. As the world demands operational and systemic changes and new material risks and opportunities arise, ESG requires leadership endorsement and budget to execute change. But, of course, the management team can't manage the business alone and relies on functional business groups and frontline workers through a distributed power and execution model. While stakeholders of all types might build a business case for change, executives are the ultimate custodians of the company's direction and must be receptive. A culture built on listening, collaboration, and trust helps employees surface these issues accordingly. In that case, the management team must foster the culture they want, where stakeholders can openly discuss ideas and escalate them through employees, employees can safely bring these considerations to light, and leaders can debate these issues with a certain level of transparency. Finally, when these executives agree, they must sponsor the change and delegate its execution, or communicate with intent and clarity why they aren't changing.

There are challenges and conflicts to the successful consideration and execution of change relating to the company's long-term value that don't necessarily have anything to do with ESG and can hinder ESG efforts. For example, the markets promote short-term quarterly financial reporting to monitor a company's performance. In theory, the board and the management team identify risks through these reports. If a company faces a poor quarter, CFOs may tighten or pull back budgets, ESG or otherwise, favoring the short-term results. This redirection away from the long-term could be for various reasons but likely intersects with near-term executive compensation models rather than shareholder value.[1]

While the CFO delivers short-term quarterly reports to appease stakeholders interested in financial performance, the board's remit covers the financials, short-term crisis management, and long-term risks and opportunities. Addressing the most pressing challenges for companies requires both a short-term and a long-term view. Boards must recognize that we live in a constantly changing world in the present while looking to a future where the company has created sustainable and lasting value. Looking at companies through the lens of ESG can shift our mindset towards recognizing the need for this balance.

Whether a company has existed for decades or is a new startup looking to solve some niche issue, ESG might not be a consideration to the company's existing business operations and culture. In the previous two chapters, we've seen how quickly the world has shifted around Environmental and Social issues. The board and management team need to figure out how to enable the company to prioritize these issues while fostering a culture that can address them. At its core, ESG attention is absent without quality Governance.

And so, if one letter represents how companies approach their business and ESG, it would unsurprisingly be Governance, which is an excellent argument for it to come first. But, as we'll find, Governance is last in the acronym because nothing, including the company's survival, will make it through poor Governance.

Governance first: Challenges to long-term growth and risk

Governance is foundational to a company as it dictates everything it does, ESG or otherwise. A structured approach is required so that boards, the management team, and employees understand the principles of a company and execute accordingly. Stakeholders can find this information in the company's Corporate Governance Guidelines for publicly traded companies, which is most of the focus of this chapter. In the guidelines, stakeholders can check if the board focuses on shareholder value only or if they've grown to understand and incorporate stakeholders as a value driver. However, the challenge with these guidelines is that legal counsel or consultants may have used boilerplate templates, following their industry or peers. Ultimately, the guidelines are just words on a page. It is only with the thoughtful adoption of the guidelines and execution by the board of directors that change occurs.

A NOTE ON PRIVATELY HELD COMPANIES

Privately held companies often have a board focused on advisory rather than fiduciary responsibilities. While this chapter is mainly about publicly traded companies and their ESG approach, many of the concepts still apply to privately held companies.

For example, privately held companies may not publish or use Corporate Governance Guidelines, but they must have principles for their operations and functions to be effective.

Private boards also have different challenges from public boards since they are primarily advisory, may consist of family and friends, and may also be beholden to the founder or CEO's whims.

To deal effectively with ESG issues, the board and management team must adhere to and actively practice solid principles. Corporate Governance Guidelines dictate these practices and typically have different parts, depending on the company. Much of the information is high-level and refers to other documentation. Some standard features include:

- General oversight policies for material matters and risks
- Board size, member term limits, director qualification, and compensation
- CEO assessment information and succession planning
- Code of Conduct, including ethical guidelines and legal compliance
- Confidentiality of board matters
- Independence of the board, meaning the number of board members that don't have a material stake in or connection to the business

- Board candidate selection and succession planning
- A board diversity statement or approach
- The committees surrounding the board and instructions on reporting to the board and/or CEO.

These issues are clearly Governance-related, but several items intersect with broader ESG matters. For example, a board diversity statement that values diversity and diverse opinions is a material matter because it can open up new perspectives on the company through varied lived and professional experiences. This example sits at the intersection with the Social.

Governance challenges to ESG issues

Even with Corporate Governance Guidelines, ESG may need to receive direct attention from the board. If a board is supposed to deliver long-term value and ESG is a mechanism to achieve that, it should be well-prepared. But the reality is that the board may overlook ESG issues due to a lack of expertise. For example, an NYU Stern analysis of the Fortune 100 found less than 5 percent of board members had material Environmental, Social, or Governance expertise in various categories.[2] Similarly, the business school INSEAD found that 70 percent of survey respondents believed that the board was moderately or not at all effectively integrating ESG.[3] So, while boards are the custodians of long-term value, they lack the expertise to do it with ESG, a long-term mechanism. To make matters worse, employees who execute the board's vision, even with ESG integrated into the strategy, may also need to understand more about ESG to drive transitional or material efforts effectively.

Compounding this lack of expertise is that, even though ESG has existed for 20 years, the board doesn't necessarily agree on its meaning. As a result, it can struggle to decide what the business should focus on regarding Environmental, Social, and Governance topics. For example, the board may look across the competitive landscape and see other companies disclosing voluntary ESG information and reporting. Then, having led with this limited analysis and expertise, it matches the disclosures without further investigation, leaving potential material risks brewing and opportunities to capture inert. In another example, a supplier might feel pressure downstream from their B2B customers to report specific disclosures and figure that they need to participate without material consideration or discussion with that customer on their objectives. This rush to comply can quickly lead to misalignment between the supplier and the B2B customer.

And so, across industries, some companies understand ESG, and others don't. It can be challenging to differentiate between the two because companies also don't distinguish disclosures from material issues well and rarely draw connections between them. As a result, there needs to be more communication about what the company does to preserve and grow the business by leveraging ESG and why.

Complicating the matter is that boards are a mix of people, often independent members with no material ties to the company. They each have unique motivations, personalities, and influence over each other in addition to this external pressure. As a result, the board may choose to do nothing with ESG. Yet, just as inaction is a form of action, the lack of ESG consideration, or its misinterpretations are Governance issues.

CEO pay

One of the more pressing Governance issues over the past few years has been the topic of CEO pay. Per As You Sow, the median CEO pay of the S&P 500 is now $10 million, well above what an individual contributor to the company would make.[4] Moreover, from 1978 through 2020, CEO compensation grew 1322 percent, outpacing the S&P's growth at 817 percent.[5] While this can be a demoralizing realization for employees and stakeholders, CEO pay is a material Governance issue well beyond the board approving it.

Some boards tie non-financial performance, often those universal table stakes issues defined through ESG disclosures and metrics, to CEO pay, which unfortunately may only drive impact for the numbers, not the outcomes. For example, driving DEI value doesn't necessarily happen in the amount of diversity you report but from supporting meaningful change or material efforts. While it is true that you can't manage what you can't measure, an executive with a particular compensation model will drive to the metrics they are managed on and may miss the outcome entirely.

And so, CEO pay is a critical material issue as the compensation model drives the behavior and strategy that the board wants to support. This lever is crucial for the board to pull when prioritizing ESG and long-term value, as the compensation model can influence the CEO's attention to these matters. The board can leverage mechanisms to support a long-term perspective such as stock options, performance-vested shares, or restricted stock that payout upon completion of service.[6]

Oversight and ESG enablement

Analysis and oversight of table stakes, values-led, and material ESG issues can occur directly from the board if ESG expertise does exist, and through existing or new committees. As Chief Sustainability and Diversity Officers might report to different organizations for the company, there isn't a one-size-fits-all approach to ESG assignments:

- ESG integration: The board understands ESG fully and integrates it across committees and the management team.
- Dedicated committee: Some boards will create a dedicated ESG committee. This committee can be a starting point to build expertise since ESG drives long-term value.
- Existing committee: A company might assign ESG oversight to an existing Risk Committee since ESG covers material risks. The responsibility could also fall to various other committees, such as Sustainability, Audit, Public Policy, or Governance.[7] Responsibility could also sit across several committees.

The goal should be to have ESG integration. As the board ramps up expertise through committees, and risks and opportunities surface, it must carefully listen across purpose, CSR, and ESG, then prioritize accordingly.

Governance doesn't only come first for ESG but for just about everything across the company's operations, management, culture, stakeholder engagement, and more. Since Governance describes the operational principles for how the company acts with its stakeholders, employees often unknowingly look to it when faced with a new challenge. For example, a Governance framework influences an employee's ability to ask thoughtful questions about their potential to execute against a challenge they are facing, whether they should take that power to act, and where ownership and accountability lie. Governance also balances priorities across the company, its stakeholders, and the ecosystem in which it operates. As a result, Governance is the first thing that comes up, regardless of your level at the company, whether you know it or not. It must be more than just words on a page.

So, while Governance should logically be first in the acronym, across expertise, misunderstandings, and the growing pressure for disclosures, boards may not deliver long-term value through ESG. Empowering these leaders to understand ESG is critical in ensuring they cover the material intersection of these topics with the business, affecting their ability to integrate ESG across the company's culture. Unfortunately, there is no time to waste as the world becomes more complex and pressures build.

ESG analysis: Stakeholders and materiality

In some ways, Governance should be in the middle of the acronym because it is critical to operations and connects everything, just like people do. Integrating ESG into the company's principles involves understanding stakeholders and materiality, which is quality Governance. While stakeholders primarily affect the Social pillar, understanding, listening to, and engaging them happens with quality Governance. Materiality helps companies understand where issues fall and whether or not they may come back to cause problems for the company.

Stakeholders are adding new levels of accountability to align with purpose-led and ESG-focused goals. However, accountability regarding ESG issues can be difficult because the boards of publicly traded companies are the custodians of fiduciary duty, and materiality around ESG matters is subject to interpretation. For example, some countries follow the business judgment rule where the board must act in good faith and in the business's best interest. Therefore, executives are not responsible for losses if they occur. However, with so much uncertainty around ESG and its long-term value, board accountability is not a black-and-white issue. Moreover, with a lack of personal liability around board decisions, ESG has little hope of using the law to drive accountability unless a misstep is egregious.

But again, as shareholder primacy gives way to additional stakeholders, emerging and changing ESG questions, especially Environmental and Social, are surfacing through purchasing power, social media influence, and even the value chain through B2B relationships. These tight stakeholder relationships are common across public and private companies. The entire flow of influence around a company to its board has transformed over the last few years as attention to ESG issues has accelerated, regardless of the board's position on ESG.

With such a vast ecosystem of stakeholders, pressure for non-material issues, like purposeful initiatives, may create conflicting priorities against material matters, especially as stakeholders look at companies to step up around primarily Environmental and Social issues as trust in more traditional institutions falls.[8] Depending on the stakeholder group, if a board ignores a stakeholder issue, material or not, there could be several consequences. For example, if a company ignores poor employee benefits or working conditions, employees may join a union for collective bargaining. Likewise, customers may band together in a boycott of goods if they feel the company isn't listening to their concerns. The board and management team cannot let short-termism, lack of ESG expertise, or conflicting personal priorities hinder listening to and servicing serious stakeholder concerns. Material accountability from the stakeholders to the risk or opportunity is needed for the company to act.

As these pressures push a range of purposeful and ESG issues into the company, driving clarity around tables stakes issues, risks, and opportunities with little expertise is challenging. However, a proactive approach with quality Governance principles can help mitigate the risks away from constant reactions to new and systemic issues. The company can leverage two ESG tools: a stakeholder mapping tool and a materiality matrix. While these tools can inform quality Governance, they are not limited to use by an assigned ESG committee, the board, or the management team. Anyone in the company or value chain can conduct this exercise for research and discussion.

Stakeholder mapping tool

As we saw in the previous chapter, companies have several groups of stakeholders to consider. Universally in business, stakeholder groups like employees, customers, and suppliers exist. Yet, each company is fundamentally so different that we quickly find that unique stakeholders within stakeholder groups need to be identified and investigated. Stakeholders are broad and deep, and their material intersections with the company are as such.

Employees and customers are the vast majority of stakeholders that the board regularly discusses.[9] However, this myopic view misses the broad internal and external stakeholders who could present risks and opportunities and, as a result, should also be up for discussion. For example, a hospital network might discuss patients as one stakeholder group. Still, caregivers and relatives are the ones who might take a patient to an appointment, give them their medicine, and make sure the bill gets paid. The caregiver influences the effect on the patient's health through their care. A hospital board examining this issue might recommend creating collaborative medical experiences built around the caregiver's needs to ensure the patient is cared for. Examples might include a simplified billing portal for the caregiver, accessible digital forms that approve caregiver access to the patient's medical records, and perhaps even a mental health hotline to care for the caregiver.

A stakeholder mapping exercise can help with this identification and expose the opportunity. This exercise can identify broad stakeholder groups, stakeholders within the group, their influence, effect, material needs that lead to value creation, and the outcomes leading to measurable metrics.

There is a simple flow around stakeholders that the board should look to discover, starting with the stakeholder groups as the broad categories, followed by more granular stakeholders to start (Figure 5.1). Once identified, the company can add several data points to develop a stakeholder thesis:

- Effect: The material effects of the Stakeholder
- Influence: Influence that the Stakeholder has over the company or other Stakeholders
- Value Creation: The value that the Stakeholder brings to the company
- Outcome: Metrics used to measure the outcome of value creation (the proof).

Let's take the example of a toy company that provides a mix of consumer and educational toys.

- Stakeholder Group: Consumers
- Stakeholders: Children, parents, adult collectors, educators, and schools
- Effect: Direct and indirect purchasing and effects on the bottom line, reputational risk, compliant marketing
- Influence: Influence across the ecosystem with peers and across programs and communities
- Value Creation: Product quality and safety, post-sale support improvements, independent social media content creation
- Outcomes: Revenue per product, the value of used goods (auctions), social media views, and educational program participation numbers.

FIGURE 5.1 Stakeholder mapping flow

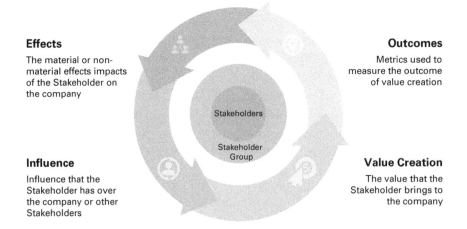

Effects

The material or non-material effects impacts of the Stakeholder on the company

Outcomes

Metrics used to measure the outcome of value creation

Stakeholders

Stakeholder Group

Influence

Influence that the Stakeholder has over the company or other Stakeholders

Value Creation

The value that the Stakeholder brings to the company

Several teams may review the results from here, such as the Marketing team, Product Developers, and others, for additional context and insights. While the board and management team can leverage the stakeholder mapping exercise for regular discussion, each related business unit should update the tool, review the results periodically, and escalate issues and insights to the board as the mapping evolves. From there, the board, management team, and business unit leaders must prioritize discussing stakeholders regularly to stay ahead of potential issues.

For example, a company with innovative engagement models and empowered employees may uncover stakeholder issues in siloes and get lucky with insights when the information is combined. Continuing the previous healthcare example, a thoughtful nurse might be more active in guiding a caregiver to patient care. Still, without an executive view and sponsorship, one nurse might pursue an active role, but another might not, leading to inconsistencies in service and care. Successfully engaging stakeholders requires all parts of the company to understand the stakeholders and the value they create.

Completing a stakeholder mapping exercise may involve other tools, like external surveys, feedback mechanisms, social media monitors, engagement models, and outcome analysis to ensure the company has a clear view of each stakeholder.

Stakeholder maps are sometimes not published or shared in CSR and ESG reports, at least in detail. Observationally, companies will select their most material stakeholder groups with a short write-up on why each matters to the company. The appearance of stakeholder groups is important to show that a company understands its value chain, but often, what is published is too high-level to be more than a platitude. A more interesting accompaniment to the report is how the company listens to and manages those groups, which reflects its Governance.

Materiality at the intersection of value creation is critical when considering stakeholders, as a challenge arises when stakeholder interests intersect in a non-material way with the company. If this happens, the company has two approaches it can take. First, the company can take a philanthropic approach and undergo charitable work, perhaps at a concession. Second, the company may integrate the non-material issue into the marketing and brand messaging. Unfortunately, the latter approach may be disjointed and alienate stakeholders, especially if leading with a specific set of values that the company cannot meet.

Materiality matrix

Some companies haven't adjusted to looking at their business through emerging ESG risks, remaining close to short-term and apparent financial risks. Per a 2022 PwC survey, most directors understand their company's ESG strategy, risk, and opportunities, yet only 57 percent see a connection to its fundamentals.[10] This discrepancy begs whether boards focus on material issues and the long-term or something else, like purpose, values, or disclosures. With this lack of expertise, the board may need to invest in formalized ESG education for its members to uncover the differences and set priorities accordingly.

A valuable tool in uncovering material issues is a materiality matrix, which can help companies understand their most pressing issues. Since stakeholders, including ESG investors, are interested in how the company prioritizes and manages these issues, companies sometimes publish their materiality matrix in their CSR or ESG reports. For investors and stakeholders, this information can help uncover alignments to priorities the company has and reveal opportunities for the former to invest in or provide lending to and the latter to execute against.

Before starting the materiality matrix, build on the intersection of stakeholder value creation and identify the Environmental, Social, and Governance issues that you believe intersect with your company. This exercise could involve researching your competitors, talking with your suppliers, checking the ESG rating agencies and the Value Reporting Foundation (VRF) for your company and industry, and asking around your company for feedback. While a competitor's disclosures are acceptable to study, be sure to ask yourself why they might be disclosing and if it is material. This exercise is less about disclosures than recognizing the company's most critical issues.

From here, map the results on a simple chart to show which issues the company should prioritize. To do this, create a 3 by 3 chart or table. The horizontal axis is the importance of an issue or risk to the company, with the risk to the company becoming more significant as it moves to the right. The vertical axis plots the importance of the issue to stakeholders. The higher an identified issue appears, the more critical it is. While mapping these out, it doesn't matter how well the company deals with the issue. The priority of the issue is what we are assessing. In other words, the further right and highest issue should be your biggest priority, regardless if the issue is well in hand. It is important to note that a crisis can quickly flip a low-priority issue to a high one.

FIGURE 5.2 Sample materiality matrix

	Low	Medium	High
High		• Product safety • License and intellectual property management • Climate risk/logistics	• Sustainable sourcing and products • Product safety • Digital safety/cybersecurity
Medium	• Accessibility • Community engagement	• Fan engagement • Promoting family-friendly workspaces • Diversity and inclusion in leadership • Sustainable packaging • Mainstreaming ESG	• Responsible and compliant marketing to children • Inclusive media and marketing • EH&S/worker safety • Forced labor in value chain
Low	Biodiversity	Responsible innovation management	Waste management

Stakeholder impact (vertical axis)

Business impact (horizontal axis)

For example, if we take a look at the material ESG issues our fictional toy company may need to deal with, it could look like Figure 5.2.

At the end of this exercise, the company's most pressing material issues appear in the upper right.

> It is worth noting that some companies will prioritize what they think their stakeholders, especially their shareholders, want to see. Like its published Corporate Governance Guidelines, a materiality matrix is also prone to universal or boilerplate issues. It is critical to populate the materiality matrix properly, otherwise material ESG risks and opportunities may go unaddressed.

There is another way to conduct a materiality assessment that involves your stakeholders more directly. In this case, you might run a questionnaire asking them about your business, which issues are the most material, and why. Combining the two efforts is worth undertaking to get the most detailed analysis possible. More advanced materiality matrices involve plotting the issues on a scatter chart similarly. Nevertheless, this rudimentary materiality matrix is a good starting point to help anyone in the company wrap their head around its most pressing ESG issues.

It is worth considering sharing your materiality matrix in your CSR or ESG report for transparency across your value chain and perhaps your competitors. While this may seem unnatural due to the level of transparency involved, solving pressing ESG challenges across the value chain alone can be difficult. Revisiting this information regularly, sharing it internally, and sharing it with your value chain has several benefits. First, these tools can propel company efforts forward with intention through open discussion and prioritization. This action moves the company from reactive to proactive as these issues are identified and addressed before surfacing. Still, it isn't enough to create a stakeholder mapping and materiality matrix and publish them. Companies must act on this information to make the exercise valuable. Otherwise, the data is as useless as boilerplate Corporate Governance Guidelines and non-material disclosures.

It is essential to recognize that not every problem is material today, and an issue may fall under dynamic materiality, meaning it becomes material over time. Even though our world is complex and crises are difficult to predict, revisiting stakeholder needs and materiality often is critical. These tools also represent data points to help investors and stakeholders understand how you see your business and to inform them of your decision-making rationale. While your company won't always please everyone, these tools can help you organize, prioritize, and make high-quality and defensible decisions.

Accountability mechanisms

Through these tools, additional perspectives of the business are created, leading to a consistent story that a management team can leverage. Defensible decisions based on material intersections can be more powerful than attempting to defend inaction in a changing world. ESG expertise and these tools can also help a company focus by not prioritizing or commenting on the latest political issue. If the company already has a tangential approach to a material issue, it is well-prepared to address controversy reactively or ignore it. Still, many problems can arise from the bottom up or outside in.

Getting board attention from outside stakeholder pressure sometimes takes a direct approach, which means working through investors, at least for publicly traded companies. Investors can set the board's priorities in targeted areas through shareholder proposals. These proposals are where a group of investors proposes a company's actions and shareholders vote. It may be non-binding if approved, but it remains a strong signal that the board should execute the proposal.

Over the past few years, there has been an uptick in the number of ESG-related shareholder proposals. The highest count of these proposals ever was in 2022 at 627 proposals; by February 2023, there were already 542.[11] However, it is worth noting that institutional support for these proposals may be waning as shareholders push for non-material ESG matters. For example, BlackRock Investment has stated that it is "more likely" to support proposals that address material risks and opportunities.[12] Of course, shareholders can vote as they like, but having powerful institutional support behind them is critical for success.

Boards participating in trend and competitive analysis of ESG issues, conducting stakeholder feedback and listening sessions, and setting the priorities for the company should not be caught off-guard by these proposals.

USE CASE: APPLE SHAREHOLDER PROPOSALS AROUND SOCIAL

For a while, stakeholder pressures on Apple had been brewing. As pressures around forced labor in China grew, Apple faced calls to do more around its involvement there. Other stakeholders were looking for proof of Apple's diversity and inclusion policies. Separately, there were concerns from one investment firm that ex-employees could not speak up freely about workplace issues after leaving the company.

All three issues became shareholder proposals for Apple during the 2022 season. While the company opposed them all, two made it through. First, shareholders voted for a civil rights audit to better inform stakeholders of Apple's approach.[13] As of April 2023, that audit is still underway. Second, shareholders approved transparency on concealment clauses. Apple consulted with counsel on the risk, who determined the risk of this move to be low. Later that year, Apple published a statement on the topic, allowing post-employees to discuss workplace issues.[14] Still, shareholders did not pass the proposal around potential forced labor in China.

During the 2023 proxy season, an anti-ESG shareholder proposal related to its Social approach went to Apple. The National Center for Public Policy Research proposed to consult with conservative groups on its approach to DEI because of a presumed bias towards white people.[15] Shareholders soundly defeated this proposal in a 98.5 percent vote.

Governance last: Nothing gets past poor Governance

So far, we've covered why Governance should come first in the acronym and considerations for operationalizing ESG through Governance in the middle. As a reminder, leading with Governance means building a solid foundation of guidelines and practices. Operationalizing Governance means investigating stakeholders and materiality to proactively identify and prioritize focus areas and drive action. However, Governance is precisely where it needs to be in the acronym. Governance must be last as a reminder and gatekeeper before we commit to decisions and act, as nothing gets past poor Governance.

In other words, Governance is the pillar that can take down a company.

Even with this incredible power, Governance is often the forgotten letter of ESG. While material and non-material Environmental and Social issues tend to garner the spotlight, press, and pages in CSR reports, executives take quality Governance for granted. Yet, companies that don't lead with ethics, compliance, or have material industry knowledge certainly would be subject to regulatory scrutiny, fines, and perhaps even a shareholder uprising. However, because boards often operate with little transparency and much confidentiality, Governance issues sometimes can go undetected until the company runs afoul of a problem. It is always much easier to see what went wrong in hindsight, as better insights are rarely available than after a company missteps and closes down. This event typically forces a level of board and executive transparency that the public rarely sees otherwise.

It's important to note that while a lack of attention to material Environmental or Social issues is unlikely to take down a company, attention to these pillars won't save a company either. However, ignoring or focusing on these pillars may erode or protect value over the long term. In the case of neglecting Governance, material divergence from company principles can be fatal.

USE CASE: SILICON VALLEY BANK

Silicon Valley Bank (SVB) was initially founded in 1983 to capture an opportunity with a unique stakeholder—startups. The approach filled a gap left by banks unwilling to accept the risk of the venture capital community. Like any stakeholder, startups have unique requirements for banking. They typically don't take out loans but rely on venture capital and investors for funding. This approach gives them a short cash runway of 12–36 months to build their platforms, go to market, secure customers, and then ask for more money.

The stakeholder model required the bank to find other ways to make money, which worked for decades. Still, a confluence of economic pressures, Governance issues, and stakeholder operations came together to take the bank down quickly.

First came a new pressure around SVB's model. A primary way banks make money is through loans and interest rates. Due to the unique operations of their stakeholders, SVB could not leverage loans because startups simply don't use them. So instead, SVB invested in long-term bonds with a fixed interest rate. When interest rates increase, the bank or investor can lose money, especially if the bank has to sell the bond.

After several years of sustained capital flows into startups, venture capital funding began to dry up in the middle of 2022 while interest rates were high. Many companies, especially financial institutions, have a Risk Committee and Chief Risk Officer to analyze events like this against the risk they present. Unfortunately, SVB was without a Chief Risk Officer for a critical eight-month period when these two issues came together, creating two effects.[16] First, startups needed to withdraw funds from their liquid pool at SVB to cover operating costs. Second, SVB had to sell bonds at a loss to cover the exposure.

Here's where the stakeholders come in. Today, startups are a tight-knit community where venture capitalists serve as advisors across the ecosystem. Unfortunately, as questions about SVB's liquidity rose, these advisors inadvertently created a run on the bank by convincing startups to pull out their money.[17] Further, digital technologies only made accessing funds easier. Technology turned a mundane table stakes operating task—quick withdrawals—into a massive risk.

As a result, California put SVB into receivership within days, sending ripple effects across the banking industry. In short, a Governance issue around risk management controls at one bank systemically impacted the startup community and global banks.

Again, hindsight is always clearer. It is worth noting that in 2015, banks were looking to roll back certain protections from the Dodd-Frank regulation. This regulation had stress-testing components to avoid financial services issues from the 2008 financial crisis. Under Dodd-Frank's Title I, any US bank with over $50 billion of assets is subject to additional regulatory scrutiny, including rules about capital losses, but more relevant here, liquidity issues.[18]

In 2015, SVB had $40 billion of assets, with the CEO commenting that regulators should raise the cap for Dodd-Frank as the bank didn't provide a systemic risk at its current level.[19] Alongside other leaders with similar concerns, the Trump administration raised the limit for this requirement to $250 billion of assets. By 2023, SVB's assets had swelled to $212 billion.

Overall, it wasn't just one thing that affected SVB, but a range of issues, including how its primary customer stakeholders operate, technology's ability to ease stakeholder access to funds, and insufficient consideration of risks around the operating model. Still, that last point around regulations cannot be overlooked, as the CEO is the one who commented on the proposed changes.

The role of regulations and externalities

Governments empower agencies to enact regulations to protect the planet and people from the negative impact of a company's operations. Typically, a prompting event, election promise, or citizen pressure leads to a government investigating and adopting regulation. For example, President Richard Nixon created the US Environmental Protection Agency in response to the 1969 Cuyahoga River Fire, where pollutants from local industries built up and caught fire from a flare. This event also led to the Clean Water Act of 1972.[20] In a similar example around a Governance regulation, Sarbanes-Oxley, a US law outlining financial recordkeeping practices, was formed after a series of high-profile accounting scandals around the early 2000s.[21]

In some cases, companies will comment or lobby against regulations because they represent a compliance cost to the company. Still, proposed and enacted regulations represent opportunities for a company to reflect on its material issues and risks, allowing thoughtful risk mitigation strategies to form.

One area where the board can lead is through attention to compliance issues in partnership with the Chief Legal Officer, General Counsel, or Compliance Officer. Compliance across Environmental, Health, and Safety (EHS), local labor laws, environmental regulations, and other external limitations and guardrails around operations are material Governance concerns. If someone at the company isn't accountable for the regulatory filings and adherence, it can lead to fines, litigation, and even the company's demise.

Again, there is limited liability for a board member due to the business judgment rule. Still, that doesn't always apply if the board has executed criminal activities through the company, willfully misled or engaged in illegal or immoral activity, or was deliberately out of compliance with certain laws, including fairly common rules related to the Environmental and Social pillars:

- Environmental regulations
- Labor practices and rights
- Consumer protections.

In many cases, regulations help manage the risks of externalities. As a reminder, externalities are costs or benefits caused by the company's operations but consigned to someone else. Business regulations often focus on negative externalities, which exist whether there are regulations around the issue or not. For example, a beverage company might leverage a community's local water source to manufacture its product. The company's depletion of that water is an externality due to its impact on the community. The community represents external stakeholders who incur a cost from the company's operations.

Today, markets don't adjust for the impact of value from externalities and, therefore, don't account for the actual cost of doing business. However, there are principles that companies can adopt around impact-weighted accounting, which can help a leadership team or investor understand the adjusted value.[22] This methodology focuses on the company's impact on the world and accounts for its positive and negative externalities. Taken further with an ESG mindset, thinking about your company's costs like this can provide insights into potential future issues and regulations that might emerge. For example, if that beverage company understood its impact on water, it could adjust its operational practices before possible regulation or lawsuits.

A crisis can bring in new stakeholders

Complicating externalities are crises that can emerge suddenly. For example, an unexpected environmental accident or high-profile safety issue could have far-reaching effects beyond a company's reputational risk. Part of having an ESG mindset is dealing with uncertainty, but that doesn't mean that your company doesn't have a plan in place for a crisis. The Governance principles set by the board should be adaptable around a solid framework to keep your company resilient.

Thinking through potential crises from a stakeholder map or materiality matrix may not uncover the impact, which can affect the company. A crisis can bring a new stakeholder front and center, one who isn't a stakeholder in the business until the situation demands it.

Suppose a manufacturing plant operates within a local community. In that case, the community is a stakeholder because employees likely live there. The plant must also consider externalities and the operational impact on the community. For the latter, this is how an issue can evolve into a material matter over time. However, for a company operating in several markets, the geographic range of its value chain may cover nearly the entire planet as goods and materials are transported and processed through local communities temporarily. If an accident happens while your company or value chain is transporting materials or goods, it can cause new stakeholders to emerge. We might refer to these people as "dynamic stakeholders." Like dynamic materiality, these stakeholders arise in the future around a crisis.

Dynamic stakeholders can be difficult to predict as many companies may not have detailed insight into their value chain's activities. For example, a chemical company might rely on a train to deliver chemicals to its plant. If that train derails in a community, suddenly the originating company and the train company may need to address new, unknown stakeholders in a new area. For example, in February 2023, a train carrying toxic chemicals, operated by Norfolk Southern, derailed in East Palestine, Ohio. Since that event, the company has answered to existing stakeholders, such as regulators and the US government. The company has also established a dedicated website to keep citizens updated on its efforts in the community, a new stakeholder. The website "Making it Right" contains the following information:[23]

- A commitment for doing what's right for the community
- Ongoing effort updates, including monetary community support
- A local Family Assistance Center
- Air, drinking, and surface water, and soil testing updates
- Incident site cleanup updates
- Contact information for air, in-home air testing, drinking water, soil, and other assistance.

These local people were not stakeholders in the company before the accident but now are due to a crisis event.

One last word on Governance

Each letter of ESG has its unique perspective and value when looking at your company. However, out of the three letters, Governance is the one that affects the company the most as it guides the company's operating principles, influences stakeholder engagement, and can ultimately protect, erode, or eliminate long-term value for all stakeholders, including those your company might not have yet.

Notes

1 Allen, J., Schacht, K., and Orsagh, M. (2020). Short-termism revisited. The Harvard Law School Forum on Corporate Governance. corpgov.law.harvard. edu/2020/10/11/short-termism-revisited/ (archived at https://perma.cc/FBK6-9DTH).

2 Whelan, T. (2021). U.S. corporate boards suffer from inadequate expertise in financially material ESG matters. *SSRN Electronic Journal*, p. 3. https://doi. org/10.2139/ssrn.3758584 (archived at https://perma.cc/KZD9-P36U).

3 Soonieus, R., Woods, W., Young, D., and Tatar, S. (2022). Directors can up their game on environmental, social, and governance issues. p. 1. www.insead.edu/ sites/default/files/assets/dept/centres/icgc/docs/directors-can-up-their-game-on-environmental-social-and-governance-issues-march2022.pdf (archived at https:// perma.cc/2B7H-KDVC).

4 As You Sow (n.d.). CEO pay. As You Sow. www.asyousow.org/our-work/ ceo-pay/ (archived at https://perma.cc/Q5Q7-W3AQ).

5 Mishel, L. and Kandra, J. (2021). CEO pay has skyrocketed 1,322% since 1978. Economic Policy Institute. www.epi.org/publication/ceo-pay-in-2020/ (archived at https://perma.cc/PT3T-M78Z).

6 CEO Worldwide (2022). CEO compensation structure, incentives and salary. CEO Worldwide. www.ceo-worldwide.com/blog/ceo-compensation-structure-incentives-and-salary (archived at https://perma.cc/L3LM-PHMU).

7 Ashley, J. and Morrison, R.V. (2021). ESG governance: Board and management roles & responsibilities. The Harvard Law School Forum on Corporate Governance. corpgov.law.harvard.edu/2021/11/10/esg-governance-board-and-management-roles-responsibilities/ (archived at https://perma.cc/ERT6-6NL7).

8 Whiting, K. (2022). Edelman report: Cycle of distrust threatens action on global challenges. World Economic Forum. www.weforum.org/agenda/2022/ 01/edelman-trust-barometer-2022-report/ (archived at https://perma.cc/3G5E-Q7HN).

9 Kors, A. (2020). Stakeholder capitalism: Translating corporate purpose into board practice. Diligent Institute, p. 9. https://web.archive.org/web/20230311112723/https:/www.diligentinstitute.com/wp-content/uploads/2020/08/20200713-Diligent-Institute-Report-Stakeholders-and-Boards-R5.pdf (archived at https://perma.cc/9J8Z-HLL4).

10 Castañón Moats, M. and DeNicola, P. (2022). Charting the course through a changing governance landscape. PwC, p. 16. www.pwc.com/us/en/services/governance-insights-center/assets/pwc-2022-annual-corporate-directors-survey.pdf (archived at https://perma.cc/4RTN-ZAFL).

11 Posner, C. (2023). Lots of shareholder proposals on ESG this proxy season—and quite a few anti-ESG proposals too. Cooley PubCo. cooleypubco.com/2023/04/12/shareholder-proposals-esg-this-proxy-season/ (archived at https://perma.cc/D65L-ZKK7).

12 BlackRock Investment Stewardship (2022). 2022 climate-related shareholder proposals more prescriptive than 2021. BlackRock, p. 1. www.blackrock.com/corporate/literature/publication/commentary-bis-approach-shareholder-proposals.pdf (archived at https://perma.cc/9W95-S82X).

13 Halaschak, Z. (2022). Apple investors vote for "civil rights audit" but reject China forced labor proposal. *Washington Examiner*. www.washingtonexaminer.com/policy/economy/apple-investors-vote-for-civil-rights-audit-but-reject-china-forced-labor-proposal (archived at https://perma.cc/XN6Z-7X5D).

14 Apple (2022). Our commitment to an open and collaborative workplace. Apple. pp. 1–3. s2.q4cdn.com/470004039/files/doc_downloads/2022/12/Our-Commitment-to-an-Open-and-Collaborative-Workplace.pdf (archived at https://perma.cc/YX5F-R96M).

15 Nellis, S. (2023). Apple shareholders reject proposals from conservative groups. Reuters. www.reuters.com/technology/apple-shareholders-reject-proposals-conservative-groups-2023-03-10/ (archived at https://perma.cc/F825-7UP3).

16 Cohen, B. (2023). It's the most thankless job in banking. Silicon Valley Bank didn't fill it for months. *The Wall Street Journal*, March 23. www.wsj.com/articles/svb-silicon-valley-bank-collapse-chief-risk-officer-f6e1fcfd (archived at https://perma.cc/QPM6-F6LN).

17 Hart, J. (2023). Venture capitalists are blaming each other for triggering the disastrous collapse of Silicon Valley Bank. Business Insider. www.businessinsider.com/vcs-blame-each-other-for-silicon-valley-bank-collapse-2023-3 (archived at https://perma.cc/BR7H-X6D4).

18 Finkle, V. (2015). Midsize banks raise warning about $50B SIFI threshold bill. *American Banker*. www.americanbanker.com/news/midsize-banks-raise-warning-about-50b-sifi-threshold-bill (archived at https://perma.cc/NUZ4-3WTM).

19 U.S. Government Publishing Office. (2015). Examining the Regulatory Regime for Regional Banks. GovInfo, pp. 117–121. www.govinfo.gov/content/pkg/CHRG-114shrg94375/pdf/CHRG-114shrg94375.pdf (archived at https://perma.cc/6B9B-5Y73).

20 Cuyahoga Valley National Park (2022). The 1969 Cuyahoga River Fire. National Park Service. www.nps.gov/articles/story-of-the-fire.htm (archived at https://perma.cc/23FC-N49X).

21 Kenton, W. (2022). Sarbanes-Oxley (SOX) Act of 2002. Investopedia. www.investopedia.com/terms/s/sarbanesoxleyact.asp (archived at https://perma.cc/424G-HPAS).

22 Cohen, R. and Serafeim, G. (2020). How to measure a company's real impact. *Harvard Business Review*. hbr.org/2020/09/how-to-measure-a-companys-real-impact (archived at https://perma.cc/7SCX-3ER2).

23 Norfolk Southern (n.d.). Making it right in East Palestine. Making it Right. nsmakingitright.com/ (archived at https://perma.cc/8UAG-C9EU).

06

The Dual Intersection Between Technology and ESG

Technology rules our lives for many of us, for better or worse. We find ourselves tethered to our phones and devices, having to take an active role in tuning out the noise of the digital jungle if we are to focus. Post-Covid, this challenge has accelerated as ubiquitous Technology access and connectivity allow for remote and hybrid work, frustrating some because it seems work never ends. Still, there are opportunities for companies as this access unlocks new diverse talent pools while allowing employees to work more or less on their terms and scaling to meet customer needs across a global market. Underpinning the infrastructure behind the scenes is each company's complex Technology stack of cloud services, servers, networking, storage equipment, and software that runs operations, services, products, and processes. Just like for many of us, there can be no doubt about just how inextricably linked Technology and modern business are, too.

It's hard to believe that the application of digital technologies in this way is a relatively recent phenomenon that has evolved exponentially over a single working generation. When I was fresh out of college, business Technology was still evolving from its early days of mainframes to networked computers. Company leaders wondered if they needed public email, domain names, and a public internet presence. The internet boomed and busted shortly after, spinning out online commerce, mobile apps, and new interconnected business applications. Web 2.0 unlocked the user-driven content we are familiar with across social media. The next Technology revolution is already upon us, where businesses are working to integrate Web 3.0 technologies like blockchain, the metaverse, and Generative AI. All of this has transpired in just the past 40 years.

Today, a company's value has shifted from physical assets to intangibles, largely built on Technology, such as intellectual property and new business processes. As of 2020, 90 percent of company value within the S&P 500 sat within intangibles,[1] accelerating at the same pace as Technology within the business. With all this value wrapped up in Technology, it is no surprise that the ongoing investment significantly contributes to the global economy. Gartner predicted global IT spend would reach $4.5 trillion in 2023.[2]

In 2003, when ESG first made its rounds, the first iPhone and the App Store were still four years from release.[3] At this time, IT teams were charged mainly with keeping the lights on and performing rote upgrades and maintenance. It is interesting to consider if the original creators of ESG would have added Technology as another pillar if they had created it just a few years later. In many ways, every company is a Technology company today. But there is more to consider regarding Technology and its use at two distinct intersections with ESG.

Adding Technology as another pillar of ESG can shift our mindset in two ways. First, companies will use Technology to solve ESG risks while creating new opportunities. Second, Technology has risks and opportunities similar to those we've seen with the pillars of E, S, and G. While companies are undoubtedly familiar with the former, the latter idea is nascent. Yet, its pace moves too quickly sometimes, and companies can be overeager to leverage it to capture opportunities. Therefore, we must always be mindful of the risks around the problems we are trying to solve and the opportunities we want to capture, lest we create more significant challenges (Figure 6.1).

FIGURE 6.1 The dual intersection of ESG and Technology

Solving ESG issues

Climate-risk models, stakeholder data and insights, operational processes

As an ESG risk (or opportunity)

Cybersecurity, responsible AI, democratized Technology access, new products/services

Technology solving ESG issues

Even though Technology sits at the foundation of the business, software developers, those building the software of this era, haven't always intended it to solve ESG challenges. Instead, Technology does what developers designed it for, running various aspects of the company's operations and processes. For example, a Human Resources system manages employee records. It may align with the US Department of Labor's EEO-1 reporting requirements and surface attrition rates but is likely unable to uncover direct insights about corporate culture or productivity. Likewise, a supply chain platform might manage supplier records, contracts, and shipments. Still, it may be unable to find acute climate risks on logistical routes in real time, or cope with the immensely challenging issue of forced labor.

With the gap between Technology and its native abilities to solve ESG issues, the board, executives, and business unit leaders struggle to understand how to weave new Technology with existing systems to solve ESG issues. The reality is that many ESG solutions must be bolted on or custom-built since existing platforms lack ESG capabilities, and the company's Technology stack and IT team may not be ready. Even worse, some IT teams are simply keeping the lights on with little investment in modernization, let alone ESG-integrated solutions. With ESG and a shift in thinking, IT leaders have a unique opportunity to move into the role of valuable business consultants and advisors, as Technology management skills are critical to creating new solutions, defining costs, and ensuring long-term supportability. However, IT leaders need not take on this challenge alone as a Technology concept exists to help.

Since around 2014, the central theme from prominent Technology vendors to address material business challenges has been "Digital Transformation." This concept applies Technology to build new digital products and experiences for customers and employees, drive efficiency in operations, and hopefully create long-term revenue growth. These concepts echo ESG. However, having watched IT teams attempt to integrate Technology into the business this way over the years, the level of success has been mixed. Instead of delivering meaningful change, many Digital Transformation efforts have ranged from simple Technology modernization to outright failure, leaving digital natives and startups to disrupt industries. In one study, BCG found that only 30 percent of Digital Transformation projects were successful.[4] The reasons these projects fail can vary significantly and are worth a review.

Legacy Technology runs rampant across many businesses, which can be costly to update due to its heavy integration across people and processes. Think of this like transition risk, which we covered in Chapter 3. As a result, these projects also run long with many moving parts due to their transformative nature, and the company's priorities can shift over the project's time window. Due to short-term thinking and predictability, executives may balk at complex IT budgets that span multiple years, another echo of ESG. In addition, IT may need new skills to connect siloed systems or develop bespoke integrated solutions, which can take time and investment. Lastly, these projects may stall if an employee's inertia and fear of change get in the way. Like any ESG issue, stakeholders need to be considered.

However, looking at Technology through an ESG mindset towards material issues and a view for long-term results can deliver on the promise of Digital Transformation. As executive leaders understand more about ESG, solving issues gives Digital Transformation something it never had—a connection to a material issue which connects to a business imperative and, therefore, access to budget. It is worth noting that Digital Transformation is coincidentally starting to get more board-level attention, as 42 percent of boards prioritized it in 2023 versus only 19 percent the previous year.[5]

To deliver on the promise of Digital Transformation and gain ESG insights to solve these challenges, a company must modernize legacy Technology, break down internal Technology and business unit siloes, and solve complex cultural fear of change. Whether digital or structurally based, internal fiefdoms will hinder the efforts, so stakeholders and quality Governance will play an important role, especially as the pressures grow for table stakes issues like disclosures. Technology, while not a panacea, can drive long-term value, not only by protecting the company from compliance issues, but also through addressing specific ESG issues and lowering related risks.

Technology and data enable disclosures and material insights

Before we look at some of the broadly applicable intersections between ESG and Technology, it is worth recalling Chapter 2 and the role that data plays in a world facing ESG disclosure pressure. While disclosures are not necessarily the most material ESG risk or opportunity a company could deal with, they represent a compliance risk, and legacy business systems struggle to understand these new requirements. Therefore, modernizing Technology systems to align with reporting requirements is good Governance.

Today, the responsibility to collect and report ESG disclosures sits across several compliance-related functions, including a company's General

Counsel, Audit and Risk Committees, Chief Sustainability Officer, and Head of Human Resources. These roles need to collaborate with IT to ensure digital systems report accurate data, conduct transparent and traceable calculations, and that audit controls exist. Whether the disclosure information is material or not, sustainability, DEI, and ESG represent opportunities to learn more about your company's processes, understand your stakeholders better, and improve on both. However, Technology and data outside of disclosures can also lead to material insights across ESG issues.

Climate risk and Technology

Collaboration is one area to consider at the intersection of the Environment and Technology beyond disclosures. It can be easy for a company to claim Environmental savings from Technology-enabled collaboration tools through employees traveling less. Still, business travel isn't very material for some industries outside of consultancies and may be more aligned with sustainability efforts. If a business trip is canceled, it can be easily moved to a remote meeting, facilitated over Teams, Zoom, or WebEx. To find how Technology can solve material ESG issues, we must look closer.

Many companies have physical facilities and a geographically dispersed value chain in our post-Covid hybrid and remote work world. From manufacturers pulling together raw materials to build a physical product, to retailers placing items on shelves, to your local coffee shop, we live and work in a physical world with risks. With climate change, acute and chronic risks impact physical locations. The prediction of these risks can be assisted with digital technologies.

Technology can uncover extreme weather event probabilities and provide companies with digital insight into these physical risks. With historical climate data and new forecasting models, Facilities and Real Estate teams can begin assessing risk to build adaptation strategies. Satellite imagery, sensor and IoT data, and AI models can be combined with specific scientific expertise to uncover climate risk. Building these Technology-based planetary insights is what a company called Earth Knowledge does with hundreds of petabytes of data.[6] It has effectively created a digital twin of the Earth to uncover long-term risk across several climate indicators. Using the models, a hotel management company might learn that three of the managed properties in California are at high risk of wildfires. From that digital insight, the company could further explore ways to adapt the land around the property for that risk through landscaping, plant cover, or other options. In this way, the digital translates back into the physical world, helping the company plan for long-term resilience.

However, climate risk is just one material Environmental issue where Technology can help. For example, a consumer goods or manufacturing company may find, through data and market trend analysis, that customers are seeking sustainable products. Addressing this opportunity might require the company to pull value chain data upstream to uncover options for changing product materials or formulas to more sustainable options. Unfortunately, this information isn't easy to discover today as the world hasn't transitioned to collecting or sharing this type of value chain data. Another Technology, proxy data, has stepped in to fill this gap. Proxy data stands in for actual data because the actuals are not available. Still, companies need to be wary because making sustainability claims against proxy data, and not actuals, can result in greenwashing, no matter how good the data is. Of course, once a Research and Development team has the quality data, it can begin to make informed decisions and drive sustainable product improvements to align with the market need.

Between stakeholders and Technology is the Social

Regarding material stakeholder management and engagement, collaboration tools mentioned previously can play a role in the Social. While people have long conducted business over email, advanced chat tools like Teams, Slack, WhatsApp, and real-time file collaboration allow high-quality interaction and content co-creation. Employees working remotely proved the material value of these tools during Covid, as new working habits developed out of necessity. Companies can build on the lessons during this time and turn to other Social matters—ensuring the retention of diverse talent through employee-to-employee connections.

Employees are one of a company's most critical stakeholders. However, building and maintaining a cohesive culture with remote and hybrid work or operating across global offices can be a massive challenge. One area is measuring employees' productivity and looking for burnout metrics through collaboration tools. Microsoft ran a report on hybrid work in 2022 where it found, through signals in its collaboration tooling, that the number of meetings per week had increased by 153 percent globally since the start of the pandemic and that 42 percent of people were multitasking during meetings—important statistics to show how employee time is being spent.[7]

Hosting Employee Resource Groups (ERGs) inside digital collaboration tools can facilitate these connections. A digital space can allow employees to foster a consistent culture and share company best practices through their passions and diversity. For example, an idea may form inside a digital group, advance into new opportunities, and translate into real-world change, which was covered in Chapter 4.

Another place Technology intersects with stakeholders is with customers. At this intersection are the signals customers create daily through digitally enabled experiences and connected devices. Research and Development, Support, and Marketing teams can reason over this data with analysis tools and visualizations to unlock opportunities with informed insights. But as always, you need diverse staff to match your customers and bring the context to make sense of that data.

To achieve any of these stakeholder insights, IT and the business must break down internal Technology and employee-based siloes. From a Technology perspective, this may involve connecting disparate systems and building new data and AI tooling to surface insights from the connections. New software is also emerging to create relationships between business systems to uncover complex data relationships and find patterns. These "control tower" solutions may remove the need for an expensive rip and replace of core business software that was fit for purpose. As an overlay, it overcomes some challenges that lead to failed Digital Transformation projects like multi-year projects that disrupt business processes.

Tech-enabled Governance

The previous Environmental and Social examples are relatively straightforward, but the universe of Digital Transformation's ability to solve ESG issues is immense. The recognition and understanding of this concept represent thoughtful Governance. Still, there are examples of Technology addressing Governance issues, and as you might expect, it happens at the highest levels of the company.

Consider the data that a CFO reasons over every day. Various Procurement, Sales, and Accounting systems funnel this information into complex spreadsheets and financial programs. These digital systems feed into a company's financial statements, balance sheets, and reporting metrics. Gone are the days of manually tracking financials in paper ledgers with manual inputs and calculations. Instead, this core business data and resulting processes reside in digital systems with computers to help with the accounting and AI models to help with forecasting. The company would be at tremendous risk if a CFO couldn't access this complex information quickly. The financials, underpinned by Technology in this way, are one mundane example of how data gathering and analysis tooling, likely with the perennial favorite software, Excel, play a role in Governance.

ESG metrics, often considered non-financials, have the same need as financials, but lack similar visibility. Beyond the table stakes ESG disclosures, standards, and compliance requirements, few business systems are built to track the mountain of material intersections with ESG issues, not to mention ongoing crises. Ultimately, executives may look to Digital Transformation to integrate ESG considerations into existing business processes and applications while reporting new ESG data. But, in many ways, there is a step companies need to take first. Getting the Technology stack to where it needs to be is an incredible Governance challenge because it will take investment, time, and the courage to transition. Leaders need to be mindful of the pitfalls of these projects and adjust accordingly.

If done well, Digital Transformation can potentially pivot the company around its most material issues, but there are benefits even in basic modernization of systems. As the company moves towards new digital systems, the data quality improves. As data quality improves, executives can make better-informed decisions based on that data, leading to improved Governance. On the other hand, suppose the business doesn't modernize around Technology, like a CFO still working in a paper ledger. In that case, executives have a myopic, fixed, or missing view of their ESG risk and opportunities, akin to deciding if a movie is good or bad from a single frame instead of the entire picture.

Regardless of what business data is available digitally, Digital Transformation and new technologies might be part of the solution, but may also introduce additional complexity and risk.

Technology as an ESG risk

Today, the power between Technology and humans can't be understated. Computers, mobile devices, and internet access can empower anyone to achieve incredible things, interact with stakeholders in new ways, and play a role in solving our most pressing challenges.

While we've reviewed how Technology is at the core of addressing a company's ESG risks and opportunities, there is another intersection because Technology is complex and rife with its own ESG-like risks and opportunities. Dr. Andrea Bonime-Blanc outlined this idea of adding Technology as a fourth pillar of ESG in her book *Gloom to Boom*, and she was prophetic in her connection. "The utterly disruptive and revolutionary impact that technology (of all kinds) is having and will continue to have on everything in the world today invites the question why technology hasn't properly been included in ESG discussions before."[8]

This is an excellent question as Technology has long been a similar risk and represented an intangible opportunity to capture. As ESG was forming in the early 2000s, computer viruses were one of the main risks around Technology. As a company digitized with software, the risk manifested across the business. These viruses were nowhere near the complex web of modern malware and phishing we struggle with today, which AI-integrated security tooling can help mitigate. Another risk back then was outages, which still plague companies. New technologies like content delivery networks that hold copies of information globally, disaster recovery strategies, and decentralized application architectures represent opportunities to solve this risk. Technology might appear to be continually working to solve its problems, but it can't solve anything without thoughtful humans understanding the risk and working towards solutions.

By the mid-2000s, remote access to work systems opened with tools like Outlook Web Access and Blackberry devices. I remember my boss asking me about the risk of cybersecurity as he wondered if it was safe to allow email from anywhere. We also explored if Research in Motion, the Canadian company that built Blackberry devices and ran the software, was a risk if emails went through their servers for inspection and delivery.

Over the past 20 years, the cloud and mobile networks have democratized access to the world's most powerful technologies and have entirely changed the landscape of modern business. As a result, the questions we ask today must also evolve, and an ESG mindset can play a role.

As Technology's footprint takes over core business processes, especially in nuanced ways with ESG integration, new threats emerge that did not exist before. In other words, more powerful technologies can mean more powerful risks. While thoughtful IT developers and engineers may consider these risks, new challenges arise when people see the promise of Technology and eagerly pursue it with abandon. Along with this tremendous power and opportunity comes unproductive pressure from executives to implement solutions quickly in the pursuit of growth or competitive advantage. Unfortunately, quick speed to market means poor implementations and possibly even additional risks, including reputational damage, product roll-backs, or even government investigations.

As the custodians of Technology, the Chief Information or Technology Officer needs to set the pace by serving in an advisory capacity at least and an ethicist at best. The latter may be an unfamiliar role for a technologist or even many of us, but as with any pillar of ESG, this approach helps reduce risk and protect opportunity.

Cybersecurity must come first

Technology touches everything from mundane business functions to inform-ing executive decisions that could determine the direction of a company. However, its mere existence across every company level is a risk because every Technology could have an attack vector that a bad actor can exploit.

The risk vectors are complex for cybersecurity experts to manage as they weigh the convenience of Technology against the risk of exposure. For example, if a computer or mobile device is compromised, every system tied to that employee's credentials may be at risk. Furthermore, these threats could quickly scale as IT breaks down data siloes and connects business systems to gain new ESG insights. In effect, modernization and connectivity introduce risks.

The range of cybersecurity threats facing companies runs the spectrum of motivations and skill sets. For example:

- A disgruntled employee might siphon corporate secrets and intellectual property off the network.
- A novice hacker might use scripts and automation tools to infect comput-ers with malware, holding them for ransom or creating chaos for fun.
- Competitors may engage in digital corporate espionage and attempt to steal trade secrets.
- Nation states may look to damage critical digital infrastructure, affecting network access and physical systems.

Even as cybersecurity continues to make its way up the board agenda, the confidence may be too high that things are well in hand. Over 90 percent of directors are comfortable that their company is staying current on cybersecurity, has identified its critical digital information, and has tested its defenses enough.[9] But unfortunately, cybersecurity requires constant vigilance and investment. Confidence, comfort, and complacency have no place here. Not only can the smallest digital entry point have ripple effects across connected business systems, but the digital consequences can spill into the physical world.

USE CASE: COLONIAL PIPELINE

The Colonial Pipeline supplies fuel from the Gulf Coast to East Coast cities in the USA. It is a critical part of America's energy infrastructure. In May 2021, the Colonial Pipeline shut down its operations in response to a ransomware attack. An attack like this is typically where computers and data are effectively locked until the victim pays the ransom. If the infected computers run the company's operations, it can halt the business. Per testimony from Colonial Pipeline's CEO, this attack occurred due to a stolen password and a VPN that did not have multi-factor authentication.[10]

Shutting down the pipeline disrupted the fuel supply and had an immediate stakeholder effect, creating fuel shortages in the eastern USA and increasing fuel prices.[11] However, the risk grew beyond even the company's stakeholders as the Biden administration took steps to protect critical energy infrastructure in the country, including setting requirements for other pipeline providers to hire 24/7 cybersecurity staff and increase reporting requirements.[12]

While not directly tied to the Colonial Pipeline incident, in March 2023, the Biden administration announced a National Cybersecurity Strategy. It focuses on defending against attacks, actively dismantling threat actors, shifting the responsibility away from those most vulnerable, and making additional investments in research and development, training, and global alliances.[13] This strategy statement has scope across both public and private sectors. By July 2023, the US SEC adopted a rule for cybersecurity disclosures that describes how the board oversees the issue, since it may be a material consideration for investors.[14]

Are your data, processes, and people ready for artificial intelligence?

One of the most revolutionary technologies over the past decade has been Artificial Intelligence (AI). This term actually can refer to several Technologies. Here are some examples:

- Automation—automating tasks digitally
- Natural language processing—enables computers to understand human language
- Computer vision—enables computers to contextualize images from the real world
- Machine learning—developing systems that can learn and adapt without human intervention
- Generative AI—a system that can produce various types of content from text, images, videos, and more.

For companies, AI tooling is like having a robust, scalable workforce at your beck and call, which can make it a threat to employees. For example, as automation grew in popularity, employees saw it displacing certain types of work, as is the case for almost any new Technology. Yet, automation can offload repetitive work, such as manual data entry, so that employees can focus on higher-value tasks. Companies must empower employees to adapt through training and reskilling as new kinds of work are needed. However, that doesn't mean that AI isn't without risks, as job displacement or disruption may happen. Executives and business leaders revel at the possibilities of AI, but company risk sits squarely in the middle of its potential.

One sustainability consideration with any new digital Technology is its energy use and carbon emissions, and AI is no different. The data that underpins the models is hosted on disks and in memory. The training models run in infrastructure and use processing power. The front-end interfaces for the models, accessed through websites and applications, are hosted on servers. However, for many companies, Technology emissions are not a material issue as the emissions do not pose a significant risk to the business. Still, it's worth noting three considerations for running infrastructure, code, and AI sustainably:

1 A quality Governance model should be developed around the implementation to contain costs and the solution's scalability.

2 Developers may want to check that their code is running optimally. The Green Software Foundation launched a Software Carbon Intensity specification to assist with this assessment.[15]

3 There is developing research around the intersection of AI model training, model accuracy, and subsequent carbon savings.[16]

Keeping these recommendations at the forefront can put IT, developers, and data scientists in the right mindset to prioritize sustainability.

Turning to AI with an ESG mindset, the material risk around AI comes into play in at least two areas: the data, processes, and people used to train the models, and the usage of the model.

The world has created galaxies of data. A company might use its internal data to train an AI model or supplement it with externally available purchased or public datasets. The data, alongside existing processes, may contain systemic or other bias as many of the systems and processes we've created for our businesses have this, unfortunately. Over time, employees may introduce bias either intentionally or unknowingly. The risk manifests when a company scales up the biased data and processes with an AI model. As you can imagine, the bias also scales.

One way to hedge against this risk is to hire diverse data scientists and AI developers and empower them to challenge and question. Data scientists can reason over the data before scaling to potentially uncover bias early. Developers must also create algorithms with stakeholders in mind and develop feedback loops and check-ins on the algorithms to avoid newly created biases.

In addition, AI is a powerful tool readily available in the cloud for anyone's use. However, the result could be harmful if layered onto a new opportunity without ESG consideration. For example, computer vision is a highly controversial area. On the one hand, manufacturing companies can use computer vision for quality control via visual inspection. This application may improve customer satisfaction through consistency. Consider the high specifications required for a piece of medical equipment, for example, which a machine may determine more accurately than a human. On the other hand, computer vision can mean facial recognition, which is wildly complex. For example, a healthcare monitoring company may use facial recognition in an eldercare facility to detect a stroke, which is helpful. Still, material ESG considerations in this use case might be related to cybersecurity and digital privacy. Further, using facial recognition as part of law enforcement may contain too much bias to be valid, causing police to arrest innocent citizens.

Despite these risks, Technology itself isn't the issue—that is the mixture of humans, systemic processes, and Technology. NIST called this challenge out in 2022 as it explored responsible AI frameworks, recognizing the need for a new socio-technical approach that considers multiple disciplines and stakeholders.[17] Like every pillar of ESG, Technology requires a lens across the pillars with people at the center. NIST recognizes the Social and Technology in its terminology and approach, but the ability to execute against this recognition also is a Governance issue.

Protecting your external stakeholders

Technology allows a company to scale its resources to give every customer a personalized experience. However, capturing this opportunity requires a company to gather personal data. An individual's right to privacy and control over the data they generate, not to mention cybersecurity concerns, surrounds this opportunity. While we often believe that the internet affords people some anonymity, the collection and correlation of different datasets across applications and services break down that façade. Companies must know how their stakeholders' personal data is stored and used, and then put Data Governance policies into place, especially as they operate in a digital and global ecosystem.

When corporates store customer information, there is always a risk that hackers may expose the data through a cybersecurity incident. My cybersecurity colleagues used to argue that, "No one wants to end up on the front page of the *Wall Street Journal*." Unfortunately, many companies have had this happen via a data breach, where a bad actor has stolen and published data online. In some cases, the government imposed fines, or the company had to make concessions to repair reputational damage. For example, after the Anthem Healthcare hack in 2015, the company offered free identity theft protection to customers.[18]

Another risk comes when companies protect customer data but leverage it without consent to build new products and services. For example, let's assume someone signs up for a social media service with their name, phone number, and email address. Even with little information, a retailer could purchase parts of the data, link it to social media networks, and target that person with specific campaigns. While this seems innocuous enough, albeit an annoyance, both the social media company and retailer could also use the data to train AI models for the company. This example is troubling because the customer produces data that someone else uses for a benefit.

So far, the EU has led the way in regulating some of these risks. For example, the EU created the General Data Protection Regulation (GDPR), one of the world's most comprehensive digital privacy laws. The GDPR regulates the use of personal data of EU citizens and how companies use it.[19] Since the regulation covers the citizens and not companies, it applies globally to all Technology services that could cover any EU citizen.

The EU is also working on AI regulation called the EU Artificial Intelligence Act or AIA. Similar to how the GDPR protects any EU citizen and is global, the AIA draft applies to any algorithmic output within the EU.[20] In addition, the draft covers prohibited AI practices, defines high-risk practices, sets transparency obligations, and sets the Governance rules for use and enforcement.[21]

Generative AI

In late 2022, OpenAI launched ChatGPT and ushered in a new era of AI computing. This model leverages large language models, a self-supervised training model that uses massive unlabeled datasets to learn. The model generates a text response to a query or prompt, hence the name Generative AI.

For example, you can ask a Generative AI a question in natural language, such as *What are the components of an ESG report?* The AI model might respond with its analysis and summarization, including breaking down sections of a sample ESG report and what they are for.

Generative AI isn't limited to text responses, either. Depending on the model, it can create audio, pictures, and videos, too. For example, when I started thinking about the book's cover, I went through several prompts with Microsoft's Bing Image Creator to help me think through designs I might like.[22] These were guided experiments between my text prompts and Bing's image-generation ability. While I used these images to ideate with a designer, Generative AI could take work away from all types of content creators.

As with any new Technology, companies need to approach Generative AI through the lens of ESG to mitigate risks that allow the company to capture new opportunities. The questions aren't necessarily different from those for other AI technologies.

- Environmental:
  - What are the carbon costs of training the models and generating content?

- o If the model addresses an Environmental challenge, are the model and data running on a sustainable infrastructure platform?
- o How much accuracy are we willing to sacrifice to save energy?
- Social:
  - o Are we training our employees to create content and other customer-facing materials using Generative AI responsibly?
  - o Are there racial, gender, age, or other social biases in the training data or results?
  - o Would hiring a diverse person rather than having an AI generate diverse content be more appropriate and authentic?
  - o Should there be age or content restrictions around the use?
  - o What skills do employees need to make responsible use of this Technology?
- Governance:
  - o What are the liability models for Generative AI?
  - o Who owns the intellectual property when a Generative AI model creates a new piece of content?
  - o Have we adequately articulated the terms of use and built Governance models around data control?
  - o Are teams monitoring the algorithm's results in a feedback loop?
  - o Are there cybersecurity protections in place across the model's intellectual property, the user's data, and the results across users?
  - o Are there controls to prevent the model from being used with malintent?

To capture the immense opportunity that Generative AI can bring, stakeholder considerations, Governance models, responsible use, and more must play a role in these questions and others. If a company ignores these basics, it may need to roll back digital products and services. The consequences could result in reputational damage, lost development time, and potential fines. Even worse, a failed launch allows competitors to learn from your mistakes and beat you to market with a responsible solution. Without thoughtfully considering these areas, a first-mover advantage around new Technologies, like Generative AI, can quickly become a risk.

From the outside in: Disinformation

The ubiquity and accessibility of Technology mean that companies need to think outside of their borders, as threats don't always target a company's internal systems. One threat focused on external stakeholders, social media, and messaging apps is disinformation. Disinformation is false information meant to mislead. In a world of Generative AI, content can easily be developed that puts your company on a defensive footing. For companies, this may mean that a bad actor or rival company is trying to persuade your stakeholders in a particular direction or simply create chaos. Unfortunately, disinformation is very hard to defend against because the narrative spreads quickly through a network outside of the company's control and via online opinions, potentially backed by an army of AI-based algorithms.

The intersection of disinformation with a particular company's risk may not be the focus of media attention or strictly reputational damage. For example, over the past few years, we've seen disinformation about 5G networks, including a bizarre claim that it was responsible for Covid-19.[23] While the disinformation campaign directly spared companies with 5G offerings, it still created a reputational issue around the Technology across the USA, UK, Australia, and Canada.[24]

The New York Times reported in May 2021 that a mysterious social media agency named Fazze popped up and offered influencers money in exchange for posting false information about the Pfizer Covid vaccine.[25] It is difficult to say if the target was the vaccine, Pfizer, or something more sinister, but the company was called out directly by the influencers who came forward.[26]

In 2019, someone launched a more direct disinformation campaign to a specific business, involving an urgent message on WhatsApp about Metrobank's financial stability. The result was a run on the bank and reactive assurance that there were no issues.[27] As a result, one of the bank's primary stakeholders, depositors, was placed at risk due to this message. A stunt like this is almost impossible to defend against because you never know where it might come from and what people might believe.

Even when the company isn't directly engaged in a particular Technology, others can use Technology to harm the company indirectly. Still, through a proactive, consistent, and transparent approach to stakeholder communication that builds trust, the company might find it easier to address these unknown risks when they arise.

Technology rating agencies and disclosures emerge

As we've seen so far, disclosures play a part in communicating ESG information to stakeholders. Technology is no different. Stakeholders want to believe that the company protects its systems and applications, personal data, ensures responsible development, and more. In addition, investors may use this information as an additional lens to test a particular investment thesis. After all, since much of a company's value resides in intangibles, the approach to its Technology stack will play a material role and may reveal Governance principles at work.

Alongside ESG rating agencies, Technology now has rating agencies to measure risks. These rating agencies attempt to use available information to assess a company's Technology risk. Let's take a look at three Technology rating agencies.

Bitsight

Bitsight helps companies understand their own and their value chain's security footprint. It does this by collecting and analyzing over 100 billion security events from the internet per day.[28] However, it also has an interesting claim. Solactive, an index provider, has built an index group based on Bitsight's ratings called the Solactive Bitsight Cyber Risk Indices. According to its research, Solactive has validated Bitsight's cybersecurity ratings and the correlation to business performance.[29] What's interesting is the logical connection between Technology risks, cybersecurity hygiene, and performance.

Bitsight also has services for the financial quantification of these risks and conducts various risk assessments.

SecurityScorecard

SecurityScorecard also helps other companies understand digital risks internally and within their value chains. It collects signals from global networks, honeypots, and sinkholes to uncover these risks. SecurityScorecard publishes the risk types it looks for and states that it layers on over 40 third-party data sources to enrich the intelligence.[30] SecurityScorecard also offers vendor management solutions and services for cybersecurity risk management and remediation.

EthicsGrade

EthicsGrade takes a different approach to Technology ratings. Rather than focusing on cybersecurity, it focuses on digital ethics and a company's digital strategy. The methodology takes in publicly available data, considers a survey that collects information from the company, and then runs the information through an internal assessment process. From there, the focus is on six pillars: Public policy, Sustainability, Structure, Technical barriers to trust, Data privacy, and Ethical risk.[31]

After the data is collected and analyzed, EthicsGrade compares the assessed company with others in its industry and the universe of public companies and outlines key digital risk factors that the company needs to be aware of, which appear to be material. In 2023, EthicsGrade launched EthicsAnswer, a Generative AI model built on OpenAI's ChatGPT to answer questions about ESG.[32]

Think of Technology like the rest of ESG

As we've seen, Technology undoubtedly has the same level of impact on a company as ESG issues. Just like each pillar can be assessed through disclosures and data, requires careful consideration and strong Governance principles, and can contribute to the long-term growth of the company, Technology can as well. Digital data provides similar insights into how the company manages the digital opportunities it is chasing, as the company builds resilience in this new world of intangible value.

Again, Technology's power in our lives cannot be overstated, but it isn't only the cutting-edge and latest developments that companies need to consider. Any Technology can play a role and intersect along the pillars of ESG.

USE CASE: CALIFORNIA POWER CONSTRAINTS

An acute climate risk hit California between late August and mid-September of 2022, blanketing the state under a heat dome.[33] This event happens when high-pressure atmospheric conditions trap heat over an area like a lid. Extreme heat events like this can cause spikes in electricity as people turn to their air conditioning and fans to cool off. The strain on the power grid hit an all-time high during this event, causing the grid manager, the California Independent System Operator, to issue a level 3 Energy Emergency Alert at 5.17 pm.[34] If the strain on the grid wouldn't improve, an event like this might signal the start of rolling blackouts, which can put citizens at risk.

At 5.45 pm, the Governor's Office of Emergency Services decided to alert citizens via a text message about reducing energy consumption to relieve pressure on the grid.[35] Texting is not a new Technology but a ubiquitous one that has existed since 1992.[36] In effect, this text reached out directly to the stakeholders of the grid. Within minutes, citizens responded and alleviated the strain on the grid.

This seemingly simple example is an excellent use case across ESG and Technology. While the State of California isn't a company, the utility providers are. The transparency built into the grid's operations through the California Independent System Operator allows close monitoring of the power grid.[37] This responsiveness and tight management could be considered a Governance principle built on public-private partnership. Technology facilitated the connection to stakeholders around the Environmental issue.

When a crisis like this hits, companies and other entities can navigate the complexities by pulling together the components of the acronym to mitigate risk.

Notes

1 Ocean Tomo (n.d.). *Intangible Asset Market Value Study*. Ocean Tomo. oceantomo.com/intangible-asset-market-value-study/ (archived at https://perma. cc/3DE3-RS28).

2 Gartner (2023). Gartner forecasts worldwide IT spending to grow 2.4% in 2023. Gartner. www.gartner.com/en/newsroom/press-releases/2023-01-18-gartner-forecasts-worldwide-it-spending-to-grow-2-percent-in-2023 (archived at https://perma.cc/KB48-ZMSD).

3 Weber, M. (2017). Today in history: Apple releases the iPhone (2007). History Collection. historycollection.com/today-history-apple-releases-iphone-2007/ (archived at https://perma.cc/5ZJZ-DRGH).

4   Forth, P., Reichert, T., de Laubier, R., and Chakraborty, S. (2020). Flipping the odds of digital transformation success. BCG. www.bcg.com/publications/2020/increasing-odds-of-success-in-digital-transformation (archived at https://perma.cc/P7LX-LM23).

5   Corporate Board Member, Diligent Institute and Chief Executive Group (2023). *What Directors Think*. Corporate Board Member. boardmember.com/whatdirectorsthink-2023-report/ (archived at https://perma.cc/62SQ-QMMW).

6   Earth Knowledge (n.d.). Our Story. Earth Knowledge. earthknowledge.net/our-story (archived at https://perma.cc/MUK8-ARXH).

7   Microsoft. (2022). Hybrid work is just work. Are we doing it wrong? Microsoft, p. 5. assets-c4akfrf5b4d3f4b7.z01.azurefd.net/assets/2023/09/a81fcdeb-860a-44f2-aaeb-0525d38358ae-2022_Work_Trend_Index_Pulse_Report_Sep-3697v2.pdf (archived at https://perma.cc/3N7K-MKWU).

8   Bonime-Blanc, A. (2019). *Gloom to Boom*. Routledge, p. 238.

9   Castañón Moats, M. and DeNicola, P. (2022). Charting the course through a changing governance landscape. p.6. www.pwc.com/us/en/services/governance-insights-center/assets/pwc-2022-annual-corporate-directors-survey.pdf (archived at https://perma.cc/853T-5D6X).

10 Kelly, S. and Resnick-ault, J. (2021). One password allowed hackers to disrupt Colonial Pipeline, CEO tells senators. Reuters. www.reuters.com/business/colonial-pipeline-ceo-tells-senate-cyber-defenses-were-compromised-ahead-hack-2021-06-08/ (archived at https://perma.cc/24U6-P2HK).

11 Dean, G. (2021). Drivers face $3 gas prices after the Colonial Pipeline cyberattack, and some gas stations have run out completely. Business Insider. www.businessinsider.com/gas-prices-colonial-pipeline-cyberattack-fuel-east-coast-2021-5 (archived at https://perma.cc/YT5P-QBK4).

12 The White House (2021). Biden administration announces further actions to protect U.S. critical infrastructure. The White House. www.whitehouse.gov/briefing-room/statements-releases/2021/07/28/fact-sheet-biden-administration-announces-further-actions-to-protect-u-s-critical-infrastructure/ (archived at https://perma.cc/88KB-AHE7).

13 The White House (2023). Biden-Harris administration announces national cybersecurity strategy. The White House. https://www.whitehouse.gov/briefing-room/statements-releases/2023/03/02/fact-sheet-biden-harris-administration-announces-national-cybersecurity-strategy/ (archived at https://perma.cc/AB2P-GWRH)

14 U.S. Securities and Exchange Commission (2023). SEC adopts rules on cybersecurity risk management, strategy, governance, and incident disclosure by public companies. U.S. Securities and Exchange Commission. www.sec.gov/news/press-release/2023-139 (archived at https://perma.cc/A4U8-5GDG).

15 Green Software Foundation (2021). Software Carbon Intensity Standard. GitHub. github.com/Green-Software-Foundation/sci (archived at https://perma. cc/N4WH-XMM9).

16 Microsoft Research (n.d.). Reducing AI's carbon footprint. Microsoft. www.microsoft.com/en-us/research/project/reducing-ais-carbon-footprint/ (archived at https://perma.cc/9FGU-UFY6).

17 Henderson, S. (2022). There's more to AI bias than biased data, NIST report highlights. NIST. www.nist.gov/news-events/news/2022/03/theres-more-ai-bias-biased-data-nist-report-highlights (archived at https://perma.cc/B36B-JBAY).

18 CBS San Francisco (2015). Anthem to offer identity theft protection after massive hack. CBS News. www.cbsnews.com/sanfrancisco/news/anthem-identity-theft-protection-massive-hack-health-insurer-blue-cross-blue-shield-cybersecurity/ (archived at https://perma.cc/W5SK-A3MJ).

19 Wolford, B. (2018). What is GDPR, the EU's new data protection law? GDPR. gdpr.eu/what-is-gdpr/ (archived at https://perma.cc/VCK8-CVLW).

20 Engler, A. (2022). The limited global impact of the EU AI Act. Brookings. www. brookings.edu/articles/the-limited-global-impact-of-the-eu-ai-act/ (archived at https://perma.cc/3DPM-9GJJ).

21 Lawson, A. (2022). EU AI Act explained. RAI Institute. www.responsible.ai/ post/eu-ai-act-explained (archived at https://perma.cc/EU3F-G9ER).

22 Image Creator from Microsoft Bing. (n.d.). www.bing.com/create (archived at https://perma.cc/2RV9-TZBT).

23 Solis-Moreira, J. (2021). How does fake news of 5G and COVID-19 spread worldwide? *Medical News Today*. www.medicalnewstoday.com/articles/5g-doesnt-cause-covid-19-but-the-rumor-it-does-spread-like-a-virus (archived at https://perma.cc/ZQH5-LE5T).

24 Jensen, M. (2020). How misinformation about 5G is spreading within our government institutions—and who's responsible. *The Conversation*. theconversation.com/how-misinformation-about-5g-is-spreading-within-our-government-institutions-and-whos-responsible-139304 (archived at https:// perma.cc/Y9TT-C559).

25 Alderman, L. (2021). Influencers say they were urged to criticize Pfizer vaccine. *The New York Times*, May 26. www.nytimes.com/2021/05/26/business/ pfizer-vaccine-disinformation-influeners.html (archived at https://perma. cc/9PSA-M3Q2).

26 Haynes, C. and Carmichael, F. (2021). The YouTubers who blew the whistle on an anti-vax plot. BBC News, July 24. www.bbc.com/news/blogs-trending-57928647 (archived at https://perma.cc/L4TU-QH2J).

27 Katwala, A. (2019). The Metro Bank hoax shows the immense power of fake news on WhatsApp. Wired UK. www.wired.co.uk/article/metro-bank-share-price-whats-app-hoax (archived at https://perma.cc/D2W3-6C6E).

28 Bitsight (n.d.). Bitsight Data Advantage. Bitsight. www.bitsight.com/security-ratings/data-advantage#tab-3 (archived at https://perma.cc/S6DF-RNGE).

29 Solactive (2020). Cybersecurity as a competitive advantage: Introducing the Solactive BitSight Cyber Risk Indices. Solactive. www.solactive.com/cybersecurity-as-a-competitive-advantage-introducing-the-solactive-bitsight-cyber-risk-indices/ (archived at https://perma.cc/3YBX-9ZFL).

30 Sohval, B. (n.d.). SecurityScorecard's scoring methodology. Security Scorecard, pp. 6–20. resources.securityscorecard.com/c/securityscorecard-sc?x=VO3MOH#page=1 (archived at https://perma.cc/449A-QHRT).

31 EthicsGrade (n.d.). Methodology. EthicsGrade. www.ethicsgrade.io/methodology (archived at https://perma.cc/6L6V-Q53X).

32 EthicsAnswer (2023). Home. EthicsAnswer. ethicsanswer.com/ (archived at https://perma.cc/9L9Q-Z9YA).

33 Newsom, G. (2022). Heat Dome Fires Request Letter. Office of the Governor, Gavin Newsom. www.gov.ca.gov/wp-content/uploads/2022/10/Heat-Dome-Fires-Request.pdf (archived at https://perma.cc/K5KQ-LDFX).

34 Calma, J. (2022). Why a text alert might have helped California keep the lights on. *The Verge.* www.theverge.com/2022/9/7/23340821/california-electricity-grid-power-outage-text-phone-alert (archived at https://perma.cc/Z5TH-YGB8).

35 Calma, J. (2022). Why a text alert might have helped California keep the lights on. *The Verge.* www.theverge.com/2022/9/7/23340821/california-electricity-grid-power-outage-text-phone-alert (archived at https://perma.cc/Z5TH-YGB8).

36 Fingas, J. (2019). The first text message was sent 25 years ago. Engadget. www.engadget.com/2017-12-03-first-text-message-25th-anniversary.html (archived at https://perma.cc/H9H8-5TVF).

37 Toohey, G. and Petri, A.E. (2022). A text asked millions of Californians to save energy. They paid heed, averting blackouts. *Los Angeles Times.* www.latimes.com/california/story/2022-09-07/a-text-asked-millions-of-californians-to-save-energy-they-listened-averting-blackouts (archived at https://perma.cc/TEQ6-FKTN).

07

Mainstreaming ESG to Improve and Innovate

Throughout the Environmental, Social, Governance, and Technology chapters, we've covered the complexity of doing business in an ever-changing world of disruption, chaos, and unpredictability outside the company's financial statement. Despite the rapid pace of change, companies have yet to develop and improve with adaptive operating models or innovate around ESG as they cling to traditional and predictable ways to deal with conventional pressures. Over the past century, companies have developed specific patterns and reactions to competitive markets, economic downturns, and uncertainty. When the stock dips in these situations, shareholder primacy creeps in, and the company pulls out its tried and tested reactive playbooks to execute. Companies appease shareholders through layoffs, selling or closing divisions, compensation adjustments, stock buybacks, or management changes.

Despite the proven reactions, companies now operate in a more complex and interconnected world, and the traditional playbook may yield different results than it once did. Part of the reason is that the nature of value has shifted from tangible assets to intangibles. In 1975, just five years after the Friedman doctrine, up to 83 percent of an S&P 500 company's value sat with tangible assets, like buildings and equipment.[1] Yet, by 2020, tangible value had dropped to only around 10 percent of a company's total value.[2] Value has now shifted to intangibles, like the application of new technologies, competitive improvements that arise from alternative material substitution, or innovative intellectual property. As a result, how a company deals with emerging pressures around its financial and ESG risks and opportunities must evolve. Traditional methods of dealing with issues when the tangible value was high may no longer work and could result in more risk.

For example, as many companies now lead with purpose and stakeholder engagement rhetoric, layoffs can quickly destroy trust and have immeasurable long-term impacts on the ability to attract talent, productivity, intellectual capital loss, and more.[3]

There are several things that companies need to be focusing on, and not necessarily in this order, but simultaneously. Companies must focus on material improvements, such as:

- Improvements to operational processes
- New sustainable product research and development (R&D)
- Higher-quality reporting.

They must also focus on material innovation that can capture new opportunities in the market as ESG issues become more prevalent. To proceed consistently and effectively requires a company to mainstream ESG across its business units and divisions and adopt new ways of protecting, growing, and creating intangible value.

Further to this, the wait-and-see era for companies entrenched in long-standing, proven business models is over. Playing catchup in a market as others make improvements and innovate can be a tricky challenge that, like climate change, gets exponentially worse the longer you wait. For example, consumer preferences are shifting so fast around ESG issues and values-driven alignment that it can be challenging for a company to innovate later, let alone execute improvements across its suppliers.[4] Trying to change an entire value chain after competitors have moved is a significant lift. It may leave the company scrambling to integrate a supplier's improvements well after its competitors have moved on. While stable and steady product approaches may have worked historically to drive long-term resilience, the same tactics may no longer apply to new intangible value, which changes quickly and is hard to quantify. This quantification can be even more challenging if the company hasn't embraced Digital Transformation and digitized its processes.

Businesses need to improve existing operational models across ESG to engage on these ever-changing issues, as the same old responses to traditional challenges may not work. Each company, unique in its operations and value chain, has fantastic opportunities for how best to meet change as only it can. However, it is worth noting that the company must still rely on quality Governance principles, data, and a strong culture to empower employees to act and drive that change. If a company casts Governance aside in its eagerness for new pursuits, it will only create more significant risks.

Companies also need new intangible solutions to capture and drive new value responsibly. To capture ESG opportunities across all company levels, the company must innovate. When companies innovate, they experiment, learn, and make the difficult but necessary change. Without innovation, the company will stand still while its peers work around it, subject to influences it refuses to engage with. But, unlike in the previous chapter, we don't need to add innovation to the acronym as another letter. Instead, improvements and innovation are the engines for how the company transforms in this new world of intangibles.

The company's ability to understand its intangibles, improve operationally, and innovate will ensure long-term value and resilience. But, along the way, the company must also mainstream ESG across intangible concepts, like data and culture, to execute effectively and drive consistency. Moreover, while the spark of innovation can light anywhere in a company, solid Governance principles from executives and business unit leaders must be in place to support and cultivate the fruit of these efforts. Still, the accountability doesn't stop at the executive level. As every industry has a material intersection with ESG issues, so does every functional business unit, and each leader and team must understand its role. These concepts may not be well understood or integrated across the business, requiring a mainstreaming effort. Mainstreaming ESG means having the different corners of the business understand ESG and intangibles, while being empowered by the executive team to build processes to surface or execute on risks and opportunities.

Intangible assets and value

The nature of business has changed over the past half of a century. As a result, companies must shift their understanding of value creation to keep up with new changes. Historically, the markets defined a company's value through physical assets and equipment. You can see this in the transition of the largest market cap companies in the S&P 500 over time. In 1975, the top companies were IBM, Exxon Mobil, Proctor & Gamble, GE, and 3M.[5] These various companies had physical assets across technology, oil and gas, and consumer goods. IBM is interesting to examine because it is now one of the world's leaders in patents, with over 122,000 filed.[6] Patents and intellectual property are examples of intangibles. Yet, this intangible plays in a mix of other factors, as by May 2023, IBM had the 114th highest market cap out of global companies.[7]

By 2020, the largest market cap companies had shifted to those with high intangible value, including Apple, Alphabet, Microsoft, Amazon, and Facebook.[8] These companies illustrate examples of intangibles, such as technology, data, algorithms, brand, and intellectual property. Here, Apple is an interesting consideration. Apple, famous for its hardware, reports services revenue, including non-hardware items, as only 20 percent of its total revenue as of its 2022 10-K filing.[9] Like IBM, a mix of factors plays into market value, as by May 2023, Apple had the highest market cap out of any company.[10] Still, intangible value doesn't just sit in patents and technology, but brand awareness and reputation, which could account for Apple's prowess. According to an Interbrand study of the Best Global Brands, Apple's brand is worth nearly $482 billion, and IBM's is worth $34 billion.[11]

Intangibles often sit off the balance sheet and are hard to define, but not always. For example, software licenses and cloud usage are primarily intangible but likely have a direct line item on a CIO's balance sheet. On the other hand, something like brand value is tough to account for. Companies protect their brands through marketing and social media strategies on budgetary line items that can be defined. Still, the Governance principles that deliver ethical operations and trust with stakeholders have value but no line item in the budget or balance sheet, yet could result in reputation risk and fines if ignored.

WHAT ARE INTANGIBLE ASSETS?

In addition to the world's largest companies and these examples, many new digital business models have been built on intangibles to drive value. Disruptive business models have emerged around digital intellectual property, software, and algorithms built on physical assets. For example, Uber and Lyft provide ride-sharing services without a physical fleet of cars, and Airbnb rents buildings that others own. Even viral and digital content creation has spun up an entirely new influencer industry with an estimated market size of $21.1 billion in 2023.[12]

Yet even in all of these examples, it is worth noting that even though intangibles lack a physical form, they can have real-world impacts at the intersection of ESG issues. Looking back to technology, a common intangible, provides an example. A new product built on data and artificial intelligence runs on physical computing hardware that had to be sourced, shipped, and connected to an energy source, all of which may have emissions (Environment). In addition, the intellectual property and applications served to customers might have been built with biased data, further marginalizing a stakeholder group (Social). Uncovering that bias might result in company fines and stricter regulations (Governance). While this example is technology-based, intangible assets permeate each pillar with real-world consequences similarly.

Addressing the tangible impacts of intangible assets requires intangible concepts, like improvements and innovation. For example, a strategy built by IT to identify and test for data bias in a deployed algorithm is an intangible improvement in processes, reducing risk. Further, while the Finance department can track the salaries of ethical AI engineers against a budget, the resulting value in the risk reduction is hard to account for.

Part of an ESG mindset is recognizing the value of intangibles without traditional financial accounting and how to leverage them to mainstream ESG. However, this idea can be challenging to execute consistently for another intangible concept: time. Over time, as the economy grows and contracts, periods of economic pressure can wipe out progress on ESG as this undefined value leads to the perception of low value. Still, the company must remember that ESG represents material issues, intangible or not. If the company slips back to shareholder primacy, it will pull away from intangibles. The results may be cut programs, stakeholder misalignment, further ESG risk exposure, lost intellectual capital through attrition, and a demoralized culture.

Instead, companies need to remain aligned with stakeholders and drive long-term value. In 2022, Deloitte published a study that called out how the next economic downturn may be different than leaders have experienced previously due to complex global issues like war, the pandemic, and supply chain issues.[13] Our world of tangible risks set against broad stakeholder considerations and new accountabilities brings new challenges, and companies must improve on existing playbooks or innovate new ones. A company must leverage intangibles such as data, culture, and mainstreaming ESG across the organization to stay consistent as it works towards new approaches to drive value.

Data, culture, and mainstreaming ESG

Improvements and innovation are the engines that drive how a company addresses its most material ESG issues in our changing world. To effectively direct employees towards an ESG mindset to foster these engines, the board and executives must leverage two intangibles—data and culture—to build a foundation that can mainstream ESG across the organization. In other words, the company must understand its position, work through its employees, and integrate ESG into its operations and business functions, not keep it separate in positions like Chief Sustainability or Diversity Officer. These roles are essential guides who serve as experts and advisors, but companies cannot rely on a single position for the broad integration of ESG considerations the company must address.

For example, a company might hire an Environmental leader to define and consult on the company's sustainability goals and projects. Still, this role can't serve as a deep expert across procurement, manufacturing processes, R&D, climate risk, building efficiency, disclosures, and reporting. Nor can a diversity leader be expected to be an expert in Human Resources activities, employee culture, human slavery, and customer engagement. ESG issues are core business issues, after all, and have a wide breadth and depth. Instead, the company needs each business unit responsible for those areas to upskill on ESG and take ownership so the company can collectively transform. In other words, a Chief Procurement Officer needs their team to understand ESG to uncover climate and supplier risk. There may be pockets where this is already happening since some ESG issues may be unavoidable for individual business units.

Diffusing ESG information across the business doesn't necessarily discount the need for a Chief ESG, Sustainability, or Diversity Officer, even over the long run, as ESG issues change and evolve rapidly. Still, to be effective and influential leaders across the organization, executives must empower employees by evaluating the company's ESG positioning through data and empowering the workforce to execute consistently through culture.

Connected data and breaking down siloes

The first intangible asset to leverage in this pursuit is data. While some liken data to oil, the analogy doesn't quite fit. Unlike oil, data is an infinitely reusable resource with nonrivalry characteristics, meaning multiple people can use it simultaneously.[14] These attributes, similarly shared across many intangibles, make data critical for comprehensive ESG analysis, but using it effectively takes careful consideration. Data works best when collected together and analyzed, just like ESG, which is not without challenges.

As company data is generated and stored, the company must consider its specific properties for it to be effectively analyzed. For example, data doesn't natively carry the context of who or what system created it, the activities that led to its generation, and for what purpose. That information isn't necessarily tracked in the data but resides in employees' intellectual capital. In other words, employees who work with the data are the ones who understand these properties. Data solely used for a single purpose is one reason companies have locked data in siloes, making it inaccessible to others they perceive as not needing access. Still, as complex and nuanced ESG issues emerge across the business, other users will want to capitalize on this data to build a complete picture.

Of course, another reason for data siloes is that, unlike a physical asset, stakeholders and bad actors can copy data repeatedly, requiring digital protections similar to paper files in a locked and monitored office or filing cabinet. This threat is another reason companies have siloed and walled off data. While cybersecurity is a responsible treatment of a technology risk and must be considered in any technology implementation, building digital architecture to protect the data but not use it collaboratively can restrict its value and hinder ESG improvements and innovation in the future.

To make the best use of company data and uncover its value, IT must break down data siloes responsibly and with robust principles, including cybersecurity considerations. IT organizations refer to these principles as Data Governance. Like Corporate Governance, Data Governance includes the responsible principles and frameworks that dictate the operations and controls around data, helping to drive reliable information to decision-makers.[15] In effect, quality data and analysis sit at the intersection of Governance and Technology.

As we saw in Chapter 2, data has a vast supply chain and can prove the company's story. While the company needs to use data to baseline, harnessing the power of the data to improve and innovate are different use cases altogether. Still, an ESG mindset can help navigate those complexities through material considerations and multi-stakeholder analysis.

Just as the transition from high-carbon activities represents an exponentially more difficult risk as time progresses, breaking down data siloes and pulling the data together has similar challenges over time. Companies must work proactively towards connected data platforms to capitalize on the value effectively while considering the properties of the data. The longer companies wait, the more challenging it will be, especially as IT and business culture may play a role in the difficulty level of the transition. Implications for business culture exist in breaking down any siloes in an organization as people look to protect their areas of control. For example, data siloes can lead to artificial fiefdoms centered around people's fear that someone is coming to take a part of their business responsibility.[16] Therefore, the company must break down internal cultural barriers and assuage fears by empowering employees to collaborate responsibly around the data.

Capitalizing on culture

The board and executives must set the tone from the top to mainstream ESG across the company. However, executing any lasting change like this throughout a company relies on another valuable intangible, a robust corporate culture, to accept the change. In turn, culture is how the company's employees further execute its purpose and mission. Governance and Social intersect with culture, as Governance principles and purpose influence the culture, but the Social is where employees reside as key stakeholders.

Unfortunately, organizational culture is challenging to quantify and understand. As an intangible, it doesn't appear as a line item on the balance sheet but has far-reaching impacts across brand value, talent acquisition, and customer engagement. As a result, companies will often use employee surveys and transparently share the results in open discussion to measure culture.[17] Despite its intangible nature and difficulty to measure, there is clear value. For example, Glassdoor, which allows employees to review their employers online, has used that data to build the Best Places to Work list since 2009.[18] Glassdoor looked at the correlation between the stock performance of leaders and the S&P 500 over 10 years and found leaders' stocks outperformed the S&P 500 by around 7.6 percent on average.[19]

Corporate culture also intersects with the employees in the context of the work styles of the company's regions. Executives must shape the communication and strategy accordingly before introducing ESG concepts but cannot consider employees outside of these efforts. Employees will want the appropriate context, support, and relevance based on how they are expected to work and perform. If this is not a consideration, the strategy will almost certainly fail to be adopted. For example, companies in the West have work cultures where employees often work independently towards results.[20] In contrast, Eastern cultures have more order and structure, working interdependently with coordination.[21] While these are broad generalizations by region, the differences will affect which employees are willing to accept the messaging and activities now being asked of them.

Yet, mainstreaming ESG doesn't mean demanding employees change their work styles. Instead, it means enabling employees to understand the material importance of ESG, where to leverage improvements, and how to innovate. The company achieves this by giving them the appropriate skills, incentives, and empowerment structures and can leverage well-established methods as a starting point. As we will see, this is a variation on improvement as executives improve the existing relationships with employees. In other words, the goal isn't for the company to change the culture to fit ESG but to leverage what already works within its culture and build on top of that to mainstream ESG across the business. Similar to the failures we saw in Digital Transformation projects in the previous chapter, mainstreaming ESG can also fail due to short-term thinking, a lack of new skills, employee inertia, and fear.[22] As before, the stakeholder mapping exercise and the materiality matrix play critical roles in helping to inform business unit leaders and their employees why the transformation is needed.

Leading into the 2020 tipping points and after, companies have a unique opportunity to engage with their employee stakeholders and across their value chain in new ways, mainly through employees' newfound sense of purpose.[23] Across employee engagement on this topic through the culture, leveraging the company's purpose and mission and consistent Governance principles, companies can capitalize on the employee shift to mainstream ESG.

Mainstreaming ESG

With how nascent consistent ESG efforts are in the corporate world and the confusion around what it is and isn't, boards and executives need to define the desired approach in Governance principles and execute enablement across the corporate culture. Then, backed by data as evidence for change, the company can mainstream ESG in anticipation of driving improvements and innovation.

Mainstreaming ESG across the culture can be a daunting task. Not many employees understand the topic or its intersection with the business. The key here is to expand an ESG perspective to fill the corners of all business units and empower them to act. Employees directly responsible for their business area should retain their responsibilities, continuing to build their expertise in their area through the integration of ESG.[24] Returning to ESG's roots shows a missed opportunity for companies and their employees. The 2004 UN Global Compact paper "Who Cares Wins," has a recommendation to "Incorporate ESG factors into mainstream research," for financial analysts and brokers, but leaves the recommendations for companies to "Lead the way by implementing ESG principles and improving reporting and disclosure."[25]

As a result, there isn't a single approach for every company to follow to mainstream ESG as all companies are different and unique. However, if your company has existing means by which it instills change and information throughout a culture, and it's working, follow that process. If there isn't a process in place or you find that change is difficult, here are five example steps as a guide to mainstreaming activities, some of which the company can complete in parallel across different business units and functions:

1 **Define, Identify, and Delegate: Define what ESG means to your company. Complete the stakeholder mapping and materiality matrix and identify the ESG issues that surround your company. Then, delegate further investigation to business unit leaders.**

The company should agree on a shared definition or approach for ESG at the board and executive levels. This definition should also include recognizing where certain related ESG activities fall. For example, if ESG refers to material change, a community outreach program might align with the company's purpose but be categorized as philanthropy. While it doesn't matter how the company classifies programs, this exercise provides context around programs and the intersection with the business to deliver a consistent message to stakeholders.

Of course, every business operates under different Governance principles and has unique and varied cultural strengths. Hence, the company needs to build around this definition to assess where things stand by gathering and examining preliminary information through a materiality matrix and stakeholder mapping exercise *(refer to Chapter 5 for how to complete these exercises)*.

The executive team should delegate further investigation to business units for identified stakeholders and materiality issues. At this stage, executives should clarify that improvement and innovations, which eager employees may rush to, are less important than uncovering additional insights that may reside inside the employees' intellectual capital.

Also, just because an issue initially appears outside the top right quadrant of the materiality matrix doesn't mean each business unit shouldn't explore it at this stage. Instead, teams should look closely at every material issue identified for intersections with their area of responsibility, providing that context back to the executives.

2 **Enhance and Assess: Enhance the initial ESG data collection with information from business units. Assess your employee engagement and culture.**

Each business unit should report back an assessment of its understanding of stakeholders, the material issues, and their intersection to executives, including potentially overlooked stakeholders and material issues and connections between them across the business. The feedback should include recommended data that can build insights into these areas. From here, executives should review, collaborate, and enhance the stakeholder tool and materiality matrix.

Also, in parallel and in preparation for employees to start looking at the company through an ESG mindset, an Employee Experience survey should be sent out, which measures how well employees understand these issues as the company defines them, their perspective on purpose, and what they think about the culture. This exercise informs the executives about the mindset overall and employee culture, assessing employees' readiness for a change. It is worth noting that these surveys can uncover cultural problems that the company must address before or as it moves forward.

The executive team and Human Resources should collect and review the results from the Employee Experience surveys, looking for cultural issues. Executives can discuss more specific ESG-related insights with the relevant business unit leads. For example, if there are material employee issues related to safety at certain sites, executives may speak with the Chief Operations Officer to investigate further and report back.

In addition to assessing the company's readiness, assess where the data exists for understanding the identified material issues in the first step and create an inventory. Engage with the Chief Information Officer to uncover ways to identify and connect datasets in preparation for analysis.

3 **Train, Engage, and Reinforce: Build a company-wide ESG training plan and/or engage through internal communications to reinforce the prioritization.**

While addressing issues with company culture outside this book's scope, working with Human Resources and business unit leaders is recommended on the survey's cultural findings.

The company may find that incoming and existing employees may need more ESG knowledge as it is a relatively new business perspective. Higher education and trade schools have yet to mainstream it into their coursework ubiquitously. Others, like NYU Stern[26] and the University of Oxford,[27] have created ESG programs, and the University of Pennsylvania's Wharton School has two ESG Master's degree programs.[28]

Yet, training employees on ESG can be a challenge because there need to be more employee-focused and scalable training programs. As a result, executives may need to upskill themselves through coursework from these programs or others, like from the Diligent and Competent Boards,[29] for example, disseminating knowledge through business unit leaders to employees. Books focused on ESG and shared business articles through a collaboration platform can also fill the broad gaps.

A company may also need to upskill some individuals more deeply on specific topics. For example, someone in R&D or Product Design needs to understand new sustainable materials, whereas someone in Recruiting needs to understand systemic biases and the latest Human Resources trends and regulations. Depending on the requirements, the company can provide this training at the group level.

Executives must also engage through clear and consistent communication, helping employees understand what's in it for them.[30] For example, companies can reinforce ESG concepts by incorporating and celebrating stories and data into their internal corporate communications at all-hands meetings, internal communications, and events. These stories inspire and help employees understand the connections between these issues and the business. Of course, incentives and rewards can also be powerful levers to get employees to pay attention, drive crowdsourcing of ESG ideas, and provide feedback from across the company.

4 **Improve and Plan: Gather feedback to improve and leverage data to inform decisions. Plan ESG targets and goals at the company and business unit level.**

As employees gain an ESG mindset, new information may surface to executives through feedback. For example, a company may institute a software platform to source employee suggestions with a team of managers to triage ideas and issues. These suggestions represent an opportunity to address material issues that may have gone overlooked and new perspectives on the company. An ad hoc management team can triage, escalate, and drive improvements from here.

The need for higher-quality and more focused data will grow as company leaders sort out material issues. The company can build on the data assessment in step 2 here. Business units must work with IT to build standard processes to collect the data, hopefully on an automated basis. Business units and IT may also need to pull disparate datasets together to create insights, as employees may see unknown connections. For example, investigating supplier climate risk may involve data from Procurement, the Risk or Sustainability office, and possibly external geospatial datasets.

It is worth noting that several business units will support some company-wide metrics and roll them up to a central office for review. For example, business units may report carbon activity data to a Sustainability office for emissions calculation. Then, depending on whether the data falls under a regulatory requirement, that office may send it to a Compliance or Legal team. In this way, the business units support the data collection, while the Sustainability office owns the calculation, and the Compliance or Legal team owns the reporting.

The company must align commitments and goals with its objectives and stakeholder desires. Don't rush to publish commitments and goals until the company gathers and analyzes feedback gathered and the data is well understood. From here, business units can plan improvements and targets. Then, executives can aggregate these goals around material themes and make broader internal and public commitments based on the data and the culture's ability to mobilize and deliver.

5 **Review, Mobilize, and Maintain: Assign accountability and review updates regularly with those accountable. Mobilize the employees to act and maintain a consistent and updated ESG program.**

As executives review the initial data and employee feedback, they should thoughtfully engage the business unit leaders on questions to improve their understanding and drive higher-quality data. For example, this exercise likely will surface the need for new business processes, possibly technology modernization, and a reshuffling of which business units are accountable or have shared accountability for metrics.

While most ESG reports are published annually, ESG data and the activities listed here are valuable outside the reporting cycle as they are material information. Accountable business units must create a cadence to monitor their material ESG data as a CFO checks financials. In other words, these business units need closer to real-time information and a watchful eye. These teams should now have the business and ESG context to analyze the data, mobilize, and address issues across people, processes, and technology before they become a crisis.

Mainstreaming ESG isn't necessarily the end state but a start. Over time, maintaining a quality ESG program means continual learning, assessment, engagement, and adjustment.

These steps (summarized in Figure 7.1) are only examples of mainstreaming ESG throughout a company and moving into an ongoing maintenance phase. But, no matter how the company reaches an ESG mindset, it must build on the foundation of its unique intellectual capital and layer on ESG and intangible concepts to remain competitive as the nature of value has shifted. The acronym itself is much less important here than the skills and perspective the company gains.

With this new understanding in hand, executives and business units can manage the issues, but there is more value the company can create through improvements and innovation. These activities are where employees execute the engine of ESG throughout the company. In fact, improvements have already appeared in these steps.

While each activity can work independently, they flow into each other like most ESG-related concepts. Of course, mainstreaming ESG isn't a requirement to improve or innovate, as individual contributors may pursue them outside of a company-wide understanding. Still, if the company doesn't mainstream ESG, it might find pockets of activity inconsistent through various disjointed approaches.

FIGURE 7.1 Steps to mainstream ESG

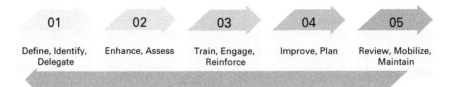

01	02	03	04	05
Define, Identify, Delegate	Enhance, Assess	Train, Engage, Reinforce	Improve, Plan	Review, Mobilize, Maintain

Improvements for what exists

Improvement is the first engine that business units and their employees can execute. It may be the most natural segue and starting point to pursue as companies are likely doing a variation of it, albeit unrelated to ESG. For example, ESG improvements can focus on existing operations and products, reporting and compliance processes, and stakeholder management. Improvements may also represent a mix of tangibles and intangibles. Since the company is tackling existing issues to improve upon, improvements may often address a risk, especially transition risks, with opportunities following close behind.

Many improvements leverage the intangible concept of R&D for tangible products in industries like manufacturing and consumer goods. To start, the company needs to ensure it fully understands the ingredients or materials in the product, which means a review of the items and corresponding data. From here, the company can understand the product lifecycle, its materials, its recyclability/reusability, and the communities from where suppliers source materials. As pressures mount to move towards sustainable alternatives and eliminate issues like human slavery in the supply chain, the cost of business as usual may increase, which is a transition risk with the potential for short-term concessions. As a result of this risk, the company needs to prepare to apply R&D to new alternative and sustainable materials and supply chains. These activities can lead to informed insights to re-engineer existing products and their packaging sustainably and responsibly.

Improvements can also apply to processes as well. For example, as a company understands its operations more effectively through mainstreaming ESG, the accuracy of the data reported may increase, and business units may find new connections between datasets. From here, risks can be better understood and mitigated. The company may also improve regulatory compliance as it understands issues more thoroughly. These new insights also can lead to more informed and improved decision-making, driving higher-quality Governance.

USE CASE: TARGET AND IMPROVEMENTS TO STAKEHOLDER ENGAGEMENT

Target is a US retailer operating in 50 states, with 75 percent of the country's population residing within 10 miles of a store.[31] From 2005 through 2019, Target's revenue grew 32 percent. Yet, in the much shorter period from 2019 through 2022, its revenue grew another 28 percent. When asked about this revenue growth, Target's CEO, Brian Cornell, attributed the success to DEI efforts, including that 40 percent of store directors are diverse.[32] Beyond that broad metric, he describes how Target engaged the local community in Inglewood, California, by hiring diverse contractors and placing Spanish-language signage to match the community's diversity.[33] Target even hired an LA-based artist, Brittney S. Price, to paint a mural.[34]

Target already has many stores, but the rationale is that this store looks and feels like the community.[35] It's an important reminder that a company has many relationships with stakeholders, but customers are among the most critical stakeholder groups, and communities, even in the same country, are diverse. The company can improve that relationship through a more informed stakeholder context and understanding.

Innovation for what's new

Innovation is the second engine that business units and their employees can execute. Innovation focuses on new products, services, markets, and engagement models. Like improvements, this may be a mix of tangibles and intangibles that hopefully disrupt an industry or create new product and service categories. But, again, since innovation covers new things, opportunities may lead here with risk mitigation following.

Innovation may be less familiar to companies as trusted playbooks tend to lead company direction and can be more easily improved upon. Large companies often struggle to innovate due to tried and true practices, products, and principles that have led to past success. But, as we've seen in this chapter, the new world of intangible value means this approach may not be sustainable. To work around this, a large company might fund a venture capital arm to connect with innovative startups, pursue new partnerships or joint ventures to spread the risk around, or create an innovation lab. However, adopting these strategies may be challenging as companies need to break with entrenched processes to innovate. While separation is important, there must also be alignment around innovation and its connection to the company's goals and objectives to be successful.[36]

Still, the board and executives may perceive innovation as a risk, and they would be right to do so. For example, investment needs to be secured as innovation takes time and resources, similar to R&D. The board and executives must adopt new Governance principles to allow innovation to be nurtured and supported, which can be an act of innovation in itself. According to a CFO.com survey, 61 percent of managers believe leadership hinders innovation.[37] Leaders must figure out the right balance and empower employees to innovate and create new value.

USE CASE: DELL AND INNOVATION AS A STAKEHOLDER ENGAGEMENT MODEL

Again, sometimes innovation comes from the company recognizing, enabling, and empowering others to innovate. According to Dell's 2022 ESG report, the company connected with factory workers through Culture of Innovation teams with new skills and methodologies to support brainstorming, prioritization, and implementation of ideas.[38]

In its Code of Conduct, Dell describes how the company believes innovation is an engine for growth, success, and progress.[39] Dell has a broad public commitment to drive sustainability improvements across its workplaces by 2030, which the company aligns with innovation.[40] It publishes the specific goals and metrics used to measure these improvements and lists the manufacturing group's Culture of Innovation program as one of the measurement tools in its 2022 ESG report. The Culture of Innovation program relies on engagement, skills, recognition, and events. The metrics Dell lists in the report are:

- Data collected by the Culture of Innovation sessions run in-house[41]
- The number of ideas implemented from this engine[42]
- The level of participation in sessions.[43]

Over three years, these efforts have resulted in 2,851 ideas implemented in-house.[44] Dell also scales the Culture of Innovation further and engages suppliers in building similar programs, with 7,763 ideas implemented across suppliers in Dell's FY22.[45]

This type of program serves as an example of the power of stakeholder engagement and enablement across employees and suppliers to facilitate innovation, including the direct connection to the Environmental pillar of ESG with Dell's goals.

As we saw in Chapter 1, one challenge to overcome is the shift in perspective from short-term concessions that might appear on the balance sheet to the long-term view of value creation. In many ways, a leadership team's ability via Governance to facilitate improvements and innovation across its employees and its value chain through the Environmental and Social is an innovation. It relies on many moving parts, such as data, to measure the metrics of the progress and a strong culture that understands its value. Even the simple consideration of an issue through the multiple lenses of ESG can be an innovation.

Notes

1 Ocean Tomo (n.d.). *Intangible Asset Market Value Study*. Ocean Tomo. oceantomo.com/intangible-asset-market-value-study/ (archived at https://perma.cc/VH26-VEQV).

2 Ocean Tomo (n.d.). *Intangible Asset Market Value Study*. Ocean Tomo. oceantomo.com/intangible-asset-market-value-study/ (archived at https://perma.cc/VH26-VEQV).

3 Sucher, S.J. and Westner, M.M. (2022). What companies still get wrong about layoffs. *Harvard Business Review*. hbr.org/2022/12/what-companies-still-get-wrong-about-layoffs (archived at https://perma.cc/KT54-8M8E).

4 Alldredge, K. and Grimmelt, A. (2021). Understanding the ever-evolving, always-surprising consumer. McKinsey. www.mckinsey.com/industries/consumer-packaged-goods/our-insights/understanding-the-ever-evolving-always-surprising-consumer (archived at https://perma.cc/P25E-3KJ9).

5 Ross, J. (2020). Intangible assets: A hidden but crucial driver of company value. *Visual Capitalist*. www.visualcapitalist.com/intangible-assets-driver-company-value/ (archived at https://perma.cc/UHS6-NJJA).

6 GREYB (2023). IBM patents Key insights and stats. IBM. insights.greyb.com/ibm-patents/ (archived at https://perma.cc/M6AG-6ZTP).

7 CompaniesMarketCap (n.d.). IBM Market capitalization. CompaniesMarketCap. companiesmarketcap.com/ibm/marketcap (archived at https://perma.cc/7MDZ-DLLT).

8 Ross, J. (2020). Intangible Assets: A hidden but crucial driver of company value. *Visual Capitalist*. www.visualcapitalist.com/intangible-assets-driver-company-value/ (archived at https://perma.cc/UHS6-NJJA).

9 Apple Inc. (2023). Form 10-K. p.21. d18rn0p25nwr6d.cloudfront.net/CIK-0000320193/b4266e40-1de6-4a34-9dfb-8632b8bd57e0.pdf (archived at https://perma.cc/3X8D-QKBU).

10 Glover, G. (2023). Apple regains a $3 trillion market cap and is on track to end the year as the world's most valuable company for the 5th time in a row. Markets Insider. https://markets.businessinsider.com/news/stocks/apple-stock-price-market-analysis-trillion-dollar-company-magnificent-seven-2023-12 (archived at https://perma.cc/AB2P-GWRH)

11 Interbrand (n.d.). Best Global Brands. Interbrand. Available at: https://ibgstaging.wpengine.com/best-global-brands/ (archived at https://perma.cc/4DB7-VCHU).

12 Dencheva, V. (2023). Influencer marketing worldwide: Statistics & facts. Statista. www.statista.com/topics/2496/influence-marketing/#topicOverview (archived at https://perma.cc/JE62-F5Y2).

13 Blau, A., Komada, E., Liu, J., Fadayomi, F., and Choi, A. (2022). Face headwinds with a business resilience strategy. Deloitte. www2.deloitte.com/us/en/pages/consulting/articles/business-resilience-strategies.html (archived at https://perma.cc/EZZ6-7SMV).

14 Collins (n.d.). nonrival. Collins. www.collinsdictionary.com/dictionary/english/nonrival (archived at https://perma.cc/Y2CR-GPAV).

15 Informatica Inc. (n.d.). What is data governance? Informatica Inc. www.informatica.com/resources/articles/what-is-data-governance.html (archived at https://perma.cc/FM8Z-P84M).

16 Ekuan, M., Zimmergren, T., Moore, G., Richards, D., Casey, L., Buck, A., Mabee, D., Blanchard, B., and Petersen, T. (2023). Silos and fiefdoms: Cloud adoption framework. Microsoft Learn. learn.microsoft.com/en-us/azure/cloud-adoption-framework/organize/fiefdoms-silos (archived at https://perma.cc/7KTS-UKQ2).

17 The Diligent Team (2019). How to measure and monitor corporate culture. Diligent Corporation. www.diligent.com/resources/blog/how-measure-monitor-corporate-culture (archived at https://perma.cc/EH64-X7YC).

18 Chamberlain, A. and Munyikwa, Z. (2019). What's culture worth? Glassdoor. research.glassdoor.com/site-us/wp-content/uploads/sites/2/2020/04/Stock-Returns-2020-Glassdoor-Final-Reduced.pdf (archived at https://perma.cc/5D4Z-CVCR).

19 Chamberlain, A. and Munyikwa, Z. (2019). What's culture worth? Glassdoor. research.glassdoor.com/site-us/wp-content/uploads/sites/2/2020/04/Stock-Returns-2020-Glassdoor-Final-Reduced.pdf (archived at https://perma.cc/5D4Z-CVCR).

20 Cheng, J.Y.-J. and Groysberg, B. (2020). How corporate cultures differ around the world. *Harvard Business Review*. hbr.org/2020/01/how-corporate-cultures-differ-around-the-world (archived at https://perma.cc/G7D3-FW4J).

21 Cheng, J.Y.-J. and Groysberg, B. (2020). How corporate cultures differ around the world. *Harvard Business Review*. hbr.org/2020/01/how-corporate-cultures-differ-around-the-world (archived at https://perma.cc/G7D3-FW4J).

22 Forth, P., Reichert, T., de Laubier, R., and Chakraborty, S. (2020). Flipping the odds of digital transformation success. BCG. www.bcg.com/publications/2020/increasing-odds-of-success-in-digital-transformation (archived at https://perma.cc/AT26-H5C4).

23 Turner, J. (2023). Employees increasingly seek value and purpose at work. Gartner. www.gartner.com/en/articles/employees-seek-personal-value-and-purpose-at-work-be-prepared-to-deliver (archived at https://perma.cc/WG99-WL7D).

24 Katz, D. and McIntosh, L. (2021). Integrating ESG into corporate culture: Not elsewhere, but everywhere. The Harvard Law School Forum on Corporate Governance. corpgov.law.harvard.edu/2021/03/29/integrating-esg-into-corporate-culture-not-elsewhere-but-everywhere/ (archived at https://perma.cc/8YDW-XB6B).

25 United Nations (2004). *Who Cares Wins*. p.v. www.unepfi.org/fileadmin/events/2004/stocks/who_cares_wins_global_compact_2004.pdf (archived at https://perma.cc/B4SN-YBYM).

26 NYU Stern Executive Education (n.d.). *Corporate Sustainability*. NYU Stern Executive Education. execed.stern.nyu.edu/products/corporate-sustainability (archived at https://perma.cc/PD8Q-7V5V).

27 Saïd Business School (n.d.). *Environmental, Social and Governance Sustainability Programme*. Saïd Business School. www.sbs.ox.ac.uk/programmes/executive-education/bespoke-business-solutions/customised-business-solutions/customised-programmes-and-propositions/environmental-social-and-governance-sustainability-programme (archived at https://perma.cc/5M5P-WBSY).

28 The Wharton School, The University of Pennsylvania (n.d.). The ESG Initiative at the Wharton School. Environmental, Social and Governance (ESG) Initiative. esg.wharton.upenn.edu/ (archived at https://perma.cc/HZ22-DSNF).

29 Diligent (n.d.). *ESG Certification for Effective Leadership*. www.diligent.com/landing/esg-leadership-certification/ (archived at https://perma.cc/2GUC-MW7M).

30 Galbraith, M. (2018). Don't just tell employees organizational changes are coming—explain why. *Harvard Business Review*. hbr.org/2018/10/dont-just-tell-employees-organizational-changes-are-coming-explain-why (archived at https://perma.cc/DN3N-CTC6).

31 Target (2023). All About Target. Target Corporate. corporate.target.com/about (archived at https://perma.cc/94HT-UQSF).

32 Fortune Editors (2023). Target CEO: DEI has "fueled much of our growth over the last 9 years". Yahoo Finance. finance.yahoo.com/news/target-ceo-dei-fueled-much-221502055.html (archived at https://perma.cc/QUG8-UVW2).

33 Fortune Editors (2023). Target CEO: DEI has "fueled much of our growth over the last 9 years". Yahoo Finance. finance.yahoo.com/news/target-ceo-dei-fueled-much-221502055.html (archived at https://perma.cc/QUG8-UVW2).

34 2UrbanGirls (2023). Target Corp. invests in community ahead of new store opening in Inglewood. 2UrbanGirls. 2urbangirls.com/2023/03/target-corp-invests-in-community-ahead-of-new-store-opening-in-inglewood/ (archived at https://perma.cc/Z2SK-YLGH).

35 Fortune Editors (2023). Target CEO: DEI has "fueled much of our growth over the last 9 years". Yahoo Finance. finance.yahoo.com/news/target-ceo-dei-fueled-much-221502055.html (archived at https://perma.cc/QUG8-UVW2).

36 Ahuja, S.B. (2019). Why innovation labs fail, and how to ensure yours doesn't. *Harvard Business Review*. hbr.org/2019/07/why-innovation-labs-fail-and-how-to-ensure-yours-doesnt (archived at https://perma.cc/7FW3-SRYQ).

37 Zaki, A. (2023). 61% of managers say exec leaders hold them back from innovation: Weekly stat. CFO. www.cfo.com/news/61-of-managers-say-exec-leaders-hold-them-back-from-innovation-weekly-sta/654501/ (archived at https://perma.cc/9BNX-DCS2).

38 Dell Technologies (2022). *Our purpose in action FY22 Environmental, Social, and Governance Report*. Dell Technologies, p. 61. www.dell.com/en-us/dt/corporate/social-impact/esg-resources/reports/fy23-esg-report.htm (archived at https://perma.cc/EN5R-ECRN).

39 Dell Technologies (2017). Code of Conduct. Dell Technologies, p. 9. www.dell.com/en-us/dt/corporate/about-us/who-we-are/code-of-conduct.htm (archived at https://perma.cc/83UR-BWPT).

40 Dell Technologies (2022). *Our purpose in action FY22 Environmental, Social, and Governance Report*. Dell Technologies, p. 28. www.dell.com/en-us/dt/corporate/social-impact/esg-resources/reports/fy23-esg-report.htm (archived at https://perma.cc/EN5R-ECRN).

41 Dell Technologies (2022). *Our purpose in action FY22 Environmental, Social, and Governance Report*. Dell Technologies, p. 38. www.dell.com/en-us/dt/corporate/social-impact/esg-resources/reports/fy23-esg-report.htm (archived at https://perma.cc/EN5R-ECRN).

42 Dell Technologies (2022). *Our purpose in action FY22 Environmental, Social, and Governance Report*. Dell Technologies, p. 38. www.dell.com/en-us/dt/corporate/social-impact/esg-resources/reports/fy23-esg-report.htm (archived at https://perma.cc/EN5R-ECRN).

43 Dell Technologies (2022). *Our purpose in action FY22 Environmental, Social, and Governance Report*. Dell Technologies, p. 38. www.dell.com/en-us/dt/corporate/social-impact/esg-resources/reports/fy23-esg-report.htm (archived at https://perma.cc/EN5R-ECRN).

44 Dell Technologies (2022). *Our purpose in action FY22 Environmental, Social, and Governance Report*. Dell Technologies, p. 61. www.dell.com/en-us/dt/ corporate/social-impact/esg-resources/reports/fy23-esg-report.htm (archived at https://perma.cc/EN5R-ECRN).

45 Dell Technologies (2022). *Our purpose in action FY22 Environmental, Social, and Governance Report*. Dell Technologies, p. 61. www.dell.com/en-us/dt/ corporate/social-impact/esg-resources/reports/fy23-esg-report.htm (archived at https://perma.cc/EN5R-ECRN).

08

Financial Services: Impact and ESG

When considering companies and their value chain, the stakeholders usually encompass upstream suppliers, employees, and downstream customers. However, as the Business Roundtable pointed out in 2019, shareholders are stakeholders, too.[1] Yet, shareholders are just one of the company's many financial stakeholders, and an entire Financial Services value chain surrounds each company across capital markets, banking, and insurance. In Chapter 1, we learned that the Financial Services perspective is the one that created ESG and remains an influence that cannot be ignored, but we've moved well past the recommendations for comparable data to get to the root of ESG and its impact on companies. As ESG has shifted how we think about companies, the nature of these financial relationships is also changing, requiring an ESG mindset shift.

Underpinning these three broad industries at the intersection of their business models and a company's model is risk management. If you are an investor, you might buy or sell securities based on risk tolerance or seek new ESG investment opportunities. A bank might weigh risk as part of its lending due diligence or lend to those pursuing a transition. Of course, insurance is entirely focused on risk management, comprised of mountains of actuarial work. As we covered in the last chapter, those relationships may be partly based now on a specific intangible asset, data. Both financial and non-financial data now inform external financial decisions around a company.

Regarding ESG, a company, and the financial firms that support it, the same conflation between non-material and material efforts in business also exists in finance. The differences and nuances between ESG, sustainability, and systemic social goals are also ill-defined across Financial Services. As it turns out, the conflation from Financial Services is one reason for so much confusion across investments and the business ecosystem. This conflation opens up various interpretations between a financial product's intent and a firm's approach. For example, when a board or CEO looks at the company's public ESG scores from rating agencies and hears about the high amount of capital inflows into "ESG Investing," they may look to capitalize on the trend, believing ESG to mean one thing, like pursuing low-carbon operations, when it is another, such as material Environmental management. As a result, the company may flail and experiment with aligning to assumptions through values-based programs when investors might value ESG risk management or something else entirely. This danger can happen across the public and private markets. In the case of publicly traded companies, shareholders have direct influence through proxy voting, as we saw with Governance. But, of course, a private equity firm with a portfolio operations team may wield similar influence over its privately owned companies.

As we saw in Chapter 4, in the early 1980s, companies and the markets subscribed to the Friedman doctrine, which put shareholders as the primary focus.[2] Even as the world has shifted towards a broader stakeholder focus, Financial Services haven't forgotten about shareholders. In his 2023 CEO letter, Larry Fink repeatedly describes delivering value and performance to shareholders.[3] Despite other stakeholder considerations, shareholders still sway the markets through publicly traded and privately held companies. Bank of America's CEO, Brian Moynihan, serves as the Chair of the Stakeholder Capitalism Metrics Initiative, which pulls together a series of non-financial disclosures for stakeholders.[4] Humana's CEO, Bruce Broussard, told JUST Capital that the coronavirus and racial equity issues in the USA have sealed the insurer's approach to stakeholders.[5] The shift towards stakeholders in Financial Services is well underway.

Yet, there's a bit of a trap regarding ESG and Financial Services. Most thinking, writing, and discussion on ESG happens through the Financial Services perspective and not the company one, but ironically the company is where the risks and opportunities lie. Despite this intense focus on Financial Services, companies are at the center of the ESG conversation, which is the primary reason for this book. This pivot away from companies may appear warranted, considering that ESG started as an idea from the capital markets, and Bloomberg predicts ESG assets may reach $53 trillion by 2025, which is no small amount.[6] Regarding transition risk, one study estimated the world needs $50 trillion for the net-zero transition,[7] which banks would need to facilitate. Climate change impacts insurance because the frequency and intensity of events are increasing and because people are moving to high-risk areas.[8]

Still, improvements, and innovations happen in companies. There are no Financial Services without companies to invest in, lend to, and protect from risk. Conversely, no company can exist without access to capital markets firms, banks, and insurers. Each is evolving in this new world of ESG, creating new meaningful relationships, building innovative products, forging new partnerships, and evaluating risk.

Capital markets as a critical stakeholder

When discussing ESG and Financial Services, it only makes sense to start with capital markets. After all, this is the perspective where ESG began, and it maintains a strong hold over the acronym's focus today. While little is black and white with ESG, the capital markets have several dualities with ESG that can creep across the executive perspective of a company and down into the employee ranks. The executive team should be cognizant of these risks as the company mainstreams ESG.

Unfortunately, the first duality is hard to work through, as it comes from the top down through the strong legacy of shareholder primacy. This perspective can get in the way of addressing ESG risks, opportunities, and long-term resilience. Many believe that shareholder primacy means chasing only profits and financial performance through extraction from natural resources and labor as the only paths to revenue and profit. Yet, we don't live on a planet with infinite resources. Eventually, this exploitative approach will present risks impacting shareholders, but the problem can be worse. Shareholder primacy may lead a company to overlook material ESG issues, intangible value, and the company's many stakeholders, compounding investor risk.

The argument for shareholder primacy is that a company needs to maximize profits for its investors and that it provides an economic return for society, but a company cannot lead with these ideas because it isn't material, nor might it align to the company's purpose. A company's purpose, typically centered around its products and services, would be a more material pursuit leading with shareholder returns. In other words, ESG isn't necessarily against shareholder attention as shareholders are another stakeholder in the mix. The focus on material ESG issues provides shareholders and all stakeholders with value.

Chasing the markets

Regardless of whether the company puts shareholders above other stake-holders or if they are in the mix, executives look to the markets to try to decipher investors' motivations and then act. One of the main ways a company interacts with investors is indirectly through reporting. Unfortunately, financial reporting cycles and executive compensation models tied to stock price movements can favor a short-term perspective. Financial regulators have to balance rules that dictate quality and timely financial reporting. Sometimes, these rules may inadvertently force a short-term outlook from the board and executives if the company must report its financials frequently. For example, the SEC requires quarterly financial reporting in the USA, Asia varies with quarterly or semi-annual reporting,[9] while the EU dropped the quarterly reporting requirement in 2013.[10] Logically, chasing quarterly numbers puts a CFO in the mindset that investors are watching performance frequently instead of the long-term trend analysis that ESG can bring. As a result, a CFO may pursue adjustments through financial reporting machinations to create short-term stock price movements, potentially even attempting to align with stock performance-related executive compensation models. For example, as the economy was slow to recover from Covid in 2023, many companies turned to legal but creative accounting methodologies to boost performance on their financials when there was no actual performance change, protecting the stock price a bit.[11] Pursuits like this are unsustainable and distract from more material issues.

It is difficult to tell whether investors adjust their perspective around the financial reporting cycle as the results are mixed. For example, a 2017 study from the UK showed no change in investing strategies when the quarterly reporting enforcement ended.[12] Yet, in another study, 34 percent of economists believed that dropping the quarterly reporting requirement would improve executives' long-term attention.[13] Nevertheless, CFOs must be mindful of the duality between investors' short-term pursuits of stock gains, such as a hedge fund, and long-term resilience of returns, like a pension, and help direct attention accordingly. As finding agreement on the financial side is difficult, locating it on the non-financial side of ESG can be equally as challenging.

Investors have long had options for investing their money as they choose, managing their risk tolerance and the returns they seek, but also with their values. As a reminder from Chapter 1, for centuries, religion played a role in advising people on variations of ethical, impact, and socially responsible investing (SRI), based mainly on what not to invest in.[14] To communicate these efforts beyond the broad strokes of vice stocks, some companies published Corporate Social Responsibility (CSR) reports to communicate the company's non-financial activities to investors and other stakeholders and to redefine success criteria as they saw fit.

Yet, from its start in the early 2000s, ESG was doing something different. ESG brought a new perspective; that investor analysis around material Environmental, Social, and Corporate Governance issues could have profound long-term effects.[15] This unique idea of ESG investing found a way to align long-term shareholder value and fiduciary duty with these seemingly non-financial factors.[16] As sustainability and purpose are separate from ESG, SRI isn't the same as ESG investing, but even Vanguard, one of the world's largest asset managers, has an ESG website which states that clients may hear these terms used interchangeably.[17] Clients may hear these terms back and forth, but that doesn't mean they have the same context, and shouldn't, but unfortunately often do. The differences can be subtle, depending on which firm offers the products and their unique definitions.

It isn't apparent what different financial products or rating agencies are attempting to measure and which behaviors they are trying to drive. Many working in Financial Services would recommend that an investor or company executives read the fund prospectus or product information and investigate the firm's website. Still, much of that language is boilerplate, which can lead to frustration.

Along the lines of clarity, three financial regulations regarding how capital markets firms approach their products via labeling are worth noting. A high-level examination can help a company consider different ESG-related objectives and perspectives. None is an exhaustive approach but they intend to bring clarity to investors by breaking down interchangeable terminology into more specific categories.

EU SFDR

The EU has implemented the Sustainable Financial Disclosure Regulation (SFDR), which describes disclosure obligations for investment and financial products such as pensions, investment products, portfolio management, insurance advice, and financial advisory services. It is worth noting that the ESG acronym does not appear in its text, but it mentions Environmental, Social, and Governance throughout. The EU also has the concept of double materiality, which considers the material effect of the world on the company (traditional ESG) and the impact of the company on the world, including the material potential on the company.

- Article 6 is the default investment category and describes a product that may or may not have sustainability characteristics. The market participant or adviser must explain sustainability risks and why or why not the products consider these risks.[18]

- Article 8 products promote quality Environmental, Social, or Governance characteristics and how the product meets those goals.[19]

- Article 9 products pursue a positive social or sustainability as its objective at the core of its offering.[20]

US SEC proposed rule around ESG investment practices

The US Securities and Exchange Commission (SEC) proposed enhancements from advisers and investment firms around ESG and impact-focused investments in May 2022.[21] The regulator recognized that certain products might look at E, S, and G issues individually or how they relate to each other. In that pursuit, the SEC describes three broad categories.

- ESG Integration: Where the product considers one or more ESG factors alongside other non-ESG factors. The product may consider ESG, but these issues alone do not drive investment selection.[22]

- ESG-Focused: ESG is a main consideration in selecting the investment, including divestment and engagement strategies.[23]

- ESG Impact: Describes investment strategies that align with an E, S, or G goal or objective in mind.[24]

ASEAN Sustainable and Responsible Fund Standards

The Association of Southeast Asian Nations (ASEAN), a political and economic union of 10 member states, has published a disclosure framework and a comprehensive list of eight possible types of investment strategies. These strategies include definitions for the following: active ownership, ESG integration, ethical and faith-based investing, impact investing, negative screening, positive screening, thematic investing, and an 'other' category.[25]

The tricky thing about the markets is that it isn't apparent what investors want, labeling and intent on products are not as clear as they could be, and different fund and portfolio managers and advisers take different approaches. Yet, labeling can be an informative way for companies and investors to consider the different possibilities and goals of the financial product.

Pressures: Divestment, proxy voting, and stewardship

Compounding the complexities of chasing the markets and the new and emerging regulations are other pressures that can arise in the nuance. For example, a religious shareholder leading with values may divest from controversial stocks to avoid risky themes. An activist investor may invest in a company leading the sustainable transition. An ESG investor might invest in an oil company managing its transition to renewables, assuming it can ensure long-term financial performance through transition risk management. In each case, pressure manifests around the company to react, continue the status quo, improve, or innovate, regardless of any financial product labeling. The company's board needs to listen to these signals and understand the difference between values-led and value-based ESG investing while remembering that long-term resilience and sustainable growth will likely prevail over short-term and extractive thinking and risky bets on investor appeasement. When considered as one stakeholder group, investors want it all, but the company cannot lose its long-term perspective.

Capital markets firms seek accurate disclosures, comparable data, and signs of progress in different areas. This progress may be a material issue like carbon intensity reductions and managing transition risk, or it could be non-material progress if the firm has a particular goal for that financial product. Again, firms may put an ESG label across either, making it difficult for investors to tell if they are saving the world or managing risk with their capital.

Historically, a divestment strategy has been employed around non-material ESG issues, similar to those used by religious investment organizations, to keep portfolios 'green' or aligned with values-based social matters. This exclusionary screening is a specific type of pressure. The goal here is not to change the company; it's simply that the investor doesn't choose to invest in that company for a thematic reason, like values. Values aren't the only reason to divest, however. Sometimes the change the company must make is so significant that the investor sees too big of a material risk.

In 2001, the largest pension fund in the USA, CalPERS, decided to divest from tobacco, citing litigation, reputational, and regulatory risks as the leading factors.[26] Over 19 years, CalPERS is estimated to have lost $3.6 billion by divesting but gained $856 million from 2017–2020.[27] Still, this is a complicated issue when considering the Social as CalPERS was also the second-largest purchaser of healthcare for government employees in 2020,[28] which likely doesn't align with tobacco from a values perspective.

The challenge is that when shareholders divest, the repeated pressure to change is lost because the investor loses access to company influence through a proxy vote or other engagement models. Only a shareholder, who owns part of that company, gets a vote. The year 2023 had the second-highest quarter of investor activism since 2019 across Europe and Asia, with a slight drop in the USA.[29] However, activism may also be values-led on broad issues, but that doesn't mean the issues aren't material or can't affect stakeholders directly. Of course, investors have the choice and don't always vote in favor of activist resolutions. Other times the company might decide to take action anyway, simply from the threat of a proxy vote.

In 2023, Key Bank received pressure from shareholders to conduct a racial equity audit, with one firm threatening to bring the issue up in a proxy vote.[30] A third party, usually a law firm, will perform such an audit to uncover systemic bias and discrimination at a company or its supply chain. On the surface, it can be challenging for an outsider to say whether this is a material issue, as these types of audits service systemic social problems rather than direct stakeholders. However, the crux of the matter for the bank was a non-profit report naming Key Bank as the worst mortgage lender for Black borrowers out of the largest top 50 in the USA.[31] One could easily see how this claim could be a material issue through stakeholder impact, potential reputational damage, and regulatory scrutiny. The bank disagreed with the report's findings but, upon reflection with its stakeholders, agreed to move forward with the audit before it came up for a vote.[32] This call was a critical Governance decision on a Social issue, regardless of where it landed. Of course, as with any disclosures or audit, the data and insights learned are essential, but only action against that information will solve systemic issues.

A third type of shareholder pressure represents an opportunity for the board and executive team to take advantage of. When an investor takes an active ownership role, which can happen in the public or private markets, they may engage in stewardship. These activities are where the firm's analysts and portfolio managers actively engage the company's leadership on ESG.

For example, an investment firm may have a stewardship team to research and investigate ESG topics by company, industry, and value chain. From there, the team might share an industry report, their materiality assessment of the company, or other information to the company in a playbook to help the company's leaders understand how the markets see the company's risks and opportunities. This information can be an invaluable perspective if the company is receptive.

Fidelity International is an investment solutions and services firm focusing on long-term growth, with offices in Europe, Asia Pacific, Japan, and Southern America.[33] The firm's 2020 report on stewardship in China tells the story of engaging with an oil and gas company on a low-carbon transition. The firm and the company discussed several topics, including the long-term energy transition, integration of renewables, compliance with government regulations, and the importance of climate disclosures on climate management.[34] Within three months of the engagement, the company set net-zero aspirations and announced plans for renewables.[35] One month after the company made the announcement, President Xi Jinping announced China's Five Year Plan for net-zero goals, and by 2021, three out of the top five power companies in China announced plans to peak emissions by 2025.[36] Engagement can make a difference.

How the board and executive team handle these types of pressure is a Governance issue for a company. A constructive approach that engages investors and examines the matter through data and transparency may reduce future risk. On the contrary, leading with investor pressure without understanding the issue is a recipe for disaster. Knowing if the investor wants you to save the world or manage risks and opportunities to pursue long-term growth can help find alignments in shared strategies. This idea presents the board and executive team with a unique ESG opportunity to work with investment firms and gain insights from them.[37] Still, if you outright ask several investment firms what they prioritize, you will get several answers due to the range of motivations. These answers are valuable for analysis and planning, but the company needs a starting point to engage with investors, develop and evolve the plan, then consistently communicate and provide updates. In his 2022 CEO letter, Larry Fink told companies that it's really up to them how to proceed with their long-term strategy and communicate it to investors.[38]

As we've seen throughout the book, a company simply cannot ignore its material issues, especially Governance ones. Yet, in parallel, companies can pursue values-based projects and value-based improvements and innovations and may even find alignment in some activities. Still, these activities may also be on divergent paths.

Shareholders want it all, but not every issue is material

Shareholders have a lot of power, different ways to engage a company, and, most importantly, different objectives. When shareholders prioritize an issue like carbon reductions or DEI, it can make the company believe it is broadly material when the nuance means it needs further examination. For example, the S&P 500 ESG Index removed Tesla in 2022.[39] Many couldn't understand how an index focused on ESG could remove an electric vehicle company. The reason was more nuanced and due to Tesla's lack of carbon reduction strategies and attention to Governance principles, claims of racial discrimination and poor working conditions, and more.[40] In other words, providing an Environmentally friendly product or service doesn't mean your company has eliminated its ESG risks. Then again, Tesla was added back into the S&P 500 ESG Index in 2023, with S&P citing the company's focus on material Environmental factors.[41]

Communication is vital when dealing with shareholders and stakeholders. As we covered in Chapter 2, many regulations, standards, and frameworks exist to guide companies in reporting ESG metrics. These often intersect with providing higher-quality and hopefully comparable data to stakeholders, including shareholders or potential private market investors. When a company collects data from its suppliers upstream, the downstream use of its products, and its internal operations and publishes it, Financial Services firms may pick that data up for analysis and feed it across the market ecosystem through financial product decisions, like an index rebalance or addition or removal from a fund.

There is an emerging trend around the disclosures where the metrics can be material due to investor pressure to report and regulatory compliance. While this is an unfortunate side-effect of data standardization and transparency, companies must still publish information. Investors want to see data as proof of ESG risk management, new opportunity development, or improvement towards a sustainable or Social goal, and regulators insist on quality data. As a company must ensure it isn't leading its purpose with investor whims, it also must be sure it doesn't lead its ESG strategy with disclosures alone because that will not appease the markets.

Banks finance change

Much attention around Environmental and Social tipping points has given way to the movement of capital to finance improvements in these areas. Banks stand ready to provide money around the change fueled by intergovernmental pledges, corporate commitments, and disclosures. Since ESG represents material risks and opportunities, funding improvements and innovation should be nothing new for a bank. Banks already serve that critical role in the company's value chain by managing cash flow and payroll, conducting due diligence on and financing complex mergers and acquisitions, providing short-term and long-term credit, and more. In these ways, banks have long focused on a company's material tangibles and intangibles, directly and indirectly. For example, a bank might provide a loan for tangible capital improvements like a new building or factory equipment. On the other hand, efficiently managing the company's cash flow and payroll transactions ensures workers are paid on time, indirectly helping to drive that stakeholder relationship through finance.

Commercial lending around ESG

Banks are playing a new and crucial role across companies, their value chains, and various ESG issues, as they now finance non-material or tangentially material ESG projects as pressure builds for companies to transform. Banks have developed new lending products as companies look to improve and innovate, especially across sustainability, net zero, and Social goals. As the company informs investors about its strategies, it must also determine the projects to take on and pursue financing in the context of materiality or other issues. Also, as in the capital markets, companies will intersect with banks around ESG data and must know the factors to get favorable lending terms, raise capital with loans, and finance transition projects. Like investors, some banks may want to save the world and fund the transition, and others might be looking to manage risk.

Three types of loans have emerged over the past few years, more aligned to values-based or ESG value than traditional lending. Companies can take advantage of these loans with guidance, principles, and external review like those agreed upon by the Asia Pacific Loan Market Association (APLMA), the Loan Market Association (LMA), and the Loan Syndications and Trading Association (LSTA).[42]

WHAT ARE GREEN, SOCIAL, AND SUSTAINABILITY-LINKED LOANS?

Green Loans refer to loans that support a clear Environmental objective, as defined and measured by the borrower. This loan might include carbon reductions through energy efficiency projects, renewables transition, conservation, green technologies, climate adaptation, and so on.[43] Sometimes, a Green Loan can support a new opportunity. In 2020, UOL Group Limited announced that it secured a $120 million loan from United Overseas Bank Limited in Singapore to redevelop the Pan Pacific Orchard Hotel with sustainability in mind.[44] The hotel opened in 2021 and featured lush greenery, solar panels, rainwater collection, and a bio-digester system, which bio-transforms food waste into cleaning water.[45]

Social Loans refer to loans that address or mitigate a Social issue, including, but not limited to, specific populations. For example, it could be a socioeconomic benefit, employment generation, an investment in affordable housing, accessibility to essential services, and so on.[46] In 2022, MUFG Bank announced that it had worked with India's Housing Development Finance Corporation (HFDC) to launch a $1.1 billion Social Loan.[47] The largest Social Loan to date, its "use of proceeds" under the principles will only finance affordable housing.[48]

Sustainability-Linked Loans are a little different from the other two types. These loans incentivize meeting ambitious sustainability goals in exchange for typically favorable economic lending terms.[49] The challenge is that this loan may not necessarily connect with an actual ESG improvement or innovation, only the metric. For example, Gildan Activewear announced a $1 billion Sustainability-Linked Loan in 2022 that will reduce or increase the lending costs around three objectives, including its SBTi-based Scope 1 and 2 reduction goals, the incorporation of recycled or sustainable materials, and gender parity at the director level and above.[50] Unless the terms state otherwise, the company can use this line of credit for any project.

Across Green and Social Loans, there is no requirement for materiality or stakeholder considerations, only the objective. With Sustainability-Linked Loans, the financing may not contribute to a material or non-material ESG issue. In this case, the loan terms connect with agreed-upon ESG metrics. As always, it is up to the company to bring the context of a worthy company investment with this loan, and companies are taking advantage. As of

September 2021, sustainable lending was more than 10 percent of the global corporate syndicated loan market, with 90 percent being Sustainability-Linked Loans.[51] Green and Sustainability-Linked Loans grew to $681 billion in 2021, a 275 percent increase over 2020.[52] This rise in lending is perhaps encouraging for activists because it signals that companies are engaging in Environmental projects. Still, with Sustainability-Linked Loans, which represent most of the market, it can be difficult to tell if ESG projects are receiving financing or if the focus is only on the metrics to improve favorable loan terms for a range of project types.

The power of corporate and finance partnerships

Sustainability and related transition work are becoming more material for suppliers as their large customers look to reduce their carbon emissions and manage their environmental footprint. Even consumers prioritize sustainability over conventionally marketed products, with a five-year compound annual growth rate of 9.48 percent for sustainably marketed products instead of 4.98 percent.[53] This trend has held steady through recent inflationary pressures as well.[54] Effective Environmental and transition management can be a differentiator impacting the bottom line for a supplier operating in this ecosystem. Sometimes companies need more expertise and processes to proceed down this path, which can be fraught with risks, as with any change. Suppliers also need financing to help transition.

Walmart is one example of engagement across suppliers in stewardship and skilling through the company's Procurement team, followed by funding the transitions in partnership with banks. Walmart announced Project Gigaton in 2017, a program focused on suppliers to remove 1 billion metric tons of greenhouse gases by 2030.[55] By 2022, the program had 4,500 suppliers enrolled with over 574 million metric tons of greenhouse gases reduced or avoided, over halfway to the goal.[56] In 2019, Walmart announced a partnership with HSBC to launch a Sustainable Supply Chain Finance (SSCF) program to drive improved financing to suppliers that can demonstrate sustainable progress.[57] In late 2021, Walmart and HSBC expanded the partnership to include CDP and now allow suppliers to get their invoices paid early by Walmart when the supplier reports into CDP, sets its targets, and reports its impact.[58]

These types of partnerships between companies and banks, or even between banks and other parties, to de-risk ESG and sustainable investments are an evolution that will lead to more creative financing to help drive the transition.

Finding materiality in loss and damage

Climate change impacts those least responsible for it, with many populations residing in developing countries. With new regulations and commitments from governments, like the Paris Agreement and the subsequent Global Stocktake, the developed world is focused on operational reductions and mitigation of future climate change impact. Meanwhile, the developing world, which is seeing heavy Environmental damage and Social tolls, is focused on adaptation.

As we saw in Chapter 3, loss and damage supports climate change adaptation by funneling money to the developing world to deal with the effects of climate change. Ideally, this money would be via grants, not loans, so the affected country doesn't need to repay the money. In other words, the developing world cannot support a loan scheme that further pushes a monetary burden on them, especially when dealing with a crisis. This money can help a developing country proactively address climate risk, plan more effectively, and conduct a recovery after an event, bringing stability and protecting potential company stakeholders. There may be a material risk depending on where a company's supply chain exists. Companies can work with banks to help fund area adaptation efforts before a crisis hits directly or through philanthropic efforts.[59] This blended finance approach allows a company to participate in the ecosystem and direct funds to where it could make a difference with its suppliers.

Insurance is about risk

If there is one industry on the front lines of ESG, it is the insurance industry. As companies face risk across Environmental, Social, and Governance factors, insurers have products backed by data and risk models to protect companies. With their broad perspective across industries, insurers also understand associated risks and may serve as risk advisors to companies on ESG matters. Insurers even have structures in place to insure each other during severe shocks to the system via reinsurance. Reinsurance is insurance for insurers to minimize the risk of losses if a crisis emerges. For example, according to the Insurance Information Institute, at least 16 insurers became insolvent after Hurricane Andrew in 1992, which caused $27.3 billion in damages (2017 adjusted numbers).[60] This event's severity changed the reinsurance landscape, with insurers now more dependent on reinsurance,[61] which should be a warning to all companies. Still, even some crises are too great for insurers. In 2023, State Farm and Allstate announced they would stop issuing new home insurance policies in California due to wildfire risk.[62]

Crises like wildfires and new extreme weather patterns can be hard to predict and might be unfamiliar territory for an insurer's models. Still, underwriters and actuaries thrive in this type of risk analysis. Also, as company value has shifted to intangibles over the past few decades, so has what needs to be insured. Whereas before, companies would only need to insure physical assets subject to risk, new intangibles, ranging from digital IP to transition risk, must also be protected.

Physical risk: Property, health, and life insurance

Climate change brings a range of physical risks to companies. As we saw in Chapter 3, extreme weather events are now more common. Flooding, severe windstorms, and wildfires can all destroy physical assets, impact global supply chains, and affect company stability. Property insurance can help a company recover from one of these disasters, but so can a proactive assessment of the physical space in which the company operates as a building sits in an ecosystem. Tools like satellite imagery, weather data, IoT sensors, and AI can help companies model their climate risk. Mitigation ahead of a disaster could help lower premiums and disruption. Still, this type of physical risk only scratches the surface.

As the climate changes, another risk presents itself along the Social. Climate change greatly affects people mentally and physiologically through disruption of nutritious food supply, extreme heat, air pollution, biodiversity loss, and even water safety after extreme flooding events.[63] These issues can materially and financially affect the company and its employees through direct impacts, like rising health and life insurance costs, and indirectly with productivity loss. Still, the intersection with insurance in these areas is developing due to the complexities around the long-term nature of the problem, uncovering statistical correlation between events and health, and variation in portfolio coverage.[64]

Transition risk: Litigation and change

Returning to TCFD's definition of Transition Risk, insurance intersects with Policy and Legal risks, as both, transitioning to a low-carbon or net-zero economy or not transitioning, carry risks. As we saw previously, a small town in Peru is suing RWE for its emissions contribution. The risk of litigation around sustainability claims and greenwashing, environmental damage with human consequences, or possibly even emissions contribution with the effects of climate change are rising.[65,66] Between 1986 and 2014, 800 cases were filed, but there was an increase to over 1,000 cases filed between 2015 and 2021, with the cases more often looking to drive a societal shift.[67] Regardless if a case is a one-off or part of a broader effort to bring attention to an issue, losing a case like this can create reputational risks for companies and increase insurance rates.

There is another indirect connection to the TCFD definition of Technology Risk, which again is more focused on sustainability-related improvements and innovation the company may pursue. Companies may need new insurance or new insurance types to support these transitions. For example, as of 2022, 40 percent of all maritime shipping was related to fossil fuels.[68] As companies shift away from fossil fuels, new insurance on those goods like renewables, biomass, and lithium for batteries will all have to be insured.[69]

Intangible insurance: Cybersecurity and intellectual property

As companies have shifted towards intangibles, new risks have emerged that can be insured. For example, technology, data, and digital systems underpin nearly every company's operations and dramatically impact business value. As we saw in Chapter 6, there are cybersecurity risks associated with this digital mode of operations. With so many potential attack vectors for hackers to pursue, cybersecurity must be a foundational consideration in technology deployment. Still, cybersecurity insurance can help minimize the costs of disruption, data breaches, digital damage, ransomware, post-incident recovery, and more. A company could even obtain insurance around a lapse in digital privacy Governance to soften the potential blow from the EU's GDPR and fines.[70]

Another intangible that can be insured is intellectual property (IP), a company's critical competitive advantage. This type of insurance can help defend a company's IP, but also as competitors bring claims against a company's IP. An Aon Insurance report stated that $3.8 billion in damages were awarded in IP litigation cases in 2021.[71] $2.175 billion was just two claims brought against Intel by VLSI Technology, showcasing the potential monetary damage an intangible can cause.[72]

Two sides of a coin in Financial Services

While understanding Financial Services is critical to managing risks and finding new financial opportunities out of non-financial activities, companies need to lead with materiality and stakeholders and not the shifting priorities of the markets. ESG is ultimately about taking care of business and managing those risks while creating new opportunities. Still, the influence of Financial Services on the company cannot be understated.

Financial Services likely scrutinize companies more than other stakeholders, including even regulators. Yet, that external lens of analysis is just one of the sides of a coin that Financial Services must consider when it comes to ESG.

On the other side, Financial Services firms must focus on their ESG efforts like other companies do. After all, each industry has considerations of materiality and stakeholders to manage. The same ESG table stakes issues exist for Financial Services firms, but each firm has unique risks they must monitor and address. An investment firm touting an impact fund needs to make sure it labels the fund and communicates to investors clearly; otherwise, it may face a Governance issue. A bank sharing its net-zero commitments might come under fire for lending to a new fossil fuel project, enraging activists focused on the Environment. Insurers must be conscious of the intersection between the Environment and the Social where their most marginalized customers live.

Even Financial Services firms can experience ESG risks and opportunities. This is one last duality, and with as much influence as firms have across the global economy, they need to lead from the front so that every company gets it right.

Notes

1 Business Roundtable (2019). Business Roundtable redefines the purpose of a corporation to promote "an economy that serves all Americans". Business Roundtable. www.businessroundtable.org/business-roundtable-redefines-the-purpose-of-a-corporation-to-promote-an-economy-that-serves-all-americans (archived at https://perma.cc/7XUW-QR6W).

2 Friedman, M. (1970). The social responsibility of business is to increase its profits. *The New York Times*, September 13. www.nytimes.com/1970/09/13/archives/a-friedman-doctrine-the-social-responsibility-of-business-is-to.html (archived at) https://perma.cc/4ZLW-MQJ7).

3 Fink, L. (2023). Larry Fink's annual Chairman's Letter to Investors. BlackRock. www.blackrock.com/corporate/investor-relations/larry-fink-annual-chairmans-letter (archived at https://perma.cc/DMV8-59VY).

4 Bank of America, N.A. (n.d.). Stakeholder capitalism metrics: Standards for measuring global sustainability. Bank of America. about.bankofamerica.com/en/making-an-impact/stakeholder-capitalism-metrics (archived at https://perma.cc/7SQX-N78H).

5 Feloni, R. and Mullineaux, M. (2020). Humana's CEO said the Coronavirus crisis has confirmed the value of a stakeholder-driven strategy. JUST Capital. justcapital.com/news/humanas-ceo-explained-how-the-coronavirus-crisis-has-confirmed-the-value-of-a-long-term-stakeholder-driven-strategy/ (archived at https://perma.cc/QN28-NGXD).

6 Bloomberg (2021). ESG assets may hit $53 trillion by 2025, a third of global AUM. Bloomberg Professional Services, February 23. www.bloomberg.com/professional/blog/esg-assets-may-hit-53-trillion-by-2025-a-third-of-global-aum/ (archived at https://perma.cc/S4U9-ETEZ).

7 Colas, J., Khaykin, I., Chitre, S., and Singh, S. (2021). Financing the transition to a net-zero future. Oliver Wyman. www.oliverwyman.com/our-expertise/insights/2021/oct/financing-the-transition-to-a-net-zero-future.html (archived at https://perma.cc/SY8W-AB3K).

8 Cho, R. (2022). With climate impacts growing, insurance companies face big challenges. *State of the Planet*. news.climate.columbia.edu/2022/11/03/with-climate-impacts-growing-insurance-companies-face-big-challenges/ (archived at https://perma.cc/57L3-3S6E).

9 Viernes, F.A.H. (2016). Asian companies' financial reporting frequency. CFA Institute, pp. 4–9. www.cfainstitute.org/-/media/regional/arx/post-pdf/2016/03/20/asian-companies-financial-reporting-frequency.ashx (archived at https://perma.cc/EG33-3FH5).

10 European Commission (n.d.). Transparency requirements for listed companies. European Commission Finance. finance.ec.europa.eu/capital-markets-union-and-financial-markets/company-reporting-and-auditing/company-reporting/transparency-requirements-listed-companies_en (archived at https://perma.cc/B456-G7EQ).

11 Foldy, B. (2023). Business is slowing. So companies are juicing profits. *The Wall Street Journal*, June 1. www.wsj.com/articles/profit-numbers-get-spruced-up-as-business-slows-8eec5017 (archived at https://perma.cc/T96T-DJ5B).

12 CFA Institute (2017). Study examines the impact of reporting frequency. CFA Institute Market Integrity Insights. blogs.cfainstitute.org/marketintegrity/2017/05/23/study-examines-the-impact-of-reporting-frequency (archived at https://perma.cc/PA6Y-VKN4).

13 Delbene, J. (2019). Reporting earnings less frequently could lead execs to make better long-term decisions, according to top economists. The University of Chicago Booth School of Business. www.chicagobooth.edu/media-relations-and-communications/press-releases/reporting-earnings-less-frequently-could-lead-execs-to-make-better-long-term-decisions (archived at https://perma.cc/P7VX-6ELL).

14 Lumberg, J. and Rhineheart, C. (2019). A brief history of impact investing. Investopedia. www.investopedia.com/news/history-impact-investing/ (archived at https://perma.cc/5A9G-UYMV).

15 UNEP Finance Initiative (2004). *The Materiality of Social, Environmental and Corporate Governance Issues to Equity Pricing*. UNEP Finance Initiative, pp. 3–4. www.unepfi.org/fileadmin/publications/amwg/ceo_briefing_materiality_equity_pricing_2004.pdf (archived at https://perma.cc/3R3N-3M46).

16 UNEP Finance Initiative (2004). *The Materiality of Social, Environmental and Corporate Governance Issues to Equity Pricing*. UNEP Finance Initiative, p. 4. www.unepfi.org/fileadmin/publications/amwg/ceo_briefing_materiality_equity_pricing_2004.pdf (archived at https://perma.cc/3R3N-3M46).

17 Vanguard (n.d.). ESG funds that reflect what matters most to you. Vaguard. investor.vanguard.com/investment-products/esg (archived at https://perma.cc/5KCR-EZEK).

18 The European Parliament and the Council of the European Union (2019). Regulation (EU) 2019/2088 of the European Parliament and of the Council of 27 November 2019 on sustainability-related disclosures in the financial services sector. Access to European Law, pp. 10–11. eur-lex.europa.eu/legal-content/EN/TXT/PDF/?uri=CELEX:32019R2088&from=EN (archived at https://perma.cc/NT9N-GD84).

19 The European Parliament and the Council of the European Union (2019). Regulation (EU) 2019/2088 of the European Parliament and of the Council of 27 November 2019 on sustainability-related disclosures in the financial services sector. Access to European Law, pp. 11–12. eur-lex.europa.eu/legal-content/EN/TXT/PDF/?uri=CELEX:32019R2088&from=EN (archived at https://perma.cc/NT9N-GD84).

20 The European Parliament and the Council of the European Union (2019). Regulation (EU) 2019/2088 of the European Parliament and of the Council of 27 November 2019 on sustainability-related disclosures in the financial services sector. Access to European Law, pp. 12–13. eur-lex.europa.eu/legal-content/EN/TXT/PDF/?uri=CELEX:32019R2088&from=EN (archived at https://perma.cc/NT9N-GD84).

21   U.S. Securities and Exchange Commission (2022). SEC proposes to enhance disclosures by certain investment advisers and investment companies about ESG investment practices. SEC. www.sec.gov/news/press-release/2022-92 (archived at https://perma.cc/5TMT-TH78).

22   U.S. Securities and Exchange Commission (2022a). *Enhanced Disclosures by Certain Investment Advisers and Investment Companies about Environmental, Social, and Governance Investment Practices.* SEC, p. 14. www.sec.gov/files/rules/proposed/2022/ia-6034.pdf (archived at https://perma.cc/6DFN-G34U).

23   U.S. Securities and Exchange Commission (2022a). *Enhanced Disclosures by Certain Investment Advisers and Investment Companies about Environmental, Social, and Governance Investment Practices.* SEC, pp. 14–15. www.sec.gov/files/rules/proposed/2022/ia-6034.pdf (archived at https://perma.cc/6DFN-G34U).

24   U.S. Securities and Exchange Commission (2022a). *Enhanced Disclosures by Certain Investment Advisers and Investment Companies about Environmental, Social, and Governance Investment Practices.* SEC, p. 15. www.sec.gov/files/rules/proposed/2022/ia-6034.pdf (archived at https://perma.cc/6DFN-G34U).

25   ASEAN Capital Markets Forum (2022). *ASEAN Sustainable and Responsible Fund Standards.* Google Docs, p. 8. drive.google.com/file/d/1zm91M_3wNvNJ4m2-TA3fhgXSUOTTpqCH/view (archived at https://perma.cc/B34N-VUGS).

26   California Public Employees' Retirement System (2014). *Towards Sustainable Investment & Operations.* CalPERS, p. 19. www.calpers.ca.gov/docs/forms-publications/esg-report-2014.pdf (archived at https://perma.cc/MHV3-KHYT).

27   Diamond, R. (2021). CalPERS rejects reinvesting in tobacco again. Chief Investment Officer. www.ai-cio.com/news/calpers-rejects-reinvesting-tobacco/ (archived at https://perma.cc/95BN-6WPM).

28   Diamond, R. (2021). CalPERS rejects reinvesting in tobacco again. Chief Investment Officer. www.ai-cio.com/news/calpers-rejects-reinvesting-tobacco/ (archived at https://perma.cc/95BN-6WPM).

29   Lazard (2023). *Shareholder Activism Update: Early Look at 2023 Trends.* Lazard. www.lazard.com/research-insights/shareholder-activism-update-early-look-at-2023-trends/ (archived at https://perma.cc/64F5-7ZTR).

30   Ramaswamy, S.V. (2023). KeyBank named "worst lender for Black borrowers" will undergo "racial equity audit". *USA Today.* www.usatoday.com/story/money/2023/05/11/keybank-worst-lender-black-borrowers-reacts-with-audit/70188905007/ (archived at https://perma.cc/6AUX-GJVX).

31 Ramaswamy, S.V. (2023). KeyBank named "worst lender for Black borrowers" will undergo "racial equity audit". *USA Today*. www.usatoday.com/story/money/2023/05/11/keybank-worst-lender-black-borrowers-reacts-with-audit/70188905007/ (archived at https://perma.cc/6AUX-GJVX).

32 Ramaswamy, S.V. (2023). KeyBank named "worst lender for Black borrowers" will undergo "racial equity audit". *USA Today*. www.usatoday.com/story/money/2023/05/11/keybank-worst-lender-black-borrowers-reacts-with-audit/70188905007/ (archived at https://perma.cc/6AUX-GJVX).

33 Fidelity International (n.d.). Our business. Fidelity International. fidelityinternational.com/about-us/our-business (archived at https://perma.cc/DP27-MWU8).

34 Fidelity International (2020). *Fidelity International China Stewardship Report 2020*. Fidelity International, p. 15. s3-eu-west-1.amazonaws.com/euissmultisiteprod-live-8dd1b69cadf7409099ee6471b87c49a-7653963/filer_public/3d/fe/3dfeed7f-74b5-42d5-9471-02fd383f4596/fidelity_china_report_2020_v6.pdf (archived at https://perma.cc/3CUN-2VDN).

35 Fidelity International (2020). *Fidelity International China Stewardship Report 2020*. Fidelity International, p. 15. s3-eu-west-1.amazonaws.com/euissmultisiteprod-live-8dd1b69cadf7409099ee6471b87c49a-7653963/filer_public/3d/fe/3dfeed7f-74b5-42d5-9471-02fd383f4596/fidelity_china_report_2020_v6.pdf (archived at https://perma.cc/3CUN-2VDN).

36 Min, H. (2021). China's net zero future. Climate Champions. climatechampions.unfccc.int/chinas-net-zero-future/ (archived at https://perma.cc/E5AJ-928P).

37 McNabb, B., Charan, R., and Carey, D. (2021). Engaging with your investors. *Harvard Business Review*. hbr.org/2021/07/engaging-with-your-investors (archived at https://perma.cc/NZ9J-3QDH).

38 Fink, L. (2022). Larry Fink's 2022 Letter to CEOs. BlackRock. www.blackrock.com/corporate/investor-relations/larry-fink-ceo-letter (archived at https://perma.cc/25FC-YJNP).

39 Dorn, M. (2022). The (re)balancing act of the S&P 500 ESG Index. Indexology Blog. www.indexologyblog.com/2022/05/17/the-rebalancing-act-of-the-sp-500-esg-index/ (archived at https://perma.cc/Y4CH-UFVK).

40 Dorn, M. (2022). The (re)balancing act of the S&P 500 ESG Index. Indexology Blog. www.indexologyblog.com/2022/05/17/the-rebalancing-act-of-the-sp-500-esg-index/ (archived at https://perma.cc/Y4CH-UFVK).

41 Kerber, R. (2023). Tesla returns to S&P 500 ESG index with more environmental disclosures. Reuters, June 21. www.reuters.com/sustainability/tesla-returns-sp-500-esg-index-with-more-environmental-disclosures-2023-06-21/ (archived at https://perma.cc/8NSS-H46N).

42 Virmani, T. (2022). New ESG guidance documents published. LSTA. www.lsta.org/news-resources/new-esg-guidance-documents-published/ (archived at https://perma.cc/6HU3-4R75).

43 APLMA, LMA and LSTA (2023a). *Green Loan Principles*. LSTA, p. 3. www.lsta.org/content/green-loan-principles/# (archived at https://perma.cc/ NSS4-X4HX).

44 Ng, S. and Ong, C. (2020). UOL secures first Green Loan of $120 million for Pan Pacific Orchard. UOL, p. 1. www.uol.com.sg/wp-content/uploads/ uol-news-releases/UOLMediaReleaseGreenLoan29Jul20.pdf (archived at https://perma.cc/5NAF-SPGG).

45 Seah, N. (2023). Why Pan Pacific Orchard is an example of sustainable hospitality and graceful luxury. *SG Magazine*. sgmagazine.com/lifestyle/ why-pan-pacific-orchard-is-the-new-example-of-sustainable-hospitality-and- graceful-luxury/ (archived at https://perma.cc/AZV9-GYNB).

46 APLMA, LMA and LSTA (2023b). *Social Loan Principles (SLP)*. LSTA, pp. 2–3. www.lsta.org/content/social-loan-principles-slp/ (archived at https:// perma.cc/D3EF-KGXE).

47 Ho, K. and Chua, H. (2022). MUFG seals landmark USD 1.1 billion social loan for affordable housing with HDFC in India. MUFG Bank, Ltd., p. 1. www.bk.mufg.jp/global/globalnetwork/asiapacific/anncts/pdf/apacnews- 20220808-01-en.pdf (archived at https://perma.cc/S6U2-LZXP).

48 Murdoch, A. (2022). HDFC's $1.1bn deal: An Indian oasis in the social loan desert. *Capital Monitor*. capitalmonitor.ai/factor/social/hdfc-social-loan- affordable-housing/ (archived at https://perma.cc/2YVU-RDG7).

49 APLMA, LMA and LSTA (2023c). *Guidance on Sustainability Linked Loan Principles (SLLP)*. LSTA, p. 2. www.lsta.org/content/guidance-on-sustainability- linked-loan-principles-sllp/# (archived at https://perma.cc/3HDG-CZJY).

50 Gildan Activewear, Inc. (2022). Gildan announces first sustainability-linked loan. GlobeNewswire News Room. www.globenewswire.com/news- release/2022/03/28/2411340/0/en/Gildan-Announces-First-Sustainability- Linked-Loan.html (archived at https://perma.cc/YA4N-FEDH).

51 Kim, S., Kumar, N., Lee, J., and Oh, J. (2022). Sustainability-linked loans: A strong ESG commitment or a vehicle for greenwashing? PRI. www.unpri.org/ pri-blog/sustainability-linked-loans-a-strong-esg-commitment-or-a-vehicle-for- greenwashing/10243.article (archived at https://perma.cc/DRB5-5LZS).

52 Virmani, T. (2022). Sustainable lending continues to surge. LSTA. www.lsta.org/ news-resources/sustainable-lending-continues-to-surge/ (archived at https:// perma.cc/8CJY-2XKJ).

53 The NYU Stern Center for Sustainable Business and Circana (2023). Research from NYU Stern Center for Sustainable Business and Circana shows sustaina- bility-marketed products continue to grow in the face of high inflation. NYU Stern. www.stern.nyu.edu/experience-stern/faculty-research/research-nyu-stern- center-sustainable-business-and-circana-shows-sustainability-marketed- products (archived at https://perma.cc/6KE2-MMUC).

54 The NYU Stern Center for Sustainable Business and Circana (2023). Research from NYU Stern Center for Sustainable Business and Circana shows sustainability-marketed products continue to grow in the face of high inflation. NYU Stern. www.stern.nyu.edu/experience-stern/faculty-research/research-nyu-stern-center-sustainable-business-and-circana-shows-sustainability-marketed-products (archived at https://perma.cc/6KE2-MMUC).

55 Stevens, P. (2019). Behind Walmart's push to eliminate 1 gigaton of greenhouse gases by 2030. CNBC. www.cnbc.com/2019/12/15/walmarts-project-gigaton-is-its-most-ambitious-climate-goal-yet.html (archived at https://perma.cc/AA9W-28AJ).

56 McLaughlin, K. (2022). Accelerating climate action: Project Gigaton marks key milestone. Walmart. corporate.walmart.com/news/2022/04/06/accelerating-climate-action-project-gigaton-marks-key-milestone (archived at https://perma.cc/FH7C-H8B5).

57 Walmart (2019). Walmart reports substantial emissions reductions in China as suppliers set ambitious targets. Walmart. corporate.walmart.com/news/2019/04/18/walmart-reports-substantial-emissions-reductions-in-china-as-suppliers-set-ambitious-targets (archived at https://perma.cc/YZ2N-KBCN).

58 Walmart (2021). Walmart creates industry first by introducing science-based targets for supply chain finance program. Walmart. corporate.walmart.com/news/2021/12/08/walmart-creates-industry-first-by-introducing-science-based-targets-for-supply-chain-finance-program (archived at https://perma.cc/G8LJ-MK2Z).

59 Bhandari, P., Warszawski, N., and Thangata, C. (2022). The current state of play on financing loss and damage. World Resource Institute. www.wri.org/technical-perspectives/current-state-play-financing-loss-and-damage (archived at https://perma.cc/PC6U-CVC5).

60 Insurance Information Institute (2017). Hurricane Andrew fact sheet. Insurance Information Institute. www.iii.org/article/hurricane-andrew-fact-sheet (archived at https://perma.cc/PS8K-FYYZ).

61 McChristian, L. (2012). *Hurricane Andrew and Insurance: The enduring Impact of an historic storm.* Insurance Information Institute, p.13. www.iii.org/sites/default/files/paper_HurricaneAndrew_final.pdf (archived at https://perma.cc/ER6A-MJBX).

62 Gall, M. (2023). Why insurance companies are pulling out of California and Florida, and how to fix some of the underlying problems. Yahoo News. news.yahoo.com/why-insurance-companies-pulling-california-122420247.html (archived at https://perma.cc/R9PB-SK2C).

63 Atwoli, L., Baqui, A.H., Benfield, T., Bosurgi, R., Godlee, F., Hancocks, S., Horton, R., Laybourn-Langton, L., Monteiro, C.A., Norman, I., Patrick, K., Praities, N., Olde Rikkert, M.G.M., Rubin, E.J., Sahni, P., Smith, R., Talley, N., Turale, S., and

Vázquez, D. (2021). Call for emergency action to limit global temperature increases, restore biodiversity, and protect health. *New England Journal of Medicine.* https://doi.org/10.1056/nejme2113200 (archived at https://perma.cc/WM6E-NE3P).

64 Ono, A. (2023). Climate change's impacts on life and health insurance lakyara vol.366. Nomura Research Institute, Ltd., p. 2. www.nri.com/-/media/Corporate/en/Files/PDF/knowledge/publication/lakyara/2023/02/lakyaravol366.pdf (archived at https://perma.cc/CSN6-QBQB).

65 Elfar, A. (2022). Landmark climate change lawsuit moves forward as German judges arrive in Peru. *State of the Planet.* news.climate.columbia.edu/2022/08/04/landmark-climate-change-lawsuit-moves-forward-as-german-judges-arrive-in-peru/ (archived at https://perma.cc/PZ9F-DBU9).

66 Djazayeri, A. (2021). Climate change litigation and its impact on the insurance industry. HDI Global. www.hdi.global/infocenter/insights/2021/climate-change-litigation/ (archived at https://perma.cc/PF5S-WM4K).

67 Setzer, J. and Higham, C. (2021). Global trends in climate change litigation: 2021 snapshot policy report. The London School of Economics and Political Science, p. 4. www.lse.ac.uk/granthaminstitute/wp-content/uploads/2021/07/Global-trends-in-climate-change-litigation_2021-snapshot.pdf (archived at https://perma.cc/KA85-XGDX).

68 Subramanian, S. (2022). Forty percent of all shipping cargo consists of fossil fuels. *Quartz.* qz.com/2113243/forty-percent-of-all-shipping-cargo-consists-of-fossil-fuels (archived at https://perma.cc/J2KM-THT5).

69 Surminski, S. (2020). Climate change and the insurance industry: Managing risk in a risky time. *Georgetown Journal of International Affairs.* gjia.georgetown.edu/2020/06/09/climate-change-and-the-insurance-industry-managing-risk-in-a-risky-time/ (archived at https://perma.cc/9QB2-YVUQ).

70 M.W., S. (2019). A quick cyber insurance guide for GDPR compliance. TechGenix. techgenix.com/cyber-insurance-guide/ (archived at https://perma.cc/X2ZH-J9W9).

71 Rose, W. (2021). *Patent Litigation Trends—2021 Year End.* Aon. insights-north-america.aon.com/intellectual-property/aon-patent-litigation-trends-2021-year-end-report (archived at https://perma.cc/AN72-YDYY).

72 Rucinski, L. and Ricci, D. (2021). $2.175 billion—with a 'B'—verdict in patent infringement case. Everything IP Under One Digital Roof. www.intellectualproperty.law/2021/03/2-175-billion-with-a-b-verdict-in-patent-infringement-case/ (archived at https://perma.cc/A9ZS-MVBS).

09

Criticism and Controversies Around ESG

While it doesn't matter what we call things, the context does matter when we use the acronym "ESG" because many use it differently. Across financial services firms and corporates, ESG isn't well defined and is poorly understood, and there is a wide range of opinions on what ESG is and isn't. With the ownership of the term sitting with the financial markets and the expansive universe of products that exist across ESG, impact, and socially responsible investing (SRI), companies are struggling to define it. Yet, as we saw in the previous chapter, regulators are attempting to put together definitions for market participants. As a result, when ESG pressure arrives at the company through shareholders, leaders don't know what to think, but they know something is up. The mere interpretation of ESG from that point forward is a Governance issue.

Unfortunately, the short acronym lends itself to a quick response from companies and stakeholders. I've talked to companies that have defined ESG as their philanthropic efforts, many who lead with disclosures and metrics as the definition, and a few who place it under the Chief Risk Officer. Some companies lead solely with the Environment and don't make it to the Social or even the most critical part, Governance. *The Economist* published a piece opining that the Environment should be split out and that companies should only focus on E for emissions.[1]

These interpretations of ESG should not be a surprise for a few reasons. The evolution of CSR and ESG, shareholder primacy to stakeholder capitalism, and Environmental and Social tipping points have been decades long. Over time, the markets have massaged and redefined these things, sometimes to capture financial and non-financial opportunities. In addition to the evolutions, many material ESG and non-material issues have become licenses to operate and flow into each other, adding to the confusion. Issues sometimes affect the company; other times, the company impacts the world and its people. Sometimes, a company deals with both at some connection point. Understanding the differences takes a systematic approach to the issues, but it is worthwhile as each has different outcomes, trade-offs, and stakeholders. The better a company understands its position, the better off it will be. Unfortunately, bridging the gap between the nuance and complexity of ESG takes time. This effort can be an immense challenge in the fast pace of the modern digital world, where issues tend to be black or white. The result is a mix of armchair and scholarly criticism, some of it valid.

You might hear a wide range of perspectives and opinions on ESG and your company's efforts, depending on which company or person you are talking to, their political persuasion, or their values. As a result, these criticisms and controversies have become ESG issues of their own through stakeholders, requiring new Governance strategies to deal with them.

Criticisms of ESG

Over the years, financial services firms and companies have tried to make ESG fit into several boxes to serve their purpose or stakeholder messaging. Of course, entirely new ecosystems like ESG rating agencies, advisory firms, and marketing experts have popped up in this wake, attempting to capitalize on the opportunity. Many valid criticisms around ESG intersect with the acronym directly, but also in the surrounding ecosystem. They are worth exploring to learn where things can improve and to watch out for pitfalls. We've already covered one criticism throughout this book—the idea of shareholder primacy, which comes up from critics often. That criticism is easy to think through with an ESG mindset as addressing material issues is something that the company should already be doing, but also one that still adds to shareholder value, at least in theory.

ESG scores

A common criticism is an overemphasis on ESG scores, sometimes to the point where critics conflate the scores with ESG. As we covered in Chapter 2, ESG rating agencies have developed over the past 20 years to surface nonfinancial information to investors, and even some companies, for more informed decision-making. Rating agencies will often tidy up the raw ESG data, layer on research and analysis, and simplify their insights into ESG scores, akin to a credit score with several ESG dimensions to the data. Credit scores have consistency between the major credit agencies, and critics hold them up as a more informed way to rate companies since they are presumed to be based on financials. However, the three largest corporate credit rating agencies, S&P Global,[2] Moody's,[3] and Fitch,[4] have published information on how they use material ESG information to inform their credit scores.

On the other hand, ESG scores, which are not credit scores, can vary between rating agencies, depending on the agency's definition and interpretation of ESG, materiality, and stakeholders.[5] While reported financials are hard and fast numbers typically, reported ESG data is not. In a 2023 survey from the SustainAbility Institute by ERM, more than half of investors and companies believed that greater consistency and comparability are needed across ESG rating agencies.[6]

In 2023, the EU took action on this criticism with a draft proposal, not aimed at normalizing the methodologies used by rating agencies but increasing the transparency and comparability of ESG ratings.[7] The objective may deal with the criticism of the black-box nature of ESG rating agencies, scores, and variability. Some think ESG scores and rating agencies play an outsized role in the markets, as some companies chase those ratings without clear understanding. Another provision of the EU draft deals with companies chasing ESG scores by removing a conflict of interest through rating agencies providing consulting services.[8] In other words, a rating agency shouldn't create the score and then sell services to a company to improve the score.

Since the draft proposal focuses on rating agencies, it doesn't prohibit companies from pursuing meaningless activities that may influence the scores, which is another criticism of ESG. Energy companies may sell off "dirty" assets like oil, gas, and coal to private equity buyers, effectively moving the transition risk and carbon emissions to another party.[9] The selling company may increase its ESG score as the asset moves into the private markets, where disclosure pressure is less, but the emissions and transition risk remain unchanged overall. While this move may seem non-material, it is a material Environmental and potentially Governance issue for an energy company, regardless if the objective is to chase scores or improve the company's transition risk.

The false narrative of win-win and chasing alpha

As ESG garnered more attention from Larry Fink's CEO letters up through Covid, the prevailing narrative from the markets, consultants, and ESG supporters was a persistent win-win. The promise was more aligned with purpose than ESG and that companies can do well by doing good, which is sometimes the case, but not always, as we've seen. ESG issues are complex, involving many moving parts requiring an ESG mindset. When a win-win isn't achieved, critics are quick to notice.

With ESG, there are often trade-offs to consider. These trade-offs can be between the three pillars or the short- and long-term horizons.[10] Take the example of an electronics manufacturer that wants to improve its product with new sustainable materials that allow for easy removal and reuse in the circular economy. Perhaps a new adhesive would be developed as part of an improvement project. The adhesive might need to be strong enough for the part to stay connected but weak enough to be removed with a certain amount of pressure. Addressing transition risks like R&D includes costs, potential product reliability testing, and functional process changes. These short-term trade-offs around cost, labor, and time may lead to long-term product sustainability and reduce the cost to catch up to competitors and change later. While the company may enjoy the Environmental benefits of this change, there are potential Social and Governance risks for those across the manufacturer's value chain. For a supplier that hasn't transitioned to sustainable sourcing, the manufacturer's pivot is its ESG risk to manage across the transition. It also must manage the economics of the change around its workers.

Aligning ESG to alpha, or outperforming stock returns, is another popular win-win scenario that ESG supporters call on. There is evidence that ESG can lead to outperformance. NYU Stern has published a meta-study that shows companies that pursue ESG maintain or have slight outperformance, which makes logical sense.[11] Companies that understand their ESG risks and opportunities and manage them well likely would at least yield market returns or do a little better. Yet, this win-win doesn't work for investors chasing short-term gains as ESG focuses on long-term resilience, and as always, one bad Governance issue can take the company down. Nothing in life is a guarantee, especially not alpha.

Tesla and tobacco: The devil is in the details

SRI or ethical investors may divest from stocks they consider vice stocks when leading with their values. These strategies typically avoid industries like weapons, fossil fuels, and tobacco and are often conflated with ESG investing, but they aren't the same. The reasons one investor over another would choose a strategy can differ, and ethics can play a leading role in the difference. With SRI and ethical investing, the investor's ethical choice or a values-based lens may inform how they wish to allocate their capital. Meanwhile, an ESG investor would consider the risk around the company's ethics and other non-financial factors to indicate a sound investment. For example, an ESG investor would look at "vice" industries and see that their core business could be subject to higher risk from regulations and negative stakeholder attention for the Environmental or Social harm they cause. Yet, they would understand that if the company has robust Governance principles in place, it might be able to manage those risks effectively.

On the other hand, a company might try to disrupt and electrify a hard-to-abate industry, like automotive, to move entire populations away from fossil fuels and garner a mix of SRI and ESG investors. This example capitalizes on the transition by creating opportunity. While pursuing its Environmental ambition, that same company might have other issues that cause it to have a high-risk ESG score. SRI and ethical investors might choose to invest along their values. At the same time, ESG investors may be more skeptical, perhaps celebrating the sustainability effort along the line of Environmental transition risks while being wary of other issues.

In June 2023, Elon Musk, CEO of Tesla proclaimed ESG to be the devil[12] as tobacco companies, whose product use has clear correlations to cancer,[13] often have higher ESG scores than Tesla. Two days after his Tweet, a pull of ESG scores from several rating agencies showed that he was right—out of the four rating agencies sampled here (Table 9.1), only MSCI and Sustainalytics gave Tesla a higher or close ESG score, putting it in the mix of a sampling of tobacco stocks.

TABLE 9.1 Sampling of tobacco company ESG scores across rating agencies

	MSCI	S&P Global	Refinitiv	Sustainalytics
	Letter-based	Higher is better	Higher is better	Lower is better
Altria Group	BBB	42	88	24.2
Philip Morris International	BBB	84	85	28.4
British American Tobacco plc	BBB	88	86	33.7
Tesla	A	37	72	27.2

Table 9.1 is an excellent example of the variability in scoring across rating agencies, a previously listed criticism, but a deeper examination is warranted as to why Tesla has lower scores here. The comparison between the two has clear undertones about the ethical differences between owning a tobacco or electric vehicle company. As we saw with CalPERS, tobacco can be subject to divestment strategies.[14] While ethics may play into the core of the business, ESG scores may not rank companies on the ethics of their business, products, or services but may consider the regulatory risks around their industry, which can appear to be the same to a casual observer.[15, 16]

S&P Global once explained Tesla's low ESG scores, at least from its perspective. One of the firm's products, the S&P 500 ESG Index, tracks 75 percent of the companies by float market capitalization across every industry and uses a Dow Jones Industrial (DJI) S&P ESG score, among other factors, for inclusion. Tesla is one of the largest companies in the world by float market capitalization, but its ESG scores, as indicated in Table 9.1, are not stellar. After spending one year in the S&P 500 ESG Index, S&P removed Tesla in 2022. The reaction from Musk at the time was a comparison to Exxon Mobile's ESG scores and the conclusion that ESG is a scam.[17] In a blog post, S&P described the reasons for rebalancing the portfolio and removing Tesla:[18]

- Lack of a carbon strategy, which considers efficiencies, but also regulatory impact
- Transparency in codes of conduct, including breach disclosure policies and anti-bribery
- Two separate events regarding racial discrimination and poor working conditions at its Fremont factory
- The handling of an NHTSA investigation related to issues with the cars' autopilot features.

In its 2020 Impact Report, Tesla published a materiality matrix based on investor and stakeholder feedback, research analysis, and more.[19] It is easy to see how an analyst could tie the issues listed in S&P's blog directly to the first five material issues, all of which Tesla placed on the higher end of the impact on its business in the matrix:

- Environmental Management, Reducing Carbon
- Quality Management—Product Safety
- Employee Workplace Safety

- Employee Attraction, Retention, Development
- Ethical Business Conduct, Integrity, Transparency.

In other words, it isn't a leap to see how the items that caught S&P's attention link to some of the same issues Tesla lists as material.

By comparison, the tobacco industry is tough to analyze, as its primary use is a massive stakeholder risk and yields strong reactions from those who have lost loved ones to cancer. In considering the tobacco industry, we see a clear example of how an ESG mindset is needed to consider these issues' complexity.

Philip Morris has the highest revenue of any tobacco company. According to its 2021 Sustainability Matrix, the top three material issues are:

- Product health impact (Social)
- Climate (Environmental)
- Innovation in wellness and healthcare (Social).

Its 2022 10K filing has an entire section that runs several pages on litigation related to healthcare risk, and it calls out the potential for adverse effects on the business.[20] In its 2022 integrated report, the company calls out that the health impact of cigarettes is the most significant externality it needs to address.[21] In recognition of these Social risks, Philip Morris announced that by 2025, it plans to have 40 million smokers switch to smoke-free products, with 50 percent of its revenue coming from smoke-free sources, investing $9 billion since 2008 to create smoke-free products.[22] The company has also announced a new Wellness and Healthcare effort launched in its 2021 subsidiary of Vectura Fertin Pharma, which it admits it does not have experience with but is part of this transition.[23]

The report makes clear the efforts the company is attempting in its transition away from cigarettes and is very clear on the metrics it uses to measure that progress and its commitments. Still, as with many things ESG-related, it depends on perspective and analysis, which is often subjective. It also depends on the outcomes, which can only be shown in evidence and over time. Still, while tobacco remains a high-risk business along the Social, it is a business that needs leaders to manage risk well. Based on the industry's ESG scores, it appears as though these companies are doing just that.

Controversy!

There's nothing inherently controversial about a company addressing its material Environmental, Social, and Governance risks in pursuit of long-term resilience. When a company examines an ESG issue, determines it to be material, and proceeds accordingly, little to no controversies should emerge, as stakeholders are well considered, and even shareholder primacy can be placated. Yet, two opposing and strangely aligned controversies have emerged among the confusion, criticism, and pressing needs of climate change, social justice issues, and business ethics.

Companies are always looking for a competitive advantage around their stakeholders. As stakeholders found new purpose after the 2020 tipping points around Environmental and Social, companies were eager to capitalize on the shift, perhaps overeager in some cases. This renewed attention to ESG and the related, but separate, push to save the world provided an opportunity to grow profits on the surface, but it aligned with one of the criticisms—the belief that a company can consistently do well by doing good. Sometimes a win-win will work, but it requires thoughtful material and stakeholder consideration.

As the idea of values leading to value bloomed, the competitive and value chain pressure built, in parallel to growing disclosure pressures. Stakeholders demanded that brands and employers support their values, and business customers added sustainability and diversity requirements to RFPs. In both cases, the pressure focused on the company's impact on the world, not the effect of the world on the company. This led to new company programs focused on the ESG pressures with a drive to capture new markets using this newfound marketing opportunity but with little substance behind it.

Meanwhile, conservative politicians in the USA found that the values touted by companies through these efforts did not align with their political platform. Conservative politicians latched on to these new company efforts to transform and address non-material values-based issues as anti-capitalism and blamed liberal politicians and Wall Street for pushing a specific progressive agenda.

While these two controversies come at ESG and values-based initiatives from two different sides, they have a shared refrain: ESG is a distraction, and companies should scrap it.

Activism: Is ESG a distraction from saving the world?

Inside stakeholder groups, there may be various stakeholders who want different things. Some consumers want a consistent product that doesn't get changed, while others may be concerned with a product's wasteful packaging. Some investors seek to ensure long-term returns, while others want to wield their capital to influence the company in the short term to perceived alpha. Still, others only want hard pivots and concessionary changes or to invest in green or socially responsible companies. For those looking to make an impact on the world through the influence of their purchasing power, either through a product or stock, ESG can appear to be a distraction from the world's biggest problems.

Broadly, these last stakeholders may be considered activists, which means a stakeholder who attempts to make a positive Environmental, Social, Governance, or possibly political change. Here, a positive change is admittedly subjective but would represent one that impacts the ESG pillars in a way that progresses its values in a manner aligned to the pillar itself. In the case of dealing with ESG topics, these people want the company to make transformational changes that connect with significant, positive systemic challenges for the planet or marginalized groups, for example, whether immediately material or not. Despite the good intentions, these changes likely have concessionary trade-offs with value, cost, stakeholders, and other business issues.

As of 2023, trust in companies outweighs trust in government,[24] and companies see the opportunity to step up. ESG can give stakeholders a false sense that the markets and companies are making progress because the storytelling around doing well by doing good is so compelling, appeasing shareholders and stakeholders. It is in capturing this opportunity that missteps can occur. For example, when a firm or company layers on promises of ESG, SRI, impact investing, or a good corporate marketing story without proof of action, it creates a recipe that will anger activists. This particular example runs parallel to another problem that activists have, which is greenwashing. Greenwashing is where a company misleads stakeholders into believing it is being more sustainable than it is. Greenwashing aligns with sustainability, and its theory can also be applied to promises made along the Social pillar. Pressures on ESG disclosures and capturing the opportunities that arise around Environmental or Social good can surface greenwashing, which activists are always on the lookout for.

Companies and financial services firms must ensure they deliver on what they say. While an ESG mindset can uncover the company's material intersections, companies feel pressure to take the change further on non-material issues as, again, business is looked to over governments to solve systemic challenges. Here, we aren't talking about issues that may fall under dynamic materiality, but even more serious systemic shifts the company may need to make, like completely upending its products or services. ESG makes a good case for involvement as stakeholder preferences are material, but many activist-raised challenges need to be part of a systemic solution that likely cannot be addressed by a company or even an industry. For example, a blended solution of finance, business, and government is needed to transition a country, its citizens, and companies to clean energy responsibly.

Some activists believe that ESG and company sustainability or social commitments are a simple distraction. The reactions range from believing that a company focus on material ESG issues blocks systemic solutions to an over-reliance on the free markets and businesses to self-correct. Activists sit within stakeholder groups and can come from anywhere, even employees. For example, Tariq Fancy worked at BlackRock from 2018 to 2019 as the firm's Chief Investment Officer in sustainable investing.[25] He's become an outspoken critic of ESG and sustainable investing, calling out that the self-correction of the market through ESG and sustainable investing pressure is a placebo for progress, especially when systemic change is needed.[26] Fancy saw massive attention on funding ESG assets, but the translation to the kind of impact governments had during Covid, for example, was missing.[27] After all, governments and regulators play a considerable role in supporting systemic change, but the markets can only influence. Still, if we stick with the definition of ESG as this book lays out, the path to impact through ESG is undoubtedly there but is indeed circuitous. Circumventing this interpretation of ESG to make a counterargument that it is about material risks and opportunities is disingenuous, as many firms and companies link the two.

Another employee activist type can be the whistleblower. A whistleblower is usually an employee but can be any stakeholder who calls out a company for a specific action, such as greenwashing or unethical behavior. A whistleblower may unwittingly understand the ESG risk to the company of the issue, attempt to surface it, and then take it to the press or a regulator or they may be out to prevent the company from engaging in the behavior to save the world. In some jurisdictions, whistleblowers are a protected group.

DWS CONTROVERSY

In June 2020, DWS, a German asset management firm, hired Desiree Fixler as its Group Sustainability Officer. In February 2021, Fixler presented to the board that sustainability was more niche at the firm than it was publicly stating, and made recommendations to correct the 2020 annual report before publishing.[28] DWS fired Fixler the day before publishing the report, and the firm did not incorporate her recommended changes. In its 2020 report, the firm claimed that half of its assets under management, at $459 billion, used its ESG Integration strategy.[29] A cursory search of the report referenced the term "ESG" a staggering 712 times, complete with references to its ESG Integration strategy, Responsible Investing Governance principles, quality management, and much more.[30] Fixler was quite vocal about the issue publicly and by August 2021, the US SEC announced a probe into the claims.[31] Then in 2022, German police found sufficient evidence to raid DWS's offices and the CEO was forced to step down.[32] There has also been a related lawsuit from a consumer watchdog group over alleged false claims.[33]

One could argue that the concerns activists raise, or when they blow the whistle on misleading behavior, are material risks. In the example of whistle-blowing, it may turn out to be a Governance issue masquerading as an ESG opportunity, as in the case of greenwashing. Yet, activism doesn't always have clear links to material issues on the surface. For example, an activist pushing the company to conduct an emissions audit of its suppliers might help to uncover transition risks in its value chain and influence that ecosystem to transform. Still, the mere existence of activism and attention from these stakeholders may make it a material issue, depending on the stakeholder and their influence. It could also be that what the stakeholder is seeking may not be material yet, but could evolve into a material issue over time, otherwise known as dynamic materiality. Overall, companies need to adopt an ESG mindset, proactively consider the issues it can uncover, and not rush to misstate their efforts to capture opportunity. Otherwise, a company may find a Governance risk of its own making.

Regardless, ESG is not a distraction from a company positively impacting the world, as a company can pursue both. As time goes on, long-term transition risk, especially around a systemic issue like climate change or social justice, will only grow and be harder to catch up on. Yet, how some have conflated ESG with saving the world as the lede means many believe it aligns with values first. This misunderstanding is a reckless path for businesses as companies may back away from ESG entirely, missing new risks and opportunities in the pursuit of long-term value. This is often referred to as "greenhushing," but it has larger implications. When a company isn't open about what it is doing around ESG, stakeholders are ill-informed and collaboration on systemic issues may be lost.

Values: ESG is a distraction from investing and business

If someone believes that ESG leads with values, and they don't agree with those values, they may believe that ESG is a distraction from the core function of a business and regress into shareholder primacy. When looking at the financial markets and the board room, questions about fiduciary duty arise. A company or individual with fiduciary duty must act in the beneficiary's interest, not their own. So, when values come into play, and a financial services firm labels a fund as ESG without strictly adhering to a consistent definition around value, some politicians may see it as working in the firm's interest, not the beneficiary's. For example, an investment firm may make a net-zero commitment. Was this to help society's adaptation to climate change, a marketing message to capture sustainable investing, or to help manage the firm's transition risk? Are these issues material for the firm, and do they lead with the beneficiary in mind when not pursuing socially responsible (SRI) or impact investing? Unfortunately, the answers are not black and white.

ESG has several interpretations, as pointed out in the previous chapter. When split apart, the first two pillars, Environmental and Social, can create potential political minefields, at least in the USA, where parties have strayed further left and right than other countries on these topics.[34] For example, per a Pew Research Center study, 78 percent of Democrats see climate change as a threat, but only 23 percent of Republicans do.[35] While citizens across the political spectrum in other countries are closer to being willing to address climate change in their personal lives, the divide is more significant in the USA.[36] Political talking points that drive election news cycles are born out of this disconnect of opinions. If politicians see trends that oppose their values, they will build new narratives.

In this way, the catalyst for the anti-ESG movement appears to have been influenced by the Environmental and Social tipping points, including the Business Roundtable's shift toward stakeholder capitalism in 2019.[37] An opposing political view developed as financial services, business, and stakeholder attention grew around ESG issues. Conservatives built a fundamental narrative around the premise that if investment firms commit to sustainability objectives, they must divest from fossil fuel companies and others to meet those goals. As a result, the conclusion was that these goals leverage client capital to pressure corporates on values-based SRI and impact investing principles. Again, these methodologies differ from ESG investing, but the difference is rarely clear at the investment product level. Unfortunately, these are logical leaps to make and have become well-funded rhetoric through conservative lobbying organizations and research firms.[38]

Anti-ESG tipping points and financial services

Anti-ESG tipping points fell shortly after 2020 for conservatives, similar to the ESG tipping points. Unlike ESG, these were less around specific crises and more around the coordinated funding effort and state legislation. Like ESG, the pushback started with an examination of the capital markets.

Perhaps the first domino to fall was the US Department of Labor which, under the Trump administration in November 2020, interpreted that the existing rules for retirement investing could only consider "pecuniary," or financial, factors.[39] This reassessment focused on the brewing attention on ESG investing, but nothing of significance changed in the new rule. A material ESG factor represents a material issue for an investment and could therefore impact the financials over the long run.[40] The US Department of Labor overturned the rule a year later under the Biden administration,[41] again not making much difference in interpreting material issues. Nevertheless, the die was cast for state legislations to attempt to thwart ESG. Conservative-led states like Texas and West Virginia began examining which financial services firms supported climate change efforts and were planning to potentially divest from fossil fuel investment.

Texas was among the first to launch anti-ESG legislation in 2021 against financial services firms, which barred the state government from doing business with firms that "boycott energy companies"[42] and requires written evidence of compliance with that strategy.[43] It is worth noting that this legislation still allows citizens to bank with whoever they choose, but large state-controlled investments and contracts like pension funds, down to smaller, cost-conscious municipalities, cannot do so. A January 2023 study estimated that within the first eight months of this legislation, municipalities might spend an extra $300–$500 million on interest alone due to the inability to work with the top bond underwriters, which the rule forced out of the market.[44]

As the groundswell continued, conservative politicians accelerated the rhetoric and supplemented it with this type of legislative action. Oklahoma followed suit a few months later with its law that requires the state to keep a list of firms that boycott energy companies.[45] Meanwhile, 19 states' Attorney Generals sent a letter to the CEO of BlackRock, Larry Fink, questioning the firm's dedication to advocating net-zero efforts, which would, in effect, eliminate fossil fuels over time while serving as a fiduciary.[46]

By May 2022, the anti-ESG campaign was in full swing with a Mike Pence editorial in the *Wall Street Journal* titled "Republicans can stop political ESG bias," which publicly drew the thread from financial services and their influence on corporates to the ballot box.[47] Here, the narrative called out an opinion that ESG represented a way to control the free markets that bypassed public elections and the will of the people. That same month, Vivek Ramaswamy, an entrepreneur and author, launched an asset management firm called Strive, leading with "excellence," or companies focused on excellent product and service delivery, over stakeholder capitalism.[48]

By March 2023, seven states had taken legislative action against ESG investing or the banks supporting ESG efforts.[49] Still, some opponents emerged as several state budget offices, advisors, and business groups analyzed the costs of these bills. For example, the Indiana Legislative Services Agency found that the proposed legislation in the state could cost pensioners $6.7 billion of returns over 10 years and restrict access to private equity investments.[50] The Indiana Governor signed the bill (HB 1008) after several amendments were made, aiming to bring that loss on returns down to $5.5 million.[51] Groups like the Indiana Chamber of Commerce[52] opposed the bill, calling it anti-free market.[53] Still, the core text of the bill contains language that states the focus on "financial" means to have a material effect on the monetary risk or monetary return of an investment as differentiated from ideologies that drive Environmental or Social movements, which is a pretty close definition to ESG.[54] After all, just as investment firms have a fiduciary duty that should consider material ESG issues, so do governments for the funds they control.

It can be easy to classify this movement as political posturing, as evidenced by Ramaswamy's announcement to run for president. ESG remains ill-defined by its many stakeholders, allowing for open interpretation to suit specific purposes. Despite this, it is essential to remember that there is a kernel of material truth in the anti-ESG movement. The risk for the planet and its people in managing long-term transition risk is a related material risk for states like Texas. The biggest exports from Texas are oil and gas, as the state accounts for 42 percent of the crude oil production in the USA.[55] An actual energy boycott would devastate the state and its people, which is not what ESG investing is about, as the impact on those people would be considered an externality. A responsible transition that considers all stakeholders, as some demand change, is more aligned with ESG. Texas appears to have it both ways, throwing its weight around political anti-ESG posturing while planning for a renewable transition. In 2021, Texas also led the USA in renewable energy projects installed at over 7,000 megawatts.[56]

The anti-ESG push continues to evolve in conservative states, with those state legislatures trying new tactics around boycotting banks and controlling which suppliers a state may choose to work with.[57] This effort continues despite voters on both sides opposing restrictions on ESG investing. Even in the highly polarized US political landscape, the majority of Democrats and Republicans were found to view climate efforts as related to their financial future and found support for long-term risk considerations.[58] While conservative politicians continue to ignore the costs to citizens and voter desires as they evolve new legislative strategies,[59] inflows into anti-ESG financial products, which started strong, have slowed down.[60] Perhaps this is a sign of the free markets at work.

Companies can use an ESG mindset as a defense

As ESG efforts accelerated from the markets to companies, so did anti-ESG efforts. As it turns out, controversies around ESG issues have always been issues. The board and the management team are responsible for being aware of long-term materiality issues, whether ESG related or not. Still, something changed around the ESG and anti-ESG tipping points in the early 2020s, causing companies that didn't understand materiality and stakeholders to flail in response to new stakeholder pressures. Companies that led with materiality and stakeholders weathered the storms well, as an ESG mindset can be a defense against controversy.

Industries and companies have always dealt with controversies. In some cases, industries came together to address the issues. For example, a year after Bowen coined CSR, the comic book industry recognized it had a brewing material Social controversy around some adult-themed content. As a result of mounting concern, it created the Comics Code Authority to self-regulate.[61] Video games followed suit with self-regulation decades later for the same reason.[62] Yet, even in cases of imposed regulation, there can be controversies. Seat belts, a material Social issue for automobile manufacturers and insurers, had a backlash that had to be managed against worries of limiting personal freedoms.[63]

Yet, as ESG efforts accelerated in recent years, companies were pressured by internal and external stakeholders to weigh in on complex issues forced into the political spectrum. In 2016, Colin Kaepernick, quarterback for the San Francisco 49ers, began to sit during the national anthem in protest of escalating police shootings against minorities in the USA.[64] After the 2016 season, he became a free agent and never returned to the game. Since Kaepernick had signed a deal with Nike a few years earlier, conservatives placed the brand in the crosshairs of an anti-ESG boycott, which became a material issue.[65] However, despite the controversy, Nike launched an ad campaign in 2018 focused on Kaepernick sacrificing everything for what he believed in. Its stock hit all-time highs shortly after,[66] showcasing that Nike understands what its stakeholders would support and staked a claim on which side of the issue it would fall on.[67]

Every issue, from civil rights to the mundane, seemingly became polarized in the USA from the Obama administration through the Trump administration as attention to the looming climate crisis and social justice issues through social media grew, and both presidents decided to weigh in on Kaepernick.[68] As a result of varying stakeholder pressure, companies were forced to take positions and reflect specific values. Since both Obama and Nike supported Kaepernick, the perspective was that the company aligned to his political values. One key to ESG success is understanding your stakeholders well enough to know what they will tolerate. In the case of Nike, consumers valued social justice values, but that isn't always the case.

In 2023, Bud Light partnered with transgender influencer Dylan Mulvaney on a marketing campaign. With the brand in decline, the company sought a new way to rejuvenate sales by targeting young drinkers, and Mulvaney had millions of subscribers on TikTok.[69] When entering new markets, a company must consider existing stakeholders and the market's current climate. In this unfortunate case, many of Bud Light's conservative drinkers reacted negatively to this campaign from a values perspective at a time when transgender rights were under fire.[70] This confluence of events further pushed the brand down and allowed another beer, Modelo Especial, to gain ground.[71] It is worth noting that both Bud Light and Modelo Especial are under the AB InBev company, which may indicate the surface value of brand recognition against conglomerate ownership and inattentive details during pushback. Regardless, Bud Light is a powerful example of how ESG doesn't align with liberal or conservative values. In this case, the ESG door swung towards what became a material issue for the company—misalignment with its stakeholders' conservative values. What matters to your customers matters to your business, regardless of whether the values lean right or left. This is why ESG is not a political issue.

The CEO of AB InBev admitted that the Bud Light campaign was not meant to divide anyone since beer intends to bring people together.[72] While this is an interesting material point at the intersection of its stakeholders, the apology didn't appease either side.[73] In contrast, in 2017, Heineken actually brought people with differing perspectives together over a beer in its "Worlds Apart" campaign to show the power of connection.[74] The award-winning campaign made consumers feel closer to the brand and increased sales by 7.3 percent for the three months following the ad's release.[75]

Companies need to be mindful of these new pressures as every complex issue increasingly becomes whittled down to black or white, at least in the USA, putting stakeholders at odds against each other. This challenge is no easy maze for a company to navigate, and it may need to accept that it cannot please everyone. Still, stakeholder attention and trend analysis can offer a company clues. As with Nike, sometimes a company can choose a side. As with Bud Light, it may inadvertently find itself on the outside.

Materiality and a deep understanding of stakeholders are especially vital in creating authenticity as it focuses the company on issues in a way only the company can address them. As Heineken showed, beer can bring people together because people came together from different political spectrums. Leading with values without regard for the material intersection of these issues with the company or its stakeholders may break stakeholder trust and lead to concessions and risk. By building on tools like a materiality matrix, stakeholder mapping, and its Governance principles, a company is better prepared to avoid controversy. In addition, the company will at least understand the criticism or controversy in the context of its brand if stakeholders force it to react on non-material intersections.

As ESG criticisms and controversies continue, companies have ways they can address material risks that surface.

Mainstreaming ESG to address controversies

Once again, a company's Governance is an outstanding indicator of how it deals with risk. Financial services firms and other companies have opportunities to lead with quality Governance principles by mainstreaming ESG throughout the organization.

Financial services firms must mainstream ESG throughout the firm to have the flexibility to pursue a range of investing and lending options to meet the needs of various stakeholders. The firm's management team must communicate a clear vision of its material obligations, such as fiduciary duty, against balancing the values and value of various transition risks and opportunities it may try to capture. Transparency around products, approaches to engagement, divestment strategy, and precise language will help drive consistency in the approach.

As for companies, they have it somewhat easier as they are outside the scope of anti-ESG legislation in the USA as of June 2023, but will still be held to global regulations that affect the value chain. Still, controversies can arise from a range of unexpected places, but especially when the company takes a stand on a values-based issue. A strong management team that has mainstreamed ESG and understands its material risks and opportunities will fare much better than others who choose to back away from these issues for fear of reprisal.

Eventually, any stakeholder group may become unsatisfied with a company's perspective on ESG, anti-ESG, or even no opinion on issues. A win-win across values, value, and stakeholders may never be truly achievable. This uncertainty represents a new type of materiality—perhaps called outrage materiality. This is where stakeholder outrage forces a company to act, making it a material issue. It is best to be prepared with a strategy for when that happens.

Notes

1 The Economist (2022a). ESG should be boiled down to one simple measure: emissions. *The Economist*. www.economist.com/leaders/2022/07/21/ esg-should-be-boiled-down-to-one-simple-measure-emissions (archived at https://perma.cc/WWS4-4JMT).

2 S&P Global (n.d.). ESG in credit ratings. S&P Global. www.spglobal.com/ ratings/en/research-insights/special-reports/esg-in-credit-ratings (archived at https://perma.cc/3G2E-NK8V).

3 Moody's Investors Service (n.d.). Integration of ESG into credit risk. Moody's Investors Service. ratings.moodys.io/integration-of-esg-into-credit-risk (archived at https://perma.cc/K7FA-VY8C).

4 Fitch Ratings (2020). *2020 ESG in Credit White Paper*. Fitch Ratings. your. fitch.group/rs/732-CKH-767/images/Fitch%20Ratings%20-%20ESG%20 In%20Credit%202020.pdf (archived at https://perma.cc/5JQ9-W6RH).

5 Berg, F., Kölbel, J.F., and Rigobon, R. (2020). Aggregate confusion: The divergence of ESG ratings. SSRN. https://papers.ssrn.com/sol3/papers.cfm?abstract_id=3438533 (archived at https://perma.cc/JFH7-X2T4).

6 Brock, E.K., Nelson, J., and Brackley, A. (2023). *ESG Ratings at a Crossroads Rate the Raters 2023*. ERM Sustainability Institute, p. 6. www.sustainability.com/globalassets/sustainability.com/thinking/pdfs/2023/rate-the-raters-report-april-2023.pdf (archived at https://perma.cc/9X57-3J8N).

7 European Commission (2023a). Regulation of the European Parliament and of the Council on the transparency and integrity of Environmental, Social and Governance (ESG) rating activities. Astrid, p. 1. www.astrid-online.it/static/upload/2306/230613-proposal-sustainable-finance_en.pdf (archived at https://perma.cc/9CLJ-JMAD).

8 European Commission (2023b). *Regulation of the European Parliament and of the Council on the transparency and integrity of Environmental, Social and Governance (ESG) rating activities.* Astrid, p. 11. www.astrid-online.it/static/upload/2306/230613-proposal-sustainable-finance_en.pdf (archived at https://perma.cc/Q4GM-P9DL).

9 The Economist (2022b). Who buys the dirty energy assets public companies no longer want? *The Economist.* www.economist.com/finance-and-economics/who-buys-the-dirty-energy-assets-public-companies-no-longer-want/21807594 (archived at https://perma.cc/6MR4-9X4V).

10 Wilkins, D. and Tett, G. (2023). Corporate Trade-Offs. Harvard Law School Center on the Legal Profession. clp.law.harvard.edu/knowledge-hub/magazine/issues/esg-and-lawyers/corporate-trade-offs/ (archived at https://perma.cc/RS3H-4WAQ).

11 NYU Stern Center for Sustainable Business and Rockefeller Asset Management (2021). Research Highlights. NYU Stern. www.stern.nyu.edu/experience-stern/faculty-research/new-meta-analysis-nyu-stern-center-sustainable-business-and-rockefeller-asset-management-finds-esg (archived at https://perma.cc/ZK9X-XY7X).

12 Musk, E. (2023). Why ESG is the devil .... X. twitter.com/elonmusk/status/1668829554448777216?s=20 (archived at https://perma.cc/35JN-XLMA).

13 National Cancer Institute (2014). Tobacco. National Cancer Institute. www.cancer.gov/about-cancer/causes-prevention/risk/tobacco (archived at https://perma.cc/H2RB-5E4W).

14 Diamond, R. (2021). CalPERS rejects reinvesting in tobacco again. Chief Investment Officer. www.ai-cio.com/news/calpers-rejects-reinvesting-tobacco/ (archived at https://perma.cc/6585-SGPC).

15 Calvert, L.S. (2021). Understanding ESG scores. Refinitiv Perspectives. www.refinitiv.com/perspectives/future-of-investing-trading/understanding-how-esg-scores-are-measured-their-usefulness-and-how-they-will-evolve (archived at https://perma.cc/DZ4E-86T4).

16 Filabi, A. (2021). ESG is not "ethical investing." And that's OK. Kiplinger. www.kiplinger.com/investing/esg/603836/esg-is-not-ethical-investing-and-thats-ok (archived at https://perma.cc/GR97-8L4C).

17 Musk, E. (2022). Exxon is rated top ten best in world for environment, social & governance (ESG) by S&P 500, while Tesla didn't make the list! ESG is a scam. It has been weaponized by phony social justice warriors. X. twitter.com/elonmusk/status/1526958110023245829 (archived at https://perma.cc/9LQZ-EABG).

18 Dorn, M. (2022). The (re)balancing act of the S&P 500 ESG Index. Indexology Blog. www.indexologyblog.com/2022/05/17/the-rebalancing-act-of-the-sp-500-esg-index/ (archived at https://perma.cc/W4QB-PL9Z).

19 Tesla (2020). *Impact Report 2020*. Tesla, p. 84. www.tesla.com/ns_videos/2020-tesla-impact-report.pdf (archived at https://perma.cc/E5EB-B77E).

20 Philip Morris International (2023). *2022 Annual Report*. Philip Morris International, pp. 127–140. philipmorrisinternational.gcs-web.com/static-files/d2370996-825f-47b8-9203-ceebbcf3a29d (archived at https://perma.cc/DWZ5-9GKH).

21 Philip Morris International (2023). *2022 Annual Report*. Philip Morris International, pp. 127–140. philipmorrisinternational.gcs-web.com/static-files/d2370996-825f-47b8-9203-ceebbcf3a29d (archived at https://perma.cc/DWZ5-9GKH).

22 Ries, T.E. (2023). *2023 Edelman Trust Barometer Global Report*. Edelman, p. 9. www.edelman.com/sites/g/files/aatuss191/files/2023-03/2023%20Edelman%20Trust%20Barometer%20Global%20Report%20FINAL.pdf (archived at https://perma.cc/SSV9-9KJ4)

23 Philip Morris International (2022). Philip Morris International launches new bonds by IQOS smoke-free device to accelerate the achievement of a smoke-free future. Philip Morris International. www.pmi.com/investor-relations/press-releases-and-events/press-releases-overview/press-release-details/?newsId=25791# (archived at https://perma.cc/8DBL-C29U).

24 Ries, T.E. (2023). *2023 Edelman Trust Barometer Global Report*. Edelman, p. 9. www.edelman.com/sites/g/files/aatuss191/files/2023-03/2023%20Edelman%20Trust%20Barometer%20Global%20Report%20FINAL.pdf (archived at https://perma.cc/SSV9-9KJ4).

25 Fancy, T. (n.d.). Tariq Fancy LinkedIn profile page. LinkedIn. www.linkedin.com/in/fancy/ (archived at https://perma.cc/26F9-Y8DS).

26 McKillop, P. (2021). BlackRock's former head of sustainable investing says ESG and sustainability investing are distractions. GreenBiz. www.greenbiz.com/article/blackrocks-former-head-sustainable-investing-says-esg-and-sustainability-investing-are (archived at https://perma.cc/F362-S4ZZ).

27 Fancy, T. (2021). Opinion: BlackRock hired me to make sustainable investing mainstream. Now I realize it's a deadly distraction from the climate-change threat. *The Globe and Mail*, March 25. www.theglobeandmail.com/business/commentary/article-sustainable-investing-is-a-deadly-distraction-from-actually-averting/ (archived at https://perma.cc/2ZLA-UWK5).

28 Brown, P.K. and K. (2021). Fired Executive Says Deutsche Bank's DWS Overstated Sustainable-Investing Efforts. *The Wall Street Journal*, August 1. www.wsj.com/articles/fired-executive-says-deutsche-banks-dws-overstated-sustainable-investing-efforts-11627810380 (archived at https://perma.cc/MXQ6-3HRK).

29 DWS Group GmbH & Co KGaA (2021). *2020 Annual Report*. DWS, p.93. download.dws.com/download?elib-assetguid=7617fa5ea7854de3a2a2ba9c371246ec&publishLocationGuid=eacbc9cf4b8e4d2189eb69cd09e2ff4f (archived at https://perma.cc/UHQ7-9RUF).

30 DWS Group GmbH & Co KGaA (2021). *2020 Annual Report*. DWS, pp. 1–282. download.dws.com/download?elib-assetguid=7617fa5ea7854de3a2a2ba9c371246ec&publishLocationGuid=eacbc9cf4b8e4d2189eb69cd09e2ff4f (archived at https://perma.cc/MN4Y-MTA2).

31 Kowsmann, P., Ramey, C., and Michaels, D. (2021). U.S. authorities probing Deutsche Bank's DWS over sustainability claims. *The Wall Street Journal*, August 25. www.wsj.com/articles/u-s-authorities-probing-deutsche-banks-dws-over-sustainability-claims-11629923018 (archived at https://perma.cc/R478-L5DQ).

32 Reuters (2022a). CEO of Deutsche Bank's asset manager steps down after "greenwashing" raid. CNN, June 1. www.cnn.com/2022/06/01/investing/deutsche-bank-dws-greenwashing/index.html (archived at https://perma.cc/J5YE-C5YK).

33 Reuters (2022b). Deutsche Bank's DWS sued by consumer group over alleged greenwashing. Reuters, October 24. www.reuters.com/business/finance/deutsche-banks-dws-sued-by-consumer-group-over-alleged-greenwashing-2022-10-24/ (archived at https://perma.cc/7JBL-FYU4).

34 Poushter, J., Fagan, M., and Gubbala, S. (2022). Climate change remains top global threat across 19-country survey. Pew Research Center's Global Attitudes Project. www.pewresearch.org/global/2022/08/31/climate-change-remains-top-global-threat-across-19-country-survey/ (archived at https://perma.cc/53VW-D2DU).

35 Tyson, A., Funk, C., and Kennedy, B. (2023). What the data says about Americans' views of climate change. Pew Research Center. www.pewresearch.org/short-reads/2023/08/09/what-the-data-says-about-americans-views-of-climate-change/ (archived at https://perma.cc/2KXC-RRGK).

36 Bell, J., Poushter, J., Fagan, M., and Huang, C. (2021). Climate change concerns make many around the world willing to alter how they live and work. Pew Research Center's Global Attitudes Project. www.pewresearch.org/global/2021/09/14/in-response-to-climate-change-citizens-in-advanced-economies-are-willing-to-alter-how-they-live-and-work/ (archived at https://perma.cc/EZ7J-TN5V).

37 Business Roundtable (2019). Business Roundtable redefines the purpose of a corporation to promote "an economy that serves all Americans". Business Roundtable. www.businessroundtable.org/business-roundtable-redefines-the-purpose-of-a-corporation-to-promote-an-economy-that-serves-all-americans (archived at https://perma.cc/B7GT-NS85).

38 Vogel, K.P. (2022). Leonard Leo pushed the courts right. Now he's aiming at American society. *The New York Times*, October 12. www.nytimes.com/2022/10/12/us/politics/leonard-leo-courts-dark-money.html (archived at https://perma.cc/59RY-ZM7H).

39 U.S. Department of Labor (2020). Financial factors in selecting plan investments. Federal Register. www.federalregister.gov/documents/2020/11/13/2020-24515/financial-factors-in-selecting-plan-investments (archived at https://perma.cc/GW5W-97HT).

40 U.S. Department of Labor (2020). Financial factors in selecting plan investments. Federal Register. www.federalregister.gov/documents/2020/11/13/2020-24515/financial-factors-in-selecting-plan-investments (archived at https://perma.cc/8A23-3BAU).

41 U.S. Department of Labor (2022). US Department of Labor announces final rule to remove barriers to considering environmental, social, governance factors in plan investments. U.S. Department of Labor. www.dol.gov/newsroom/releases/ebsa/ebsa20221122 (archived at https://perma.cc/945N-8E4A).

42 Comptroller of Public Accounts, Texas (2023). List of financial companies that boycott energy companies: Frequently asked questions. Texas.gov. comptroller.texas.gov/purchasing/docs/divest-energy.pdf (archived at https://perma.cc/75LE-4Z9C).

43 Birdwell, B. (2021). 87(R) SB 13: Committee report. Bill analysis. Texas Legislature Online. capitol.texas.gov/tlodocs/87R/analysis/html/SB00013H.htm (archived at https://perma.cc/BVS9-LCS4).

44 Garrett, D. and Ivanov, I. (2022). Gas, Guns, and Governments: Financial Costs of Anti-ESG Policies. *SSRN Electronic Journal.* https://doi.org/10.2139/ssrn.4123366 (archived at https://perma.cc/7ASZ-U2M2).

45 McBride, O'Donnell, West (Kevin), Bashore, and Roberts (Sean) of the House and Allen, David, Bullard, and Bergstrom of the Senate (2022). House Bill No. 2034. http://webserver1.lsb.state.ok.us/cf_pdf/2021-22%20ENR/hB/HB2034%20ENR.PDF (archived at https://perma.cc/RE77-HHEM).

46 Brnovich, M. and Paxton, K. (2022). Texas Attorney General. www. texasattorneygeneral.gov/sites/default/files/images/executive-management/ BlackRock%20Letter.pdf (archived at https://perma.cc/JMV8-MZDE).

47 Pence, M. (2022). Opinion: Republicans can stop ESG political bias. *Wall Street Journal*, May 26. www.wsj.com/articles/only-republicans-can-stop-the-esg-madness-woke-musk-consumer-demand-free-speech-corporate-america-11653574189 (archived at https://perma.cc/4RTD-T48L).

48 Strive Asset Management (2022). Depoliticizing corporate America: Strive Asset Management launches to advance excellence capitalism over "stakeholder capitalism". Strive Asset Management. www.strive.com/depoliticizing-corporate-america-strive-asset-management-launches-to-advance-excellence-capitalism-over-stakeholder-capitalism (archived at https://perma.cc/7HXT-4EJP).

49 Houston, C., Holland, E.B., and Malone, L. (2023). ESG battlegrounds: How the states are shaping the regulatory landscape in the U.S. The Harvard Law School Forum on Corporate Governance. https://corpgov.law.harvard.edu/2023/03/11/esg-battlegrounds-how-the-states-are-shaping-the-regulatory-landscape-in-the-u-s (archived at https://perma.cc/ZS33-3KQ8).

50 Kerber, R. (2023). Anti-ESG bill could cut Indiana pension returns by $6.7 bln. Reuters. www.reuters.com/business/sustainable-business/anti-esg-bill-could-cut-indiana-pension-returns-by-67-bln-analysis-2023-02-07/ (archived at https://perma.cc/8CVE-PUNR).

51 Thiele, R. (2023). Anti-ESG bill passes Indiana House with fewer losses expected for state pensioners. WFYI Public Media. www.wfyi.org/news/articles/anti-esg-bill-passes-indiana-house-with-fewer-losses-expected-for-state-pensioners (archived at https://perma.cc/7T2X-RPR6).

52 Ellis, G. (2023). Wins for energy and environmental matters: Anti-free market measures mitigated. Indiana Chamber of Commerce. www.indianachamber. com/wp-content/uploads/2023/05/Ellis.pdf (archived at https://perma.cc/7YCX-4GV5).

53 Thiele, R. (2023). Anti-ESG bill passes Indiana House with fewer losses expected for state pensioners. WFYI Public Media. www.wfyi.org/news/articles/anti-esg-bill-passes-indiana-house-with-fewer-losses-expected-for-state-pensioners (archived at https://perma.cc/2QWA-SXNZ).

54 Indiana General Assembly (2023). House Enrolled Act No. 1008. iga.in.gov. https://iga.in.gov/pdf-documents/123/2023/house/bills/HB1008/HB1008.06. ENRS.pdf (archived at https://perma.cc/8WY3-HN69).

55 U.S. Energy Information Administration (2023). Texas profile. EIA. www.eia. gov/state/print.php?sid=TX (archived at https://perma.cc/HPR5-TQ9F).

56 Newburger, E. (2022). Texas led the country in new renewable energy projects last year. CNBC. www.cnbc.com/2022/02/18/texas-led-the-country-in-new-renewable-energy-projects-last-year.html (archived at https://perma.cc/D5H3-U4ED).

57 Pleiades Strategy (2023). *2023 Anti-ESG Statehouse Report on legislative attacks on the freedom to invest responsibly and their opposition.* Google Docs. https://drive.google.com/file/d/1t38kmUxWFK43NZQxc-m_ EbQADUk8cbPb/view?pli=1 (archived at https://perma.cc/RPB4-937D).

58 Wolman, J. (2022). An unpopular crusade against sustainable investing. *Politico.* www.politico.com/newsletters/the-long-game/2022/12/08/an-unpopular-battle-00073004#:~:text=Sixty-three%20percent%20of%20 respondents%20E2%80%94%20majorities%20in%20both (archived at https://perma.cc/95LR-KLDY).

59 Pleiades Strategy (2023). *2023 Anti-ESG Statehouse Report on legislative attacks on the freedom to invest responsibly and their opposition.* Google Docs. https://drive.google.com/file/d/1t38kmUxWFK43NZQxc-m_ EbQADUk8cbPb/view?pli=1 (archived at https://perma.cc/H2FE-W2XM).

60 Stankiewicz, A. (2023). The anti-ESG fad might be over before it got going. Morningstar. www.morningstar.com/sustainable-investing/anti-esg-fad-might-be-over-before-it-got-going (archived at https://perma.cc/68B2-89PL).

61 Rittenberg, J. (2021). A look into the history of the Comics Code Authority. Book Riot. https://bookriot.com/comics-code-authority-history/ (archived at https://perma.cc/7FTX-Q3FJ).

62 ESRB (2014). ESRB celebrates 20 years of rating games and apps. ESRB Ratings. www.esrb.org/blog/esrb-celebrates-20-years-of-rating-video-games-and-apps/ (archived at https://perma.cc/98FH-C8KJ).

63 Roos, D. (2020). When Americans resisted seat belt laws. History. www.history.com/news/seat-belt-laws-resistance (archived at https://perma.cc/5GPQ-JB8V).

64 Jennings, P. (2017). Colin Kaepernick: From one man kneeling to a movement dividing a country. BBC Sport, October 11. www.bbc.com/sport/american-football/41530732 (archived at https://perma.cc/8DD4-XMXT).

65 Abad-Santos, A. (2018). The Nike boycott over Colin Kaepernick, explained. Vox. www.vox.com/2018/9/4/17818148/nike-boycott-kaepernick (archived at https://perma.cc/VHF9-H2UA).

66 Berr, J. (2018). Nike stock price reaches all-time high after Colin Kaepernick ad. CBS News. www.cbsnews.com/news/nike-stock-price-reaches-all-time-high-despite-colin-kaepernick-ad-boycott/ (archived at https://perma.cc/F737-6M92).

67 Youn, S. (2018). Nike sales booming after Colin Kaepernick ad, invalidating critics. ABC News. https://abcnews.go.com/Business/nike-sales-booming-kaepernick-ad-invalidating-critics/story?id=59957137 (archived at https://perma.cc/L2WR-8FFA).

68 Time (2017). The difference between President Trump and President Obama's reactions to the NFL kneeling movement. *Time*. https://time.com/4955050/trump-obama-nfl-nba-kaepernick-kneeling/ (archived at https://perma.cc/HE7W-3U25).

69 Frank, C. (2023). Bud Light marketing VP behind Dylan Mulvaney partnership replaced. CF.ORG. www.cf.org/news/bud-light-marketing-vp-behind-dylan-mulvaney-partnership-replaced-by-senior-exec/ (archived at https://perma.cc/GD3F-ZAHT).

70 Petri, A. (2023). Anti-trans backlash against Bud Light has executives on the hot seat. What's going on? *Los Angeles Times*, April 25. www.latimes.com/business/story/2023-04-25/anti-transgender-backlash-against-bud-light-explained (archived at https://perma.cc/HKS2-MYQ5).

71 Associated Press (2023). Bud Light dethroned as America's top-selling beer after backlash to trans-inclusive campaign. *Billboard*. www.billboard.com/music/music-news/bud-light-not-top-selling-beer-backlash-trans-campaign-kid-rock-1235354603/# (archived at https://perma.cc/W7TR-N29Y).

72 Romero, D. (2023). Anheuser-Busch CEO says Bud Light partnership with trans influencer wasn't meant to divide. NBC News. www.nbcnews.com/nbc-out/out-news/anheuser-busch-bud-light-dylan-mulvaney-trans-influencer-rcna79810 (archived at https://perma.cc/3ZHG-LDWY).

73 Power, S. (2023). Anheuser-Busch statement slammed amid Bud Light boycott: "No apology". Newsweek. www.newsweek.com/bud-light-boycott-anheuser-busch-statement-apology-1807552 (archived at https://perma.cc/D4UC-3T3D).

74 Segarra, L.M. (2017). Heineken ad pairs up strangers with opposing views. *Time*. https://time.com/4757540/heineken-ad-worlds-apart-commercial/ (archived at https://perma.cc/8DKX-KG44).

75 Edelman (2019). Worlds Apart. Edelman. www.edelman.com/work/heineken-worlds-apart (archived at https://perma.cc/X932-NKPS).

10

Interconnected ESG Risks and Issues

While many companies disclose ESG metrics and project information, they don't typically discuss their approaches directly, yet they constantly deal with ESG risks and opportunities. Sometimes, they may not even know it, as the terminology matters less than the action and subsequent outcomes. For example, a company's IT organization may manage cybersecurity risks, protecting IP from being stolen, or an Operations team might drive equipment efficiencies to save energy costs. These represent targeted internal material efforts that hit one particular pillar of the acronym and address a threat or work towards a specific goal; in these cases, Governance and Environmental, respectively. As we've seen throughout this book, issues like these are material, and companies must always deal with these issues to maintain stable and resilient operations as part of normal business, regardless of the controversies covered in the previous chapter. However, as we've learned, modern business is anything but normal as a universe of financial and ESG issues surround a company, and stakeholders are varied and complex.

As globalization increased and the Environmental and Social tipping points fell around the early 2020s, the sheer volume of new and connected external issues had compounding impacts across local and global levels. Different emerging problems each had significance to companies and multiple connections to other issues, forcing companies to react to a murky, incomplete picture of several crises at once. Some companies reactively dealt with the problems, favoring a targeted activity to a specific crisis rather than a more systemic or thoughtful approach, as we saw with DEI programs built around a Social tipping point. Yet, many found that the continuous disruption, a term co-opted by technology firms to represent positive opportunities during a period of growth, was no longer a catchy marketing term but a series of intense systemic shocks. These unexpected shocks were, and continue to be, challenging to address due to their multifaceted and relentless nature, even for those companies with robust long-term plans.

In his paper, *The End of ESG*, Alex Edmans of London Business School argued that ESG shouldn't be treated as niche because addressing long-term factors is something all companies and investors should strive to do and is therefore important and nothing special.[1] In other words, ESG isn't special because the management team and their companies should already be doing the work to pursue long-term resilience and stable growth. Edmans is right, of course, yet, in talking with numerous companies and firms about these new types of challenges, there is value in ESG as an acronym in a different way, at least observationally. If considered together with a receptive mindset, ESG empowers a company, its management team, and its employees to think about the interconnected nature of issues and crises and the activities that will address them toward successful outcomes.

The term *interconnected* here is different than *connected* in that ESG issues connect with business and stakeholder issues through multiple connections, not always one linear risk associated with a single activity and subsequent outcome. Not only do the Environmental and Social tipping points have cascading and interconnected relationships on the side of table stakes issues,[2] but so does ESG. While singular risks still exist and can be addressed by a company directly, a recent phenomenon has emerged—a complex web of interconnected risks that impact the company in multiple ways. The World Economic Forum (WEF) first noted this risk trend in its 2006 Global Risks report,[3] and it again became a central theme of the report in 2023 after the numerous tipping points we've examined, plus others.[4] Matching risk analysis and mitigation, improvements, and innovation equally through the interconnected nature of ESG and other factors can help companies plan for disruption and react appropriately. There is no one way to examine and connect these issues logically. Still, there are unique ways to consider them in collaboration with others, depending on the complexity of the challenge. As expected, even collaborative efforts that drive towards opportunities to solve ESG issues can introduce new risks. Regardless, when addressing interconnected issues, an ESG mindset is an idea whose time has come. To get there, we must build perspectives that extend from internal ESG materiality to external crises to a polycrisis.

Internally material: The interconnected nature of ESG at the pillar level

Due to the urgent climate crisis, its quantitative nature, and emerging regulations, attention tends to focus on the Environment, with Social issues gaining the next highest level of attention and Governance issues coming in last, at least in public discourse globally and awareness. Part of an ESG mindset uncovers the connections across the pillars to gain a complete picture of related issues. Looking across the pillars is the starting point for understanding the interconnected nature of ESG.

In a singular perspective, a simple view of an ESG issue means a direct point-to-point connection between the material issue identified and the efforts. An example might be a fabric company leveraging water in its dye process. The Chief Operations Officer may start a project to measure water consumption and discharge with the goal of water reduction. On the surface, this example is an Environmental activity that drives an outcome from Point A to Point B. Yet, due to the nature of ESG, issues are more interconnected and may span the acronym. Someone looking at the issue from the myopic lens of water, such as an expert who has depth on the topic, may only see the Environmental connections but not the breadth across the acronym nor the multiple links to other considerations. Re-examining the same issue through a broader lens changes the way we think about it. Using the example of water usage, a company may:

- Examine the local watershed and weather patterns to determine natural replenishment (E)

- Using those estimates, monitor its water consumption, recycling, and discharge (E) to understand better its operational use and contribution to the local watershed

- Decide to lower water usage in the manufacturing of its product or switch to dry dyes (E, G) and address the issue in partnership with its suppliers while continuing to work on improvements

- Study the local biodiversity and the impact of the legacy and the new processes (E, G) while monitoring the local community's health related to the watershed (S, G).

- As a result of its observations, the company may decide to advocate for quality water regulations and measurement standards (G) to drive consistency across its industry and value chain, protecting itself from litigation.

In other words, this single water management issue has multiple facets across ESG that connect to each pillar in different ways, uncovering more material issues. Looking across the acronym to discover an issue's interconnected relationships with the company and its stakeholders is only the starting point. The company may also uncover non-material or dynamic material issues for future consideration in this approach. For example, it may not be immediately apparent that stakeholders will appreciate the sustainability benefits of a shift towards saving water, which can drive a closer relationship between consumers and the brand. The employees who live locally would certainly appreciate this effort as it may impact the health of their families who drink the local water.

This particular example is intentionally limited, serving as a baseline for thinking about the relationships and complexity within a single issue. Yet, one concept management teams should be aware of is that by managing this issue well, the company can avoid reputational risk, including potential litigation for environmental or social damage. In this case, policy advocacy can result in true market leadership and prove that the company understands its material risks well, which some investors may value. On the other hand, stakeholder trust may break if the company greenwashes and leads with marketing or metrics over action. In today's world of social media attention and accountability, your story is only as good as the actions that back it. The company may experience reputational damage and litigation if it proceeds without evidence.

External pressure: The interconnected nature of outside ESG risk

Even though a single ESG issue may intersect in multiple ways across each pillar with a deeper investigation, external ESG issues can also place material pressure on stakeholders and the company in a connected way. Here, the interconnected nature of our world delivers an external and perhaps unrelated ESG force to impact the company materially.

Since the 1990s, rapid technological advancements have made our world more connected, allowing new collaborations that have driven globalization.[5] This era accelerated through intense hyper-globalization up to the 2008 financial crisis. However, after and through the tipping points of the early 2020s, companies and countries shifted towards stagnation and slowing globalization. For example, some companies began reshoring supply chains to manage the risk of several external factors that globalization introduced.[6] But even with this slowdown appearing as a protectionist strategy against complex global risks, it is likely too late to be effective as value chains connect in unseen ways and interconnected ESG issues transcend borders, even at a personal level.

In the summer of 2023, there were wildfires in Quebec wreaking havoc on forests and biodiversity locally.[7] The Air Quality Index in the eastern United States was Code Red, which is highly unhealthy as particulates were in the air. As a result, I had a headache day after day, which lowered my work productivity and caused me to stay indoors, not exercise, or even run out for a coffee. In addition, the smoke and the related lack of outdoor activities may have long-term effects on my family's physical health and mental well-being, which could increase our insurance costs and overrun local healthcare providers in our area. As a result of staying inside, I'm also not spending money in my local community. This geographically unrelated Environmental risk has created a material Social risk that healthcare providers, insurers, actuaries, and local governments must now account for.

For companies of all kinds, wildfire smoke represents a material risk at the intersection of their employee and customer stakeholders. Employees might be less likely to commute to the office, as wildfire smoke and extreme weather could augment personal risks when commuting. The result could be more remote work, which has a range of outcomes, from positive employee health and better work-life balance to less in-person collaboration and stranded office buildings. Human Resources departments and managers must consider the Social impact on the company's culture and productivity, while real estate managers must be mindful of their physical assets' usage.

For retailers and restaurants, customers might stay home and choose to shop online, which translates to potential revenue loss and risks for warehouse and delivery workers who cannot work from home. The situation was similar during Covid when these workers had to make decisions between personal safety and making a living.[8]

While these are somewhat hypothetical situations, the Quebec wildfires have affected tourism in Canada,[9] shuttered 14 mining operations,[10] and have, ironically, closed a sawmill, affecting lumber prices.[11] These examples are straight lines from cause (smoke) to effect (protecting employees from danger) to outcome (varying business impacts). In these situations, a company may have enough information in a rudimentary assessment to understand the primary driver and connect it across the Environment to the

Social implications, executing its Governance principles to address it. Yet, understanding the internal short-term impacts of the issue, even across the breadth of ESG, may not go far enough.

A board and the management team need to consider other seemingly unrelated external forces that may compound the effects of wildfire smoke in the unique moment it happens, as other issues can exacerbate and worsen difficulties for the company. For example, in addition to customers staying home from the smoke, a company may also consider how the cost of living, a key risk identified in WEF's Global Risks report, has increased over the past few years, which may have a multiplier effect on the pullback in consumer spending.[12] Specifically for restaurants, hospitality, and the broader food industry, food costs have increased due to climate change and the Russian invasion of Ukraine.[13] The compounding issues of wildfire smoke, customers staying home, and cost of living increases can intersect around a company and its stakeholders, resulting in exponential pressure.

Not every industry is impacted by the compounding effects of the same external forces. Industries may find different combinations of outside pressure where proximity matters and therefore cannot move to remote work, including warehouse, logistics, delivery, grocery, and food service. If the company can safely remain open, it may provide workers with masks to protect them from the smoke, as with Covid. Yet, health risks may still develop over time. If this happens, another external force will compound the issue. The two largest healthcare suppliers in the USA expect the cost of healthcare to rise through the 2020s,[14] likely triggering an increase in premiums on top of health risks that might manifest from the smoke. Canada isn't immune either to rising healthcare costs,[15] nor is the rest of the world, as healthcare costs have increased in the past 10 years as a percentage of GDP.[16] Whether taxpayers or individuals pay for healthcare, these costs are increasing, and climate change will impact people's health adversely.[17] Companies need to balance these issues around the employee, and efforts may manifest in additional costs like higher salaries or competitive healthcare coverage to attract and retain talent.

And on and on it goes. Compounding issues interact with each other and pressure businesses in various ways. ESG isn't necessarily special here, as companies have always had to plan for and react to crises, to Edmans's earlier point. Still, the interconnected nature of risk behind the backdrop of globalization is new, and an ESG mindset can lay a foundation for thinking about the complexity. Each of these issues alone represents a difficult material challenge to overcome, but the company can find its unique impacts in the interconnected nature of ESG. Unfortunately, considering how these crises intersect around a company and the impact can be exhausting and requires an exhaustive strategy, including potentially new value chain and stakeholder engagement models, collective action, and policy advocacy.

There is no one solution or approach to these external issues. Still, a multifaceted approach led by the relevant business unit, perhaps in consultation with an ESG or topic expert, is a good starting point until the problems and their relationships are better understood. From here, the business unit can inform the management team to secure buy-in for a more robust approach and coordinate with others across the company for a consistent effort. Without executive sponsorship and a coordinated cross-discipline attempt, the company will likely find itself continually dodging or putting out incoming fires reactively one at a time, unable to avoid business disruption as it flails. Mainstreaming ESG will help ease these conversations across every level of the business and could expedite a proactive approach.

An updated view on materiality for the company level

Building on this examination of individual ESG issues, external forces, and the impact across the acronym, a company can uncover new insights by re-examining its materiality matrix and stakeholder mapping tool through the lens of interconnected risks, opportunities, and stakeholders. Just as business units collaborate on complex systemic company issues and external problems, known material ESG issues intersect and must be addressed similarly. Again, this should be what companies are working on already, but the lens of ESG materiality affords companies a framework to examine these issues with a different mindset.

Revisiting our fictitious toy company's materiality matrix shown in Figure 10.1, we can look at one particular material issue and examine how several related issues in the matrix interconnect. For example, the bold lines represent direct connections to Fan engagement, with the thinner lines representing secondary connections. Let's examine the interconnected relationships from Fan engagement to Responsible and compliant marketing to children and clockwise around the matrix.

FIGURE 10.1 The interconnected nature of material issues

	Low	Medium	High
High		• Product safety • License and intellectual property management • Climate risk/logistics	• Sustainable sourcing and products • Product safety • Digital safety/cybersecurity
Medium	• Accessibility • Community engagement	• Fan engagement • Promoting family-friendly workspaces • Diversity and inclusion in leadership • Sustainable packaging • Mainstreaming ESG	• Responsible and compliant marketing to children • Inclusive media and marketing • EH&S/worker safety • Forced labor in value chain
Low	Biodiversity	Responsible innovation management	Waste management

Stakeholder impact (vertical axis)

Business impact (horizontal axis)

While the company may have adult fans of the physical product as collectors, children represent a core stakeholder group to engage outside the tangible product with new digital experiences and content creation. In many jurisdictions, children are a protected group with specific rules for marketing. If the engagement happens over digital means, this topic also connects to Digital safety/cybersecurity, as there are similar rules for protecting and storing a child's data, making both of these issues compliance related, a material Governance issue that may be overlooked through a singular lens. Already, the company has found value in this exercise, as this new perspective helped uncover a related material issue and a new perspective that can inform a path forward. In the meantime, the company must build Fan engagement to capture or maintain revenue while addressing these compliance concerns.

The next three issues relate to the opportunity to capture a diverse group of fans and potentially new markets through Inclusive media and marketing, Diversity and inclusion in leadership, and Accessibility along the Social pillar. For example, the company may explore making its characters more inclusive and representative of the market and its stakeholders. An executive or individual contributor who understands inclusive product design can work with Marketing, DEI champions, and communities to bring sensitivity and empathy to the new product creation and launch. These all connect to deliver a unique ESG opportunity.

That finally brings us to a connection with Sustainable sourcing and products, which may be of interest to a range of fans and connects to Product safety as product changes may result in quality control adjustments. Waste management, Responsible innovation management, Sustainable packaging, and Product safety are also connected here, as these changes have upstream and downstream impacts that R&D teams and other business units need to consider.

In mapping out the relationships, we can see that two outsized material issues surrounding Fan engagement have emerged. First, Sustainable sourcing and products, one of the higher material issues, has several connections across the matrix at the next level. The company may already prioritize this topic to address transition risk due to its location on the matrix, but it should also empower business leaders to address the issue in coordination across the company. Similarly, Diversity and inclusion in leadership, a material issue in the middle, likely has several connections to issues across the matrix. Again, the company may look to leaders to impact this topic broadly, alongside other groups, to capture the opportunity in the various ways it connects.

Let's take the example further to show how a collaborative effort can form. With a cursory glance at Fan engagement, the management team may assign Marketing or Brand Management as the owners of Fan engagement at the company. Understanding stakeholders through research is likely a first step. Yet, this team needs to be empowered to gain support from across the company in its pursuit. This new interconnected perspective on the materiality matrix connects to IT, Human Resources, R&D, Quality Control, Operations, and Procurement. The management team also found a new connection to compliance through careful analysis, leading to General Counsel. To effectively execute a strategy around Fan engagement, all internal stakeholders must understand the priorities and relationships to support the work. In other words, ESG must be mainstreamed so internal stakeholders can effectively prioritize and come together. With the management team on board, perhaps an executive sponsor would be assigned to navigate the internal business politics to help secure cross-functional support and a budget to fund the necessary projects. Without mainstreaming ESG and the structures to facilitate an interconnected execution of strategy to match the challenges, the matrix is effectively inert, and the company may struggle to solve any material issue.

Internal issues, external crises, and systemic problems: Polycrisis!

Multiple external crises are brimming over from long-standing system problems, building around companies and their internal issues in new and interconnected ways. This confluence can bring detrimental shocks as crises interact unpredictably, making proactive risk management nearly impossible. In its 2023 Global Risks report, WEF lists a term that perfectly captures these risks' interconnected nature and confluence: a polycrisis.[18] What is particularly challenging about a polycrisis is that, like related issues from external ESG forces that can compound problems, these crises impact across the pillars and with material and non-material systemic issues, including those the company should already address around sustainability and DEI. Companies must foster a well-organized response from within, organize across their industry, gain capital support from financial services, and seek regulatory guidance to effectively address a polycrisis or its component crises.

Commercial real estate in the 2020s provides an excellent example of a brewing polycrisis. As we've covered, many companies that could adopt hybrid or remote working models during Covid did so. This necessary internal tactic had an unfortunate externality, straining the economic viability of cities, as remote workers were no longer coming in to spend their money. Some cities offer tax incentives to companies around the promise of employees commuting and the subsequent spending revenue and taxes within the city. Cities typically structure the tax benefits around some percentage of company workers in the office. Historically, the checks on occupancy have been unenforced, as it was a long-standing assumption that a company leasing or owning buildings would have its workers show up.[19] But as Covid waned, companies found that employees still preferred to work remotely, yet the buildings and related tax incentives remained.[20] Across the USA, Europe, and Asia, remote workers moved to smaller towns and even other countries in the same time zone.[21] Until May 2023, building occupancy in New York City sat at under 50 percent, increasing to only 50.5 percent in

June, with Bloomberg estimating the cost to the city as $12 billion annually.[22] The effects of remote work in a metropolitan area have interconnected risks across tax revenue, tourism, local merchants, and real estate value. Still, this is only one crisis that companies, real estate, and cities face.

Another crisis is on the horizon for office buildings. Through 2025, the commercial real estate market is heading towards $1.5 trillion of loans that must be refinanced.[23] Interest rates remain high, increasing borrowing costs for companies. These financial pressures come at a time when not only are the buildings half empty, but building owners and real estate managers are conscious of their facilities' carbon footprint, requiring short-term retrofitting projects to meet ESG market pressures to adopt sustainable operations. Environmental-related building improvements are no small transition, as existing buildings generate 27 percent of global emissions.[24] Without better occupancy rates, it can be difficult for companies to continue to invest in retrofitting and making improvements without financial or government assistance.

Singapore may have staved off this aspect of the polycrisis through a good example of how a private-public-sector effort can help with transition risk. Through a multi-step program that targets retrofitting 80 percent of existing buildings, making 80 percent of new buildings super low energy, and 80 percent energy efficiency through financing and green certifications, Singapore has become one of the most sustainable cities in the world.[25] In contrast to other global cities, Singapore's occupancy rates were also close to 95 percent in 2023.[26] Still, not every country or city offers such an approach, and as we've seen, occupancy rates are not ubiquitously high.

Balancing refinancing without a support system against remote work and sustainability updates is a losing financial proposition, but it gets worse because there may not be a way out for companies. With many feeling this pain, buildings may not sell. Selling a building is even more difficult in this new world of remote work, and analysts predict values will potentially depreciate up to 40 percent.[27] Climate and transition risks, perhaps not considered when companies originally took loans out, can compound depreciation, negatively impacting a building's valuation.[28] This polycrisis has so many interconnected issues that companies may simply walk away from the debt, the building, and any tax incentives.

San Francisco is one example of a localized polycrisis, where internal, external, and systemic factors impacted commercial real estate. Layoffs in the tech industry due to the economic pressures, tourism declines from

Covid, increasing crime, and homelessness have led to city-wide loan defaults.[29] As a result, the influence of this problem is a new external crisis that stretches into the banking industry, specifically as buildings become worth less than their loans, and banks may be left with low-value assets.

One mechanism to hedge against this risk is financial stress testing exercises. The European Banking Authority and the US Federal Reserve have both run these exercises with banks, which included several factors, including recognition of the challenging commercial real estate markets and planning for drops in value.[30, 31] Regional banks make up 68 percent of commercial real estate loans,[32] so there could be significant impacts on the financial markets in localized areas, similar to the Silicon Valley Bank collapse outlined in Chapter 5. As with Silicon Valley Bank, the confluence of issues could ripple across economies globally and have far-reaching consequences as credit becomes constrained. The impact could pass from the regional banks to the bigger banks and impact companies, landlords, city governments, and potentially everyone, similar to the 2008 financial crisis.

The collapse of the commercial real estate market is a hypothetical risk. The example showcases the interconnected crises that can quickly accelerate. The issues that intersect around commercial real estate, including remote work, the impact of transition risks, and sustainability efficiencies, are ESG crises that combine with other factors, such as refinancing with high-interest rates, to create the polycrisis. In addition, a commercial real estate crisis, while a polycrisis for borrowers and lenders, could be another crisis that connects with other material crises across the banking industry and impact the global economy in unknown ways.

There can't be one solution to a polycrisis, as this is a confluence of crises and systemic issues. Yet, an internal and external multi-stakeholder approach that matches its complexity and breadth can help. For example, in addition to stress testing, the EU Central Bank,[33] several US agencies, and the Federal Reserve[34] released updated guidance for banks working with commercial real estate borrowers during financial stress. The recommendations range from looking at credit data to creating short-term accommodations to address potential ESG issues like disasters or other national and international events to workouts that restructure the loan to minimize adverse long-term events. Even though these recommendations are outside a company's control, the management team should understand the guidance to better prepare for tough conversations with lenders. Banks should review and heed this predictive guidance and be ready to collaborate with companies to ensure they can pay off the loans, even if they need to trade short-term concessions for long-term assurance to recover or protect the loan. While a brewing commercial real estate polycrisis may not impact every company, it illustrates how these crises connect and potential considerations for addressing them.

A NOTE ON SYSTEMIC PROBLEMS, MATERIALITY, AND TIME

A polycrisis represents an important nuance for supporters of ESG who lead with materiality and a long-term view because, over time, the confluence may align values to value. Globalization has compounded systemic issues and risks with issues like child welfare, climate change, forced labor, equity and justice, and so on, which have led to many of these crises. The only option left is to deal with the systemic issues and work to solve them. In the future, the more systemic crises intersect in a much more material way where these issues and their solutions will shift businesses forward into the unknown. Companies must recognize, against a short-term mindset, that these long-term interconnected crises will become material to every company over time, despite the goals and commitments set.

There is simply no bypassing these systemic threats on the horizon, requiring dramatic adjustments to the business, financial markets, and governments, therefore making today's table stakes issues of saving the world and its people a dynamic materiality opportunity. As companies wake up to this reality, they need a new interconnected approach to lower their risks while facilitating the necessary systemic changes required to ensure entire industries and value chains make changes responsibly. It will take new partnerships to be successful, but addressing these systemic risks are worthwhile pursuits to build long-term business resilience.

Partnership on ESG: Antitrust laws and the dangers of greenhushing

Behind the UN's Sustainable Development Goals (SDGs) are whispers of ESG, even though material, long-term business resilience isn't the intention. The SDGs remain a useful and easy-to-understand guidepost towards material issues. Some companies co-opt some of the more material SDGs, align them with the other frameworks and standards, and list them alongside relevant project work and commitments in their CSR reports. While the SDGs focus on what many consider admirable values-based ideas like peace and prosperity, each goal can have a material impact on the company and represent unavoidable issues for management teams to address over the long term.

One SDG is required when it comes to interconnected issues and a polycrisis. SDG17 is named "Partnership for the Goals" and largely focuses on partnerships aimed at improving the developing world from the perspective of developed countries. The idea of loss and damage funded by a coordinated effort across public-private partnerships and philanthropic companies, covered in Chapter 3, is an example of this type of effort, although one that has remained underfunded. Inside SDG17 are two targets, 17.16 and 17.17, which describe multi-stakeholder approaches to public-private partnerships considering civil society's needs, knowledge sharing, funding, technical support, and so on.[35] Like other SDGs, companies can co-opt SDG17 to address more systemic challenges that can't be solved alone, intending to solve them before they manifest in a crisis or contribute to a polycrisis. Again, this long-term proactive approach is where values eventually align with value.

As these brewing crises and long-standing systemic problems threaten a company's long-term strategy and resilience, it should engage multiple stakeholders in a coordinated approach. Similar to the interconnected materiality matrix, finding the relationships across stakeholders in the context of brewing crises may yield similar improved perspectives and deepen the understanding of which stakeholder groups to engage on what issues and how they can help. A company may find that stakeholders connect unexpectedly, and it has a unique opportunity to either pull them together as a leader or participate in a coordinated effort. While governments, financial services, suppliers, employees, customers, and philanthropies represent these important stakeholders, the company must not overlook its competitors. Solving individual or even interconnected internal ESG issues may mean a competitive advantage for one market player, but systemic problems are too big to solve alone, and it will likely fail to do so. Competitors in the same industry represent a key stakeholder group that can help improve or solve material systemic challenges.

Throughout the book, there have been references to consortiums that attempt to organize companies around change. In Chapter 3, we looked at the Beverage Industry Environmental Roundtable (BIER), which mobilizes the industry around material Environmental issues like water. Chapter 4 closed with Paramount's Content for Change, inviting others to join its Social efforts. The Green Software Foundation, in Chapter 6, works across the industry to lower the carbon emissions of technology through efficient software development. Industry calls and consortiums organize around topics to drive material changes.

An effective consortium should not restrict participants from joining, work with a level of transparency, have clear objectives, not lock participants or their value chain into self-serving action, and be in service to stakeholders. The resulting collective action will make more of a difference than if participants act alone.

Unfortunately, some companies have left consortiums to pursue their own ESG path. In December 2022, Vanguard, one of the world's largest asset managers, pulled out of the Net Zero Asset Managers initiative (NZAM). In its announcement, it recognized that climate change would have far-reaching economic consequences, is part of material risk identification, and that there is much confusion with collective goals.[36] Similarly, the Net Zero Insurance Alliance (NZIA) had many members leave.[37] Both groups focus more on reducing carbon emissions, a long-term goal best serviced through collaboration, as one firm cannot meet this planetary objective alone. Aside from the political pressures in the USA, one of the speculations as to why companies have left these climate consortiums is due to potential antitrust issues.[38]

Antitrust has long focused on preventing companies from colluding around market control, monopolies, and price-fixing issues. For example, Canada Bread colluded with other industry bakers to fix the price of bread over 16 years in the companies' favor.[39] Historically, antitrust has focused on monitoring the financial aspects of competition alongside consumer protection in this way. Antitrust worries have become a growing consideration for these consortiums or any group of companies collectively driving ESG improvements and innovation, regardless of whether or not the objectives are material. This concern could mean that industries cannot solve their most systemic problems, ultimately hurting the company and its stakeholders.

In the USA, sustainability and ESG have drawn the government's attention. Antitrust was called out in the Republican State Attorney Generals' anti-ESG letter from August 2022, citing potential ESG pitfalls, including boycotting, trade restraints, and reduced dealmaking for non-participants as part of their concerns.[40] While companies may employ these strategies, they are less likely to be related to ESG as they don't result in impact. Impact is a key stakeholder concern as companies manage metrics and need proof through action, not punitive adjustments. The anti-ESG perspective affords much interpretation, so companies must be mindful of their individual and collective approaches. For example, suppose a company switches suppliers from dirty to green to meet its sustainability commitments alone. In that case, it has done nothing to address the long-term systemic problem, only serving a short-term reporting requirement without meeting the real intention of its goals. In other words, this myopic approach may be considered greenwashing because the problem persists. The legal system and regulators may consider it an antitrust issue if a consortium of companies does this at scale, punishing suppliers instead of engaging in the upstream risks.

This sentiment has translated into real-world probes. In 2019, several automakers, including Ford, Honda, BMW, and Volkswagen, agreed to California's proposed emissions standards, which exceeded the efficiencies set by the federal government.[41] As a result, the Justice Department, reportedly outside the White House, investigated whether the automakers violated antitrust laws.[42] Ultimately, the Justice Department dropped the case after determining the companies broke no laws.[43] While this is encouraging for companies working in consortiums or in concert around these issues, which are again required to solve some of their industry's crises, it would also be wise to consult a lawyer.

Backing away from collective action due to antitrust concerns would certainly reduce the sharing of best practices, knowledge, and influence through engagement. However, similar to how crises intersect around a company, another pullback is brewing around anti-ESG efforts, augmenting the reduction in collaborative efforts.

Companies began stepping away from the ESG acronym and communicating their efforts as the term made news in anti-ESG congressional hearings in 2023, conservative states filed new bills against ESG, consumer outrage created new controversies, and activists argued that efforts aren't going far enough. As we saw in the previous chapter, various types of outrage materiality can force a company to react when addressing a material risk or opportunity. Companies cannot seem to try new things or take risks on these issues for fear of getting things wrong when reporting their metrics and actions. Even BlackRock CEO Larry Fink announced that he would be backing away from using ESG as a term but remarked he still favored "conscientious capitalism."[44] The result may be that companies stop trying to take risks, but it is perhaps more likely that they will be less vocal about any efforts and therefore may be unable to solve more interconnected challenges, even material ones.

When companies no longer share their data or actions around ESG and related efforts, it is called greenhushing. Some believe greenhushing is an acceptable path towards progress as companies will continue managing their transition risks and drive progress around systemic problems. When considering interconnected issues that need a collective approach, however, greenhushing will slow progress at best but have devastating inertia at worst. When industries aren't working together, it is extremely challenging for pockets of single players to affect change at the scale needed. Since systemic problems aren't handled, the timeline to dynamic materiality, where it suddenly impacts every company through a systemic shock, may be shortened. In addition, the company would not engage stakeholders as it is silent about its efforts, leaving stakeholders, including shareholders, with an opaque picture of challenges and solutions. Also, if a company doesn't communicate its ESG efforts when projects go right, finding new ways to meet its goals through improvement and innovation, the knowledge remains locked away, and others cannot learn from what's come before.

There are a lot of talented people working on ESG issues who don't explicitly call out the acronym. The work and communication are more important than the acronym, and this is not greenhushing. While the work and its outcomes are certainly more important than the term, if these efforts aren't transparent or openly communicated, they cannot inform an industry struggling to deal with complex interconnected crises, let alone individual business impact and material issues. Companies must find ways to work across multiple stakeholders, including their competitors, to transform their industry and value chain around material risks and opportunities.

Notes

1 Edmans, A. (2023). *The End of ESG*. SSRN, Rochester, NY, pp. 2–5. papers. ssrn.com/sol3/papers.cfm?abstract_id=4221990 (archived at https://perma.cc/ E2JW-HTGY.)

2 OECD (2022). *Climate Tipping Points: Insights for effective policy action.* OECD iLibrary. Paris: Organisation for Economic Co-operation and Development. www.oecd-ilibrary.org/environment/climate-tipping-points_ abc5a69e-en (archived at https://perma.cc/9FV7-Z7A5).

3 World Economic Forum, Global Risk Team, Mercer Oliver Wyman, a Marsh & McLennan Company, Merrill Lynch, SwissRe and The Wharton School (2006). *Global Risks 2006.* World Economic Forum, pp. 4, 11. www3. weforum.org/docs/WEF_Global_Risks_Report_2006.pdf (archived at https:// perma.cc/D9W7-9TLU).

4 Heading, S. and Markovitz, G. (2023). *Global Risks Report 2023: The biggest risks facing the world.* World Economic Forum. www.weforum.org/agenda/ 2023/01/these-are-the-biggest-risks-facing-the-world-global-risks-2023/ (archived at https://perma.cc/BU8W-MYQ4).

5 Jayakumar, V. (2020). How technology shapes globalization. The Hill. thehill. com/opinion/technology/517375-how-technology-shapes-globalization/ (archived at https://perma.cc/2TKM-8BWC).

6 Keller, C. and Marold, R. (2023). Deglobalisation: Here's what you need to know. World Economic Forum. www.weforum.org/agenda/2023/01/ deglobalisation-what-you-need-to-know-wef23/ (archived at https://perma. cc/7VHH-GDZW).

7 The Canadian Press (2023). Smog, air quality alerts in place across much of Quebec as wildfires continue to burn. *Toronto Star.* www.thestar.com/news/ canada/smog-air-quality-alerts-in-place-across-much-of-quebec-as-wildfires-continue-to-burn/article_f371125a-a195-5d2a-9b85-018db9772895.html (archived at https://perma.cc/S382-BEC6).

8 Kirkham, C., Levinson, R. and Bose, N. (2020). Warehouse workers risk COVID-19 to ship Gucci shades, face cream, sofas. Reuters, April 11. www. reuters.com/article/us-health-coronavirus-retail-workforce-i-idUSKCN21T0P9 (archived at https://perma.cc/4W7U-NN7K).

9 Mills, S. (2023). Quebec forest fires shutter businesses during lucrative fishing season. CBC. www.cbc.ca/news/canada/ottawa/quebec-forest-fire-smoke-business-economy-1.6875172 (archived at https://perma.cc/T7X2-A5HG).

10 Reuters (2023). Wildfires halt mining operations in Canada. Reuters, June 8. www.reuters.com/world/americas/wildfires-halt-mining-operations-canada-2023-06-06/ (archived at https://perma.cc/5MTE-3JUF).

11 Nickel, R. (2023). Analysis: Canadian wildfires shutter sawmills, drive up lumber prices. Reuters, June 12. www.reuters.com/business/environment/ canadian-wildfires-shutter-sawmills-drive-up-lumber-prices-2023-06-12/ (archived at https://perma.cc/5XA2-ZCHA).

12 Heading, S. and Zahidi, S. (2023). *The Global Risks Report 2023* 18th edition. p. 7. World Economic Forum. www3.weforum.org/docs/WEF_Global_ Risks_Report_2023.pdf (archived at https://perma.cc/T7AY-7N9V).

13 Heading, S. and Zahidi, S. (2023). *The Global Risks Report 2023* 18th edition. p. 15. World Economic Forum. www3.weforum.org/docs/WEF_ Global_Risks_Report_2023.pdf (archived at World Economic Forum.https:// perma.cc/T7AY-7N9V).

14 Balasubramanian, S. (2023). Healthcare costs will increase significantly over the next decade. Forbes. www.forbes.com/sites/saibala/2023/06/20/healthcare-costs-will-increase-significantly-over-the-next-decade/?sh=48de24506c6b (archived at https://perma.cc/CSY9-K47Z).

15 Jones, D. (2023). Opinion: Canada's other health care crisis: Costs are on a vicious spiral—a looming economic mess. *The Globe and Mail*, June 21. www.theglobeandmail.com/business/commentary/article-canadas-other-health-care-crisis-costs-are-on-a-vicious-spiral-a/ (archived at https://perma.cc/53DC-RENR).

16 OECD (2019). OECD Health Statistics 2019. OECD. www.oecd.org/health/health-data.htm (archived at https://perma.cc/B6YK-8SY2).

17 Lenton, T.M., Xu, C., Abrams, J.F., Ghadiali, A., Loriani, S., Sakschewski, B., Zimm, C., Ebi, K.L., Dunn, R.R., Svenning, J-C., and Scheffer, M. (2023). Quantifying the human cost of global warming. *Nature Sustainability*, 6, pp. 1237–1247. https://doi.org/10.1038/s41893-023-01132-6 (archived at https:// perma.cc/8S94-VSGM).

18 Heading, S. and Zahidi, S. (2023). *The Global Risks Report 2023* 18th edition. p. 57. World Economic Forum. www3.weforum.org/docs/WEF_ Global_Risks_Report_2023.pdf (archived at https://perma.cc/T7AY-7N9V).

19 Constanz, J. and Holder, S. (2023). Tax breaks threaten remote work if cities start enforcing them. Bloomberg, February 21. www.bloomberg.com/news/ features/2023-02-21/another-threat-to-work-from-home-tax-breaks (archived at https://perma.cc/2TPB-V4AZ).

20 Gonzales, M. (2022). Nearly half of workers are "definitely looking" to work remotely. SHRM. www.shrm.org/resourcesandtools/hr-topics/behavioral-competencies/global-and-cultural-effectiveness/pages/nearly-half-of-workers-are-definitely-looking-to-work-remotely.aspx (archived at https:// perma.cc/JVR5-K9KX).

21 Smith, M. (2023). Remote jobs are moving overseas and to smaller U.S. cities: "The same skills for 60% of the cost". CNBC. www.cnbc.com/ 2023/06/09/remote-jobs-are-moving-overseas-and-to-smaller-us-cities.html (archived at https://perma.cc/4QTQ-XKG6).

22 Constantz, J. (2023). New York office occupancy breaks 50% for first time since pandemic hit. Bloomberg, June 12. www.bloomberg.com/news/ articles/2023-06-12/new-york-occupancy-breaks-50-for-first-time-since-pandemic-hit (archived at https://perma.cc/FUR2-H2V8).

23 Fox, M. (2023). Commercial real estate is the next shoe to drop for regional banks and the stock market. Markets Insider. markets.businessinsider.com/ news/stocks/commercial-real-estate-debt-regional-banks-risk-stock-market-cre-2023-3 (archived at https://perma.cc/A7VB-LW5Q).

24 Architecture 2030 (n.d.). Why the building sector? Architecture 2030. architecture2030.org/why-the-built-environment/ (archived at https://perma. cc/789V-YBGE).

25 Chan, K. (2022). How the Singapore Green Plan 2030 is creating Asia's most sustainable city. *South China Morning Post.* www.scmp.com/country-reports/ country-reports/topics/singapore-national-day-2022/article/3188126/how-singapore (archived at https://perma.cc/ANR7-SFLH).

26 Bloomberg (2023). Singapore stands out with climbing office rents, occupancy rates. *South China Morning Post.* www.scmp.com/news/asia/southeast-asia/ article/3225387/singapore-stands-out-climbing-office-rents-occupancy-rates (archived at https://perma.cc/W22N-MHUN).

27 Tayeb, Z. (2023). Commercial real estate prices could crash 40% from their peak in a worse disaster than the financial crisis, Morgan Stanley strategist warns. Markets Insider. markets.businessinsider.com/news/stocks/commercial-real-estate-prices-outlook-crash-financial-crisis-morgan-stanley-2023-4 (archived at https://perma.cc/NN2B-YXXJ).

28 PRI (2021). TCFD for real assets investors. PRI. www.unpri.org/infrastructure-and-other-real-assets/tcfd-for-real-assets-investors/7495.article (archived at https://perma.cc/XU3H-JFG9).

29 Kinder, T. (2023). Defaults raise alarm over stability of San Francisco's commercial property. *Financial Times*, June 17. www.ft.com/content/ d0c0fd7b-e2fc-4da3-a698-4b959efa1bfd (archived at https://perma.cc/ M3SZ-CBEB).

30 European Systemic Risk Board (n.d.). ECB-PUBLIC Macro-financial scenario for the 2023 EU-wide banking sector stress test. European Banking Authority. www.eba.europa.eu/sites/default/documents/files/document_library/Risk%20 Analysis%20and%20Data/EU-wide%20Stress%20Testing/2023/Scenarios/ Updated%202/1053809/2023%20EBA%20Stress%20Test%20adverse%20 scenario%20%28updated%2020%20March%202023%29.pdf (archived at https://perma.cc/E3XE-UJ88).

31 The Federal Reserve System Board of Governors (2023). 2023 stress test scenarios. The Federal Reserve. www.federalreserve.gov/newsevents/pressreleases/ files/bcreg20230209a1.pdf (archived at https://perma.cc/GK2U-WNMM).

32 Fox, M. (2023b). Commercial real estate is the next shoe to drop for regional banks and the stock market. Markets Insider. markets.businessinsider.com/ news/stocks/commercial-real-estate-debt-regional-banks-risk-stock-market-cre-2023-3 (archived at https://perma.cc/A7VB-LW5Q).

33 Ryan, E., Horan, A., and Jarmulska, B. (2022). Commercial real estate and financial stability—new insights from the euro area credit register. European Central Bank. www.ecb.europa.eu/pub/financial-stability/macroprudential-bulletin/html/ecb.mpbu202210_4~0aa7d44e15.en.html (archived at https:// perma.cc/8GPF-EXUH).

34   Federal Reserve (2022). Final policy statement. The Federal Reserve. www.
     federalreserve.gov/newsevents/pressreleases/files/bcreg20230629a1.pdf
     (archived at https://perma.cc/LXD4-WEGM).

35   United Nations (n.d.). Goal 17 | Department of Economic and Social Affairs.
     Sustainable Development. sdgs.un.org/goals/goal17#targets_and_indicators
     (archived at https://perma.cc/D2Y8-FX8U).

36   The Vanguard Group, Inc. (2022). An update on our engagement with NZAM.
     Vanguard. corporate.vanguard.com/content/corporatesite/us/en/corp/articles/
     update-on-nzam-engagement.html (archived at https://perma.cc/K46T-29Q6).

37   Insurtech Insights (2023). Lloyd's withdraws from Net Zero Insurance
     Alliance, joining growing list of major players. Insurtech Insights. www.
     insurtechinsights.com/lloyds-withdraws-from-net-zero-insurance-alliance-
     joining-growing-list-of-major-players/ (archived at https://perma.cc/
     C67D-AQ99).

38   Gasparini, M., Haanaes, K., and Tufano, P. (2022). When climate collabora-
     tion is treated as an antitrust violation. *Harvard Business Review*. hbr.
     org/2022/10/when-climate-collaboration-is-treated-as-an-antitrust-violation
     (archived at https://perma.cc/WA5R-A2SH).

39   Evans, P. (2023). Canada Bread agrees to $50M fine for role in bread price-
     fixing scandal. CBC. www.cbc.ca/news/business/canada-bread-price-
     fixing-1.6883783 (archived at https://perma.cc/M22A-NA6M).

40   Brnovich, M. and Peterson, D. (2022). Letter. Attorney General of Texas. www.
     texasattorneygeneral.gov/sites/default/files/images/executive-management/
     BlackRock%20Letter.pdf (archived at https://perma.cc/6U6Y-NEPF).

41   Shama, E. (2019). Ford, BMW, Honda, and Volkswagen agree to California
     emissions framework. CNBC. www.cnbc.com/2019/07/25/ford-bmw-honda-
     and-volkswagen-agree-to-california-emissions-rules.html (archived at https://
     perma.cc/BPJ3-PXJR).

42   Puko, T. and Foldy, B. (2019). Justice Department launches antitrust probe
     into four auto makers. *The Wall Street Journal*, September 6. www.wsj.com/
     articles/justice-department-launches-antitrust-probe-into-four-auto-makers-
     11567778958 (archived at https://perma.cc/VVT7-RHAC).

43   O'Kane, S. (2020). DOJ drops antitrust probe into automakers that want
     cleaner cars. *The Verge*. www.theverge.com/2020/2/7/21128684/doj-antitrust-
     investigation-closed-trump-ford-vw (archived at https://perma.cc/NB57-33SZ).

44   Worland, J. (2023). Larry Fink takes on ESG backlash. *Time*. time.com/6291317/
     larry-fink-esg-climate-action/ (archived at https://perma.cc/8TAZ-P698).

11

All Well and Good

Since the tipping points around 2020, activists have received much attention from management teams and investors. One of the biggest criticisms of ESG comes from activists, who are understandably upset that ESG focuses companies on disclosures, data, and material issues while the world and its people suffer. This criticism is somewhat valid, as saving the world and its people is not what ESG is about. However, there are multiple connections between the two, and focusing on the company's risks and opportunities doesn't mean efforts won't generate impactful progress outside of its walls, nor does it mean that the company can't pursue altruistic objectives around its purpose. While it's likely that the company's ESG efforts will not assuage activists' concerns, a company that leads with ESG can ensure a responsible transition while perhaps doing good in the world too. Yet, if a company attempts to capture opportunities without doing the work, otherwise known as greenwashing, activists are standing watch to call it out, aided by new forms of digital accountability.

ESG, especially quality Governance, supports the company to help it remain viable and resilient so that it may be around long enough to help drive impact. In this chapter, impact is an umbrella term that captures the company's impact on the world. Addressing and improving on these issues have become licenses to operate, often intersect materially with the company through regulations and stakeholders, and represent the baseline of what the company should already be doing, especially as it prepares to manage long-term transition risk.

Today, companies have little choice but to move past operational improvements into impact. While impact may appear to be a choice the company makes, in a world growing in complexity and accountability, the pressures that influence the decision to engage on impact are rapidly increasing. Environmental and Social tipping points will no doubt accelerate, and the future effects may be unpredictable, forcing companies to react in unknown ways, even potentially deconstructing extractive economic and capitalist institutions and rebuilding new systems. While this prediction is a bit dysto-pian, new interconnected risks have emerged that could facilitate highly disruptive shifts. Companies have the opportunity to work within existing systems to influence transitions that could change the course of the world's biggest problems, which would certainly protect and return value to them over the long term.

Companies must keep this long-term view in mind as it can be easy to focus on quick short-term connections between ESG and impact through shifting stakeholder preferences. Stakeholders, whether socially responsible investors, mindful employees and consumers in younger generations, or governments and regulators, all now expect companies to engage in positive change around these crises and act with haste. As before, the definition of "positive change" or potentially "doing good," as we saw in Chapter 9, is objective. Here, it means that the ESG progress improves along its pillars. In other words, the efforts and outcomes align with achieving what one might consider the positive Environmental, Social, or Governance ideals, not those that necessarily return positive financials. However, as companies feel pres-sure to create this idyllic balance from their stakeholders, it compels them to act, and that movement generates value through financial or reputational support from stakeholders. Still, this stakeholder connection only scratches the surface of value creation around the move towards positive change.

If a company builds on this pressure and has mainstreamed ESG through improvements and innovation, it may start seeing the opportunity to improve its impact on the world and its people. The range of potential here can be vast, depending on the company's position. For example, a company can take a more active role in local community issues and scale its efforts to address some of the world's most pressing problems through its value chain. Impact is highly dependent on outcomes but approaches to get there can take place across little things that make a difference to highly ambitious and systemic shifts.

In addition to serving as a primer on ESG and helping to think through those challenges, this book serves as a precursor to ambitious and inspira-tional change, as an ESG mindset can help a company move its business and stakeholders forward responsibly and with intention. A company that main-streams ESG is well-positioned to lead impact outward or participate in systemic efforts because it can build on what it has learned to execute more effectively while inspiring and taking action with others.

The intersection of impact issues at its stakeholders and the business's purpose is an effective place to start since the company should build on its existing expertise. This approach adds efficacy and allows for a more accessible defense of projects when controversies arise since the company is engaging in what might be considered philanthropy but through the lens of topics it understands best (Figure 11.1). As always, it is essential to note that a win-win may be unlikely as any project or change can be challenging for a business to adapt without some short-term concessionary costs and even more so to pursue non-material systemic changes.

With proven or in-progress ESG and impact projects underway or completed, a company can communicate outcomes to stakeholders and then use the goodwill generated to scale impact through others or address related projects across its value chain, similar to its approach in addressing long-term transition risks. In this forward-looking view, we have finally arrived at the complex connection between ESG and impact, both now fundamental to operating a business in civil society. Here, seemingly less material short-term impact investments become material long-term ESG-driven value.

In 1999, Kofi Annan addressed the World Economic Forum in Davos, encouraging business leaders to take action towards a new sustainable economy that also protects human rights.[1] The world needs today's companies to build resilience through addressing their material ESG issues while engaging

FIGURE 11.1 The path to impact's defensibility flows through ESG

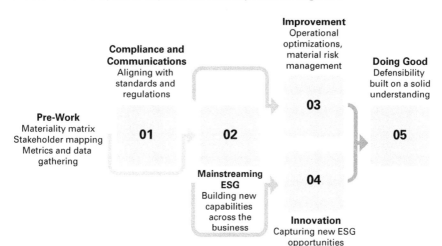

in the long-term perspective regarding impact to achieve that vision. These companies will find they are well-equipped to tackle new crises and react better to disruption by completely understanding their place in the world.

Considering the scope: From global impact to local

There can be no argument that business is changing around the potential of impact, with many stakeholders looking to companies to solve these challenges. As early as 2038, the world may experience catastrophic climate tipping points that will know no borders.[2] On the Social side, around 12 percent of people worldwide identify as LGBT+,[3] although some severe risks exist for those self-identifying in some countries. Globally, an estimated 1.3 billion people identify as having a significant disability.[4] Combine these statistics with survey results showing that 79 percent of consumers want to interact with brands that share their Environmental, Social, and inclusiveness values,[5] and it is no wonder impact is becoming more material to value.

Driving impact is no easy task. The rise of globalization means that businesses now operate in a more complex and interconnected world. Upstream supply chains to downstream stakeholders are global, making driving meaningful change exponentially more difficult across these systems. Still, stakeholder sentiment is shifting and pushing companies to engage in their values, and simple data reporting and internal operational improvements are insufficient. Companies must embrace this challenge because 40 percent of consumers have said they would permanently boycott their favorite brand if it doesn't agree with their values.[6] Yet, there is little global consensus on shared values, making capturing a global market through a single purpose complicated. Local nuance can quickly be lost, and an impact effort can quickly shift to risk.

Globalization and market capture around purpose require a tight balance between supporting impact and doing it alongside local context and laws. For example, in the Muslim-majority country of Malaysia, sexual activity between two same-sex partners is illegal under Penal Code 1936.[7] In May 2023, the Malaysian government confiscated rainbow-colored Pride watches made by the Swiss company Swatch.[8] Shortly after, the company sued to recover the watches.[9] With controversies generated by values, a company can't consistently manifest wins across markets. The management team must take a nuanced approach to ensure an impact campaign doesn't threaten market value as it proceeds. Of course, global impact efforts may stem from a company's purpose. In that case, the management team must be consistent in its values and prepare to engage in any repercussions, including exiting markets or managing reputational backlash with stakeholders internally and externally.

Conversely, the company may realize that local attention can drive significant impact, as crises affect regional areas and their people. Local impact is, after all, the idea behind loss and damage, as we saw in Chapter 3, where Global South communities are asking governments and companies based in the Global North to take financial responsibility for localized climate change disasters.

Still, not every local effort needs to center around the rise of disasters. The local focus on communities is where global impact can happen at scale. For example, Warby Parker, the eyeglasses company, has a unique "Buy a Pair, Give a Pair" program at the center of a material Social issue, affordable eye care. It distributes eyeglasses and empowers underserved and low-income communities by educating people to conduct basic eye exams, sell glasses at ultra-affordable prices, and provide vision care and eyeglasses through partnerships.[10] The program has given away 13 million eyeglasses and runs in over 50 countries.[11]

Whether global or local, impact efforts can have long-term planetary and social benefits such as driving inclusion and empowering individuals, helping struggling populations deal with a crisis, or increasing the ability for people to earn a living wage. A company may appear to have values, but it is its internal stakeholders that manifest them through Governance principles. As we've seen, employees are now often ready to support and work around these efforts. Yet, challenges remain.

Regardless of whether the outcome stems from material issues, extreme activists may see these corporate efforts as a bit of a cheat because the focus is often still on the company and not the bigger issues facing the world and its people. Depending on their passion, activists may ask companies to unnaturally engage in areas where they lack expertise, or rail against existing institutions, like capitalism, since the exploitation of labor and resources has caused many crises. Companies should be mindful of these pressures and work through their intellectual capital, areas of expertise, existing systems, and spheres of influence to deliver change. By leading with what matters to the company, what it knows, and leveraging its lessons learned for inspiration and influence, a company can more easily drive impact by working to help others rather than being randomized through non-material attention.

Inspiration and impact through an ESG mindset

With employees filled with a newfound sense of purpose coming out of the Environmental and Social tipping points, one of the best opportunities a company has around impact projects and activism can be found by focusing on its intellectual capital and unique area of expertise. Sorting this out is no easy task, as balancing employee expectations for impact against the realities of running a business is an exercise in stakeholder care and management. Too much freedom may result in budget excess, which shareholders will question, and too little impact or reductions during tough economic conditions might yield a demoralized workforce.

Many companies approach brewing employee expectations with perennial volunteer programs and charitable contributions. These programs, while laudable, are too transient to harness company purpose and often don't take advantage of the company's unique ESG and business positions. As Warby Parker's "Buy a Pair, Give a Pair" program shows, there can be a powerful impact at the intersection of a company's business and an impact goal. This approach augments the power of volunteerism and philanthropy, turning it into something that lasts and can feed back an effect on the company positively. There are many examples to explore that show this impact out and back in again.

While monetary donations to various charitable causes are one approach, there is power in working with material intent. Novo Nordisk A/S, the global healthcare company focused on chronic diseases, makes multimillion DKK donations to the World Diabetes Foundation and Novo Nordisk Heamophilia Foundation,[12] but also takes its philanthropy further around its business and Social mission. The Novo Nordisk Foundation, created from the two organizations' separate foundations in 1989, provides research and humanitarian grants worldwide.[13] The grant listings are online and transparently available for stakeholder review.[14] The requests range from financial support to Diabetes Centers, grants to support medical research, and more. Besides the grant funding, a time, personnel, and Governance component exists as staff must review the grant applications, which signifies the investment required.[15] Many companies run philanthropy arms or foundations like this for a specific purpose, often separate but related to the company and supported by its profits. The Novo Nordisk Foundation organizes its philanthropy around three broad themes, which appear to intersect materially with the company's work: Health, Sustainability (which affects people's health), and Life Sciences.[16]

Not all philanthropy is financially focused through a foundation but may still have costs through volunteer time or other structured program attributes. If done thoughtfully, the company may recognize a non-financial return, however. SAP, the enterprise application company, runs a unique pro-bono program that allows employees to engage in social impact projects on a short-term basis. The SAP Social Sabbatical program started in 2012 and has had over 1,400 participants impacting over 6.4 million people in the first 10 years.[17] It brings together diverse teams of employees, allowing them to leverage their enterprise expertise alongside non-profits and social organizations in emerging markets.[18] SAP realizes benefits to the company through the program as employees build leadership, gain cultural awareness, and better understand emerging markets.[19] In other words, this effort has a charitable mission, but the company benefits via stakeholder learning and growth.

Part of philanthropy may be solving a global challenge that helps empower a broad set of stakeholders. Big tech companies, including Microsoft, Amazon, Google, and IBM have launched various technology skilling programs ranging from understanding AI, cybersecurity, the cloud, and more. These, often free, programs aim to fill a talent gap to keep corporate customers consuming technology responsibly while staying well-protected. Empowering people to earn a living wage with high-tech jobs is a generous opportunity and intersects materially across the Social and Technology pillars. These efforts have a material and commercial component as the programs create a labor force capable of supporting and growing technologies.

While many technology skilling programs focus on modernizing and reskilling an existing workforce, Dell's Student Tech Crew program is a fascinating example that targets potential workers even earlier. Through this program, Dell offers high school students a chance to build their technological skills by serving as their school's technology support, giving them hands-on repair experience.[20] Not only does the program lead to Dell Tech certifications, but the tools that students work with are the same as the tools an enterprise IT group would use.[21] This connection gives students a direct line from their educational path into the workforce. The result goes beyond digital inclusion, allowing students to enter the technology job market at graduation or gain options for future technology study.[22]

In each example, the thread from the business to the impact and back again is easy to find. Each company leads these efforts with a consideration of its core expertise and stakeholders to drive impact. Arguably, these companies make an impact in the unique way they can, revealing the intersection between ESG and more philanthropic endeavors. Many of these programs also have a thread from the global perspective to the local, creating stakeholder inspiration through a material approach. As the company works through its improvements and innovations and turns the intellectual capital towards philanthropy, stakeholders may be inspired, affording a reputational boost. Inspiration can also come from recognizing the company's unique place in society and taking action with stakeholders and their needs.

Engaging downstream customers with impact

It's no secret that quality customer service is critical to running a successful business. A company has a direct opportunity to create value downstream for customers through product and service improvement and innovation, which we covered in Chapter 7. Pulling at the thread of the company's intellectual capital and purpose a little more will reveal opportunities to engage customers on impact.

In 2019, the Netherlands conducted a study on loneliness and found that around 26 percent of people sometimes feel lonely, but that number jumps to 33 percent when looking at people over the age of 75.[23] The country's Ministry of Health, Welfare, and Sport created a "Together against Loneliness" campaign focused on these older adults to address this challenge. Jumbo, a Dutch supermarket chain that attempts to create an enjoyable shopping experience,[24] decided to take action. Frontline workers noticed that elderly patrons coming in to shop also enjoyed chatting with employees and taking the time to do so. They escalated the observation to the head office, which recognized the impact opportunity and created a new program.[25] In 2019, Jumbo piloted a program called "kletskassa," which means "chat checkout,"[26] starting a slower checkout lane to service elderly patrons wanting to spend time talking with someone. By 2021, the head office supplemented the program with a field-worker handbook to provide guidance and then expanded the program to 200 stores.[27] The program continues to grow and now includes a "chat corner" for people who want to chat with others in their community while enjoying a cup of coffee.[28]

Jumbo recognizes its stores are the heart of the community and that local impact can come from them.[29] The idea of a company taking on a Social issue at the intersection of its stakeholders and around the core of its business function is wildly inspirational. That inspiration is certainly hard to measure, as are many Social efforts, but Jumbo connects customer satisfaction data to its programs to track and forecast progress.[30] Kletskassa is no simple customer service program with philanthropy and impact layered on. By recognizing the company's unique place in the community and aligning with a known need around a stakeholder group, Jumbo can make a difference with individual shoppers and the broader community.

There's an interesting intersection between examples like this and ESG, which runs through impact and stakeholders. A company may lead with a philanthropic project that has an impact through a connection to its purpose. As a company does this independently and stakeholder preferences align positively, the program or project work may become a material concern for other companies in the industry, leading them to follow suit while scaling up the impact. After all, inspiration for customer stakeholders may translate to a brewing reputational risk for a competitor who isn't leading with impact. Of course, in certain jurisdictions, an adverse reaction from stakeholders may have the opposite effect, leaving the reputational risk sitting with the company that attempted a change.

Intention through public benefit corporations and B Corps

Questions about a company's philanthropic or volunteering activities may arise from shareholders or those watching the company's financials closely. After all, the Friedman doctrine remains well entrenched in business culture and the markets. Yet, philanthropy and volunteerism can lead to both inspiration and value when considering materiality and when they are in the interest of stakeholder growth or care.

As stakeholder capitalism took hold, an option to address this concern at the center of clear intent presented itself. Starting in 2010, the state of Maryland in the USA, and then expanding to a limited amount of jurisdictions including other US states,[31] Italy,[32] Columbia,[33] and British Columbia, Canada,[34] designated that for-profit companies can be a public benefit or benefit corporation. This designation in these jurisdictions allows a for-profit company to engage in value across stakeholders, not just in the sole focus of financial growth. Incorporating as a for-profit public benefit company may offer a path to address long-term ESG issues at the intersection with impact with fewer questions and less scrutiny around investments in short-term projects, as the company's intention and purpose are clear.

Since 2007, companies have had a separate yet related option to obtain certification around a focus on Environmental and Social goals through the B Corp certification process. This process, run by B Labs, involves a rigorous assessment of the company's impact, a risk review, and even re-evaluation as business situations evolve and change.[35] An interesting requirement is legally recognizing that the company is accountable to stakeholders, not just share-holders.[36] B Labs operates fairly transparently with company scores on a scale of 200, with a score of 80 to become certified. The scores are openly available for all 7,000 certified companies online.[37]

Becoming a benefit corporation or a certified B Corp is not necessarily easy and doesn't speak to a company's understanding or handling of its material issues, but it does refocus attention to stakeholders. While a benefit corporation represents the company's incorporation and B Corp is a certifi-cation, some companies will pursue both. Either vehicle will signal to your stakeholders that you consider impact, a broader set of stakeholders, and that you are not obligated to maximize shareholder returns solely.

EXAMPLE: TONY'S CHOCOLONELY

One Dutch B Corp-certified company is Tony's Chocolonely, whose mission is to free the chocolate supply chain from exploitation.[38] The company has been B Corp certified since 2013 and has two special callouts from its B Lab certification. First, Tony's Chocolonely is mission-locked with a business model designed for a specific outcome for a stakeholder group.[39] Second, B Lab also lists Supply Chain Poverty Alleviation as its particular focus under the Community category of its scoring.[40]

The company is on a journey in this effort across its cocoa suppliers, which are 100 percent cooperative-based.[41] In 2019, it launched Tony's Open Chain, which brings together various supporters and participants to focus on equity and equality in the cocoa supply chain. The initiative calls out five integrated, or interconnected, parts to focus on to solve this specific challenge, including traceable beans, a premium to enable farmers to earn a living wage, creating new opportunities for farmers in new markets, engagement in five-year commitments with cooperatives, and supporting farmers' collaborative efforts to improve yield.[42]

Some questioned this purpose after the company published its 2020–2021 annual report as it noted that instances of child labor in the supply chain had increased to 1,701.[43] A spokesperson commented that Tony's is transparent in its reporting and that these numbers, largely due to the addition of two new cooperatives, show the company takes responsibility for the issue, pointing to the long-term reductions in child labor issues.[44] It's worth recalling that a company can continually improve its value chain if engaged to drive material improvements and impact. Divestment from suppliers puts them outside the company's ecosystem, which means that the company and its program cannot influence them. Logically, a company cannot meet its stakeholder goals with divestment, so it must remain engaged.

Tony's Chocolonely is an example of a company working across its value chain to drive impact through improvement, engagement, and cooperation. Yet, companies don't have to be a certified B Corp to manage these types of impact issues. Ultimately, deciding to pursue any impact-related project is a matter of Governance between the board of directors and the management team. As we've seen, there can be unique opportunities to impact at the intersection of material ESG business issues and create positive impact returns to the company. Still, the opportunity to drive impact across a value chain is worthy because it can scale that impact across a broad ecosystem if the company remains engaged. To embark on this path requires new scaled engagement models, which coincidentally align with the mechanisms for ESG influence.

Influence, impact, and value chain improvement

As it turns out, stakeholders connect accountability across industries, between companies, with their upstream suppliers, and the downstream use of their products and services. The logic is pretty straightforward, as a company cannot function without its value chain. Therefore, stakeholders ascribe the activities in that value chain to the company or, in the case of investments and lending, the financial services firm providing capital. For example, fast fashion is known for low wages and overtime issues across suppliers in the garment industry.[45] Those Social issues translate to the final fashion brand as safety, forced labor, and other human rights concerns grow.[46] The culmination of value chain risk is the company's reputational risk. If a financial services firm invests in this company, the way stakeholders perceive this investment may be also affected.

These connections can similarly surface in how ESG and sustainability standards organizations construct reporting frameworks. For example, the GHG Protocol aligns accountability between a company and its suppliers through Scope 3 carbon accounting. As a result, companies contact their suppliers to get their upstream Environmental data for their reporting. Proxy proposals also connect and bring shared accountability through activities like racial equity audits within a company's supply chain to uncover forced labor or other Social issues, such as equity.

Stakeholders, including customers, employees, and investors, will use information about a company's value chain, part of its intangible IP, to form opinions or make decisions about the company, translating into reputational risks and opportunities. The opportunity for a company is to engage in impact through its influence across its value chain. This critical path combines positive change and managing an ESG risk.

This intersection may cause companies to stumble as the mashing of values and value is complex and runs through many interconnected relationships across the value chain. Still, those companies not engaged in internal operational improvements or externally impacting their externalities will find it difficult to foster change from their upstream suppliers as they will have few examples to lead with.

ESG and impact are similar to what we're told before takeoff on an airplane, "In case of cabin pressure loss, put your mask on before helping others." In other words, companies must first work towards their issues at the intersection of their unique expertise and ESG to build high-quality, resilient projects that improve, innovate, or drive impact. Reporting metrics will not be enough to garner action beyond convincing suppliers to share similar disclosures. Only after a company can prove or at least start the journey to impact can it inspire others in its value chain to do the same, which is a powerful way to use influence. Effectively wielding two unique intangibles—namely established ESG credentials and a positive reputation—into impact means that companies must move past disclosures and into action.

Data, divestment, and engagement

The Procurement team plays a critical role in influencing impact across the value chain, as this team has the existing relationships and expertise needed as financial contracts, renewals, and RFPs integrate more ESG and impact criteria. In Chapters 3 and 4, we covered some ways that Procurement teams can interact with the supply chain to gather data or understand what their suppliers are doing around Environmental and Social efforts. The management team must be clear in its guidance to the Procurement team as many ESG and impact-related activities spin up, depending on the company's goals. For example, does the management team lead with risk mitigation, impact, or a bit of both? As a result, Procurement may need to ramp up quickly on the differences and nuance between ESG and impact. From there, the team and its leadership can build a vision for strategy supplier execution. For instance, Procurement may start with collecting basic supplier ESG metrics and supplement the data with risk information and context through dialogue and analysis with suppliers. From there, the team may circle internally, perhaps in consultation with a Chief Sustainability Officer and their team, to consider how well the supplier aligns with the company's goals and then examine how it can support the suppliers' impact or risk mitigation strategy through the work the company has gone through or is engaged in.

The Procurement team will play a critical role in the ESG and impact approach across the value chain. While this section covers impact, a company can employ similar strategies to meet supplier goals around ESG risk mitigation and creating opportunities. There are a few broad strategies that a Procurement team can use in its efforts and considerations for each:

- Data collection: This is the starting point for assessing and understanding your supplier's position. It includes metrics and contextual impact information around the supplier's strategy, the ability to execute, and its expertise. Here, Procurement can baseline and benchmark its suppliers but must recognize that data alone with action cannot drive influence on impact.

- Divestment: Dropping the supplier due to underperforming impact information or action.

- Engagement: Engaging the supplier on impact, mentoring the supplier, connecting the supplier to broader ecosystems and financing, and sharing best practices.

Some Procurement teams may stop at data collection until their company can create a more refined strategy or choose never to take additional action with suppliers if impact isn't a priority and the focus is on reporting and compliance. Other Procurement teams will baseline suppliers to understand their position and sort their suppliers into material and non-material.

Categorizing suppliers in this manner can uncover where the company can make the most significant impact. Regardless of the intention across data collection, ESG, or impact, the company may move into divestment or engagement strategies to drive the desired change.

As we've seen repeatedly, divestment from a supplier works the same way as it does with financial services. Once the company drops a supplier, there is no opportunity to influence its position. This strategy is best employed as a last resort for the company because it focuses solely on improving the company's stance, not lifting the value chain. Suppose a company stops working with a supplier. In that case, it has put no effort into that supplier's transformation, allowing it to continue operating, perhaps against the intent of the company's stated impact goals, while improving metrics only. A company that repeatedly punishes suppliers through divestment to game its metrics may earn a poor reputation, making divestment a potential Governance risk. In addition, without the company's influence at work, the supplier's transition risk may compound over time, and potentially harmful behaviors will perpetuate and grow. Even if the supplier makes a positive adjustment, the company that walked away didn't contribute to the impact.

On the other hand, there may be valid reasons to divest from a supplier around impact. First, if the supplier outright refuses to engage or actively fights against improvements and the company's purpose, the company may have little choice but to walk away due to purpose misalignment. The second reason is that, as with transition risk, time can affect a material issue. The supplier's inability to change or drive impact may represent a dynamic material risk to the company, increasing its costs or subjecting it to reputational risk. These movements are tricky, however. Suppose a company makes a sustainable component change in its product, and its existing suppliers must shift to meet new demand and retire legacy materials. The company has a choice. It can attempt supplier engagement to drive positive change or divest and pick up new suppliers. Engagement shows that the company understands the way in which it can make an impact.

While a company's Procurement team has influence over its supply chain, the Sales team sits along the receiving end of these issues from the company's business customers. Sales has a unique opportunity to partner with the Procurement team to expand its understanding of these customers' new requirements. Procurement can enable Sales to be responsive to ESG and impact-related requests, understand the company's positioning and differentiators, and support customer's efforts. In effect, this Procurement and Sales connection represents a way to capture a new ESG opportunity and revenue and must not be overlooked.

Engaging at scale through industry collaboration

For any engagement strategy, communication and adaptability are key. The company must communicate its impact positioning, goals, metrics, the intention behind pursuing it, and what it hopes to achieve. For example, an 80 percent carbon reduction in Scope 3 emissions is a goal with metrics aligned. The intention behind an impact effort might be to support suppliers to address their transition risk, allowing them to stay competitive while building resilience. The messaging helps frame the context for a supplier that may not have expertise in this area and needs help understanding the motivations behind these new goals.

While companies may build new programs, financing vehicles, and mentoring strategies for suppliers, the plan must be flexible enough to support those who need it, recognize that there are likely no quick wins, and understand that larger suppliers run similar programs and can address impact how they see fit. Focusing on suppliers needing help drives impact, as their lack of expertise can perpetuate inertia and misunderstanding, delaying change. For example, suppose the company examines its supply chain and finds that many suppliers lack expertise in determined targeted impact areas. In that case, it may engage suppliers directly through dedicated impact specialists in the Procurement team alongside digital tools and a programmatic approach. The company that prefers engagement will need to invest in taking this approach.

As we saw with interconnected risks in the previous chapter, collaboration can be a powerful tool to address crises and ESG issues at scale. Collaboration works similarly across impact, as engagement is a preferred option to empower impact across existing suppliers and ecosystems, especially if the company understands these topics well and the Procurement team can support solutions for its suppliers, such as financing, education, or mentoring. However, as with ESG and philanthropy, this isn't a win-win scenario, as the company will need to invest time and money in others. Again, this concern may surface with shareholders seeking only financial returns since they may not want the company to invest its resources in this manner as impact appears more charitable than material. The company can build on a defensible foundation if it mainstreams ESG, approaches impact through its expertise, and collaborates within its industry openly for supplier assistance and support. An open approach is essential because it can help allay fears of antitrust concerns. These actions create a shared defense by aligning with the long-term value of resilient suppliers in an industry through a material consideration, rather than focusing on the myopic view of short-term, transient costs and a purely charitable approach. In effect, impact can become material through a long-term position.

In a shared supply chain, the supplier may become overwhelmed by the range of bespoke and siloed impact approaches from its customers' Procurement teams. Every company's goals and requirements will vary, potentially requiring the supplier to report the same or different information into the same or different digital tooling. Smaller suppliers cannot deal with the volume and variability of these requests and may lack a way to respond at all, let alone efficiently. Industry players may find that organized collaboration across the shared supply chain in a consortium or collective engagement effort may help overcome this challenge. For example, Tony's Open Chain attempts to pull players in the cocoa industry together in this unified manner. This approach augments the industry's power while distributing the costs and resources across multiple participants to match the breadth and complexity of the supply chain.

In 2021, Mars, Pepsi, McCormick, and the consulting firm Guidehouse announced a new supplier-focused consortium named Supplier Leadership on Climate Transition (Supplier LoCT) to bring educational resources to suppliers to help empower suppliers to launch their own science-based targets and action plans.[47] This consortium has grown to include a path to impact through disclosures and abatement, with more brands joining, such as Coca-Cola, Estée Lauder, Nestlé, and others. The resources include a climate school with expert instructors, help-desk support, networking opportunities, and certificates and badges to show progress.[48] In the previous chapter, we co-opted SDG17, Partnership for the Goals, to help address systemic ESG issues. Here, it returns to its original intention to show how companies can band together for impact in a collaborative manner. As of April 2023, there are now over 600 suppliers participating in the Supplier LoCT program.[49]

With a shared engagement model, the industry can lead suppliers to understand ESG risks and opportunities through impact first, the inverse way proposed throughout this book. Suppliers can learn about impact projects through education and enablement, allowing for straightforward discussions with each company about its ESG risk and new opportunities. An exercise in scaling impact through industry collaboration is a material gain for each company and its suppliers.

Notes

1 United Nations (1999). Secretary-General proposes global compact on human rights, labour, environment, in address to World Economic Forum in Davos. UN Press. United Nations Meetings Coverage and Press Releases. press.un.org/en/1999/19990201.sgsm6881.html (archived at https://perma.cc/HNM9-NX6S).

2 Turner, B. (2023). Catastrophic climate "doom loops" could start in just 15 years, new study warns. Live Science. www.livescience.com/planet-earth/climate-change/catastrophic-climate-doom-loops-could-start-in-just-15-years-new-study-warns (archived at https://perma.cc/382Y-VXBS).

3 Ipsos (2023). Pride month 2023: 9% of adults identify as LGBT+. Ipsos. www.ipsos.com/en-us/pride-month-2023-9-adults-identify-lgbt (archived at https://perma.cc/6B8M-VYPF).

4 World Health Organization (2023). Disability. World Health Organization. www.who.int/en/news-room/fact-sheets/detail/disability-and-health (archived at https://perma.cc/M8NZ-NN83).

5 Capgemini Research Institute (2020). *How sustainability is fundamentally changing consumer preferences*. Capgemini, p. 7. www.capgemini.com/wp-content/uploads/2021/02/20-06_9880_Sustainability-in-CPR_Final_Web-1-2.pdf (archived at https://perma.cc/97Y8-UKBF).

6 Buonfantino, G. (2022). Data shows shoppers prioritizing sustainability and values. Google Cloud Blog. cloud.google.com/blog/topics/consumer-packaged-goods/data-shows-shoppers-prioritizing-sustainability-and-values (archived at https://perma.cc/SHB3-VNFD).

7 Human Dignity Trust (2023). Malaysia. Human Dignity Trust. www.humandignitytrust.org/country-profile/malaysia/ (archived at https://perma.cc/7AJC-AKMQ).

8 Reuters (2023). Rainbow Swatch watches confiscated in Malaysia-company. Reuters, May 24. www.reuters.com/world/asia-pacific/rainbow-swatch-watches-confiscated-malaysia-company-2023-05-24/ (archived at https://perma.cc/JAD4-DQQS).

9 Reuters (2023). Swiss watchmaker Swatch sues Malaysia for seizure of Pride watches. NBC News. www.nbcnews.com/nbc-out/out-news/swiss-watchmaker-swatch-sues-malaysia-seizure-pride-watches-rcna94649 (archived at https://perma.cc/KDE9-57A9).

10 Warby Parker (2019). The whole story begins with you. Warby Parker. www. warbyparker.com/buy-a-pair-give-a-pair (archived at https://perma.cc/ Y44M-4DL6).

11 Warby Parker (2019). The whole story begins with you. Warby Parker. www. warbyparker.com/buy-a-pair-give-a-pair (archived at https://perma.cc/ Y44M-4DL6).

12 Novo Nordisk Global (n.d.). Social. Novo Nordisk. www.novonordisk.com/ sustainable-business/esg-portal/social.html (archived at https://perma.cc/ NWV8-5XL2).

13 Novo Nordisk (n.d.). Our heritage: Driving change. Novo Nordisk USA. www.novonordisk-us.com/about/our-heritage.html (archived at https://perma. cc/5US8-5QVT).

14 Novo Nordisk Foundation (n.d.a). List of grant recipients. Novo Nordisk Fonden. novonordiskfonden.dk/en/grant-recipient/ (archived at https://perma. cc/NQ2L-Q8FL).

15 Novo Nordisk Foundation (n.d.b). What are grants? Novo Nordisk Fonden. novonordiskfonden.dk/en/how-we-work/what-are-grants/ (archived at https:// perma.cc/2SCZ-4Z3E).

16 Novo Nordisk Foundation (2022). *Strategy*. Novo Nordisk Fonden, p. 2. novonordiskfonden.dk/app/uploads/Novo-Nordisk-Foundation-Strategy-EN.pdf (archived at https://perma.cc/LJ33-HHQV).

17 SAP (n.d.). Bringing our best to the world. SAP Global Sabbatical. www.sap. com/dmc/exp/2017_03_46558/enUS/ (archived at https://perma.cc/8BNB-GDAW).

18 SAP (2023). *SAP CSR Annual eBook 2022*. Issuu, p. 13. issuu.com/ sapleadingwithpurpose/docs/sap_2023_ebook (archived at https://perma. cc/49EX-E7Q6).

19 SAP (n.d.). Bringing our best to the world. SAP Social Sabbatical. www.sap. com/dmc/exp/2017_03_46558/enUS/ (archived at https://perma.cc/8BNB-GDAW[).

20 Dellesline III, N. (2022). Students get hands-on learning with Dell's Student TechCrew. ZDNET. www.zdnet.com/education/computers-tech/students-get-hands-on-learning-dell-student-tech-crew/ (archived at https://perma.cc/ M9CS-695G).

21 Dellesline III, N. (2022). Students get hands-on learning with Dell's Student TechCrew. ZDNET. www.zdnet.com/education/computers-tech/students-get-hands-on-learning-dell-student-tech-crew/ (archived at https://perma.cc/ M9CS-695G).

22 Dell Technologies (2022). Dell Student TechCrew expands ten-fold, equipping the next generation with the digital skills needed in a rapidly transforming world. Dell. www.dell.com/en-us/dt/corporate/newsroom/announcements/detailpage.press-releases~usa~2022~09~09122022-dell-student-techcrew-expands-ten-fold-arming-the-next-generation-with-digital-skills-needed-in-a-rapidly-transforming-world.htm (archived at https://perma.cc/Y5ZB-AQU4).

23 Statistics Netherlands. (2020). Nearly 1 in 10 Dutch people frequently lonely in 2019. Statistics Netherlands. www.cbs.nl/en-gb/news/2020/13/nearly-1-in-10-dutch-people-frequently-lonely-in-2019 (archived at https://perma.cc/EFC6-GTV3).

24 Jumbo Supermarkten (n.d.a). De missie van Jumbo. Jumbo Supermarkten. https://web.archive.org/web/20230129001600/https:/www.jumbo.com/service/het-bedrijf-jumbo/missie (archived at https://perma.cc/UUS9-QKLW).

25 Jumbo Supermarkten (n.d.b). Onze winkels zijn meer dan alleen een plek om boodschappen te doen. Jumbo Supermarkten. www.eentegeneenzaamheid.nl/deelnemer/onze-winkels-zijn-meer-dan-alleen-een-plek-om-boodschappen-te-doen/ (archived at https://perma.cc/5LDL-69CG).

26 Massey, J. (2023). Grocery store introduces "slow checkout lane" for people who enjoy talking in line. UNILAD. www.unilad.com/news/slow-checkout-lane-netherlands-supermarket-205944-20230109 (archived at https://perma.cc/M9RG-8FJK).

27 Jumbo Supermarkten (n.d.b). Onze winkels zijn meer dan alleen een plek om boodschappen te doen. Jumbo Supermarkten. www.eentegeneenzaamheid.nl/deelnemer/onze-winkels-zijn-meer-dan-alleen-een-plek-om-boodschappen-te-doen/ (archived at https://perma.cc/5LDL-69CG).

28 Jumbo Supermarkten (n.d.b). Onze winkels zijn meer dan alleen een plek om boodschappen te doen. Jumbo Supermarkten. www.eentegeneenzaamheid.nl/deelnemer/onze-winkels-zijn-meer-dan-alleen-een-plek-om-boodschappen-te-doen/ (archived at https://perma.cc/5LDL-69CG).

29 Jumbo Supermarkten (n.d.c). Lokale betrokkenheid. Jumborapportage. www.jumborapportage.com/Aandachtspunt_lokaal-betrokken (archived at https://perma.cc/BA5D-3SGE).

30 Jumbo Supermarkten (n.d.c). Lokale betrokkenheid. Jumborapportage. www.jumborapportage.com/in-cijfers/lokale-betrokkenheid (archived at https://perma.cc/6AMT-VME9).

31 UpCounsel (n.d.). B Corp states: Everything you need to know. UpCounsel. www.upcounsel.com/b-corp-states (archived at https://perma.cc/F23D-G4ZE).

32 Valsan, R. (2017). The legacy of B Lab: Italy's Società Benefit. The ECCLblog. www.ecclblog.law.ed.ac.uk/2017/03/31/the-legacy-of-b-lab-italys-societa-benefit/ (archived at https://perma.cc/JHT3-THUG).

33 The Columbian Congress (2018). LEY 1901 DE 2018. SUIN-juriscol. www. suin-juriscol.gov.co/viewDocument.asp?ruta=Leyes/30035321 (archived at https://perma.cc/2JX4-WHJK).

34 Gillis, M. and Siracusa, D. (2020). Benefit Companies: New British Columbia corporate form combines profit and public purpose. McCarthy Tétrault. www. mccarthy.ca/en/insights/articles/benefit-companies-new-british-columbia-corporate-form-combines-profit-and-public-purpose (archived at https:// perma.cc/3RTB-CELF).

35 B Corporation (n.d.a). B Corp Certification demonstrates a company's entire social and environmental impact. B Corporation. www.bcorporation.net/en-us/ certification/ (archived at https://perma.cc/M9DX-Z6AS).

36 B Corporation (n.d.a). B Corp Certification demonstrates a company's entire social and environmental impact. B Corporation. www.bcorporation.net/en-us/ certification/ (archived at https://perma.cc/M9DX-Z6AS).

37 B Corporation (n.d.b). Find a B Corp. B Corporation. www.bcorporation.net/ en-us/find-a-b-corp/ (archived at https://perma.cc/YRM6-5H9T).

38 Tony's Chocolonely (n.d.). Our mission. Tony's Chocolonely. tonyschocolonely. com/us/en/our-mission (archived at https://perma.cc/8GRC-6NAS).

39 B Corporation (n.d.c). Tony's Chocolonely. B Corporation. www.bcorporation. net/en-us/find-a-b-corp/company/tonys-chocolonely/ (archived at https:// perma.cc/Q87Q-CKTB).

40 B Corporation (n.d.c). Tony's Chocolonely. B Corporation. www.bcorporation. net/en-us/find-a-b-corp/company/tonys-chocolonely/ (archived at https:// perma.cc/Q87Q-CKTB).

41 Tony's Chocolonely (2022a). *Disclosure Materials*. p. 1. s3.amazonaws.com/ blab-impact-published-production/9oVKMJhaC0t6s61OO49b3H7jORDgzkDE (archived at https://perma.cc/3258-2H4T).

42 Tony's Open Chain (n.d.). 5 Sourcing Principles. Tony's Open Chain. www. tonysopenchain.com/sourcing-principles/#traceable-beans (archived at https:// perma.cc/KU8M-LL48).

43 Tony's Chocolonely (2022b). *Report*. Tony's Chocolonely, p. 200. tonyschocolonely.com/storage/configurations/tonyschocolonelycom.app/files/ jaarfairslag/2020-2021/jfs_2021_en_binw_13.pdf (archived at https://perma. cc/XT8J-69TL).

44 Green, W. (2022). Tony's Chocolonely admits to 1,700 cases of supply chain child labour. *Supply Management*. www.cips.org/supply-management/news/ 2022/february/tonys-chocolonely-admits-to-1700-cases-of-supply-chain-child-labour/ (archived at https://perma.cc/UV23-BJWF).

45 Rosalez, R. (2023). The exploitation of garment workers: Threading the needle on fast fashion. U.S. Department of Labor blog. blog.dol.gov/2023/03/21/ the-exploitation-of-garment-workers-threading-the-needle-on-fast-fashion (archived at https://perma.cc/G4N7-GFDQ).

46 Goodman, P.S., Wang, V., and Paton, E. (2021). Global brands find it hard to untangle themselves from Xinjiang cotton. *The New York Times*, April 6. www.nytimes.com/2021/04/06/business/xinjiang-china-cotton-brands.html (archived at https://perma.cc/J738-UP9A).

47 Mars (2021). Mars launches new coalition to mobilize suppliers & accelerate climate action. Mars. www.mars.com/news-and-stories/press-releases/mars-launches-new-coalition-to-accelerate-climate-change (archived at https://perma.cc/U8MG-DFV8).

48 Supplier LoCT (n.d.). Supplier LoCT. Supplier LOCT. supplierloct.com/ (archived at https://perma.cc/44DK-KSAY).

49 Mehta, S. (2023). It will take teams of rivals to save the planet. Fast Company. www.fastcompany.com/90880066/it-will-take-teams-of-rivals-to-save-the-planet (archived at https://perma.cc/9WU4-6F6Z).

12

The Future of ESG

Looking into the future of any topic is a challenge, yet ESG fundamentally focuses on the long term, so it should be simple. If you skipped ahead to the end of the book, however, nothing with ESG is simple.

The short period that ESG has been an acronym and the confusing narratives surrounding it compounds the difficulty in making accurate predictions, especially in a world of increasing intangible value, globalization, and interconnected crises. For example, in the early 2000s, could any business leader have anticipated that the world would shut down for a global pandemic, throwing entire industries, the nature of modern work, and supply chains into disarray? With increasing extreme weather events perpetually pummeling the planet and its people, the next global crisis is already here, with unknown business disruption close behind.

The pressure to manage non-financial ESG and Technology factors is not letting up, nor are the impacts from outside the company slowing down. Now that ESG has become a mainstream investment strategy worldwide, moving capital towards ESG risk mitigation and new opportunities for improvement and innovation, companies must be ready. To be prepared, a company must mainstream ESG into its long-term business strategy, but dealing with material ESG issues is something that companies should already be doing. Still, if ESG were in broad practice and mainstreamed, there wouldn't be much debate, and management teams would continue with business as usual. The fact that it is widely discussed hints at its value, but companies still struggle to define it consistently, which is understandable.

ESG has had multiple iterations. It began as a perspective for financial services to drive capital into investments, with many firms pulling the lever of risk further down to drive impact along the pillars. Along the way, it became matched to a company's CSR efforts and reporting, which accelerated an alignment to information, data, and metrics. The idea of ESG materiality and long-term value was lost for some and remained for others. As Technology advanced, so has the expectation from financial services firms for quality and comparable data. The push for transparent and consistent data has manifested in emerging standards and regulations. And so, ESG has evolved again to align with the need for financial services to have consistent and transparent investor-useful information, focusing on the markets. Unfortunately, this latest iteration appears to be over-focused on the data aspect of ESG because companies may miss connections to improvements and innovations in the pursuit of uncovering data from existing systems and processes. Yet, despite all of the changes, consistency cannot be found, so the term possesses multiple catch-all meanings.

If there are two things the future of ESG must have, they are a clear definition of ESG and action that follows the data. The definition needs to afford flexibility to account for the role of impact over time. Perhaps a new definition of ESG might incorporate double and dynamic materiality:

ESG: The material Environmental, Social, and Governance issues that impact a company today and drive towards long-term resilience and sustainable growth, including the systemic issues that the company can influence, which may return material impact over time.

This definition accounts for the nuance between ESG and impact. While it isn't in use today, it could inform the perspective of management teams along both paths, providing defensibility along material and non-material efforts. Companies, after all, should be able to pursue both but must understand the differences and how to communicate each to stakeholders. Without this baseline, companies will struggle to progress in the way that stakeholders want while protecting the business, the world, and its people. Companies must address material issues to improve and innovate and engage their stakeholders, including financial markets and governments, to create resilience and impact our world's most challenging problems.

However, to embark on this path, the ownership of ESG needs to move from the financial markets to companies because that is where much of the work happens.

Companies need to own ESG to fulfill its purpose

One of the biggest challenges with ESG is that it relies on companies to understand and integrate it into the overall company strategy, but the custodians of ESG, those in financial services, remain outside the company's walls. The language used around ESG derives from financial services and floats between the effect on the company and the company's impact on the world and never quite lands as cleanly as the definition just proposed. As a result, countless articles, podcasts, and social media posts start with ESG and meander aimlessly into impact, ignoring the ambiguity, uncertainty, and connections that exist, as if the author and audience only understand black-and-white binaries.

While socially responsible investing stretches back 200 years to investors who led with religious interpretations, values, and divestment strategies, the concept of ESG similarly started as a financial concept, but only in the early 2000s. ESG integrated critical material factors around the three pillars and focused on risks and opportunities to uncover long-term investment resilience. This mindset approach to value remains a compelling explainer to help financial firms analyze which companies understand the effect of ESG issues on them and, therefore, their business best.

This investing focus has led to much confusion as ESG's lack of consistent definitions have left a critical gap for companies to fill, further perpetuating the challenge. This inconsistency stems from the term being used to fit for purpose. Returning to *Who Cares Wins*, companies are expected to provide ESG and impact information to firms via investor relations, quickly whittling down a company's participation to metrics. Still, the paper does not mention educating boards or management teams on ESG outside of the fund managers and analysts at the financial firm.[1] This lack of education has proved to be a miss as years later, when the tipping points finally fell, some management teams emerged confused about what ESG is and isn't, what to do about it, and even where to start. In retrospect, it is as if ESG was a mechanism to uncover which companies were already doing ESG well without telling other management teams what it is. Ultimately, companies were never the target audience for ESG but were still the target for the outcomes.

As new crises emerge, the focus has only increased to serving investors better with data and information, and still not educating companies on mainstreaming ESG or addressing their critical risks and opportunities. As intangible value continues to grow, this refocus of ESG on disclosures and away from its core purpose is a perpetuating miss for companies. Unfortunately, the regulations and standards surrounding ESG are where companies see the next iteration of ESG. Some list materiality, but this is often an overlooked aside in the pursuit of the data. These reporting mechanisms focus on bringing investor-quality data around non-financial metrics to stakeholders and aligning that information with financial data through integrated reporting. Yet, required or voluntary datasets alone will not snap management teams into understanding the complexity and nuance of ESG or the unique ways a company can deliver value or drive impact. Gathering ESG data, which remains in the domain of individual contributors, surely will not help employees understand ESG or enable the company to leverage theirs and its purpose to help improve and innovate. Of course, companies must still comply with regulations, but leading ESG efforts with compliance and regulations will not deliver value; it only delivers data to ever-eager financial services firms, who themselves often struggle to make sense of it.

While financing ESG improvements and innovation is a critical function, and financial services firms need data to inform those decisions, the ownership and narrative of ESG must shift to companies if they are to progress material ESG and impact issues, especially at scale.

Unfortunately, ESG still has a way to go until the business world takes ownership of the acronym and moves past reporting into an agency to act. In the meantime, some individual companies will take ownership alone, and it will likely be those who have been on this journey for some time. If other companies solely focus on disclosures and don't mainstream ESG in parallel, they will find themselves at the mercy of reacting to trends rather than proactively being in control and ready, putting them at serious risk at least or at a competitive disadvantage at best. When those management teams wake up from the fog of solely measuring their ESG data for financial services firms and stakeholder communications, they will quickly realize that they've made little progress and stakeholders had expected them to take action towards outcomes all along.

It is time for businesses to take control of ESG, decide their material pursuits and where to drive impact, and communicate intent and progress back to the financial markets rather than trying to hit the moving targets of investors' ESG needs. If this sounds like an empowering statement, it is meant to be one, but let's go further. Companies must run their business, understand their material issues, work on selected purpose-driven impact initiatives, and learn to decline non-material data requests and stakeholder initiatives that are irrelevant or possibly distracting. If they do this well, they should be better positioned with a new intangible, an ESG mindset, to help deliver future value.

ESG moves from data to Technology

Many equate ESG to data, which is reasonable considering much of the world correlates ESG to ESG investing. In this context, data is helpful for investment risk and opportunity analysis, but there is much more a company can do with an ESG mindset, the data, and Technology.

As we covered in earlier chapters, Technology has a role to play with ESG through enablement across the pillars and as its own ESG risk and opportunity. Unfortunately, with so much confusion around the acronym and a lack of a global governing body that controls it, it seems unlikely the business world will adopt it as an official fourth pillar. Still, companies must remember to consider Technology's implementation, management, and application thoughtfully because ignoring Technology and its Governance creates risk. As we saw in Chapter 6, Technology-related scores are emerging, so there is brewing attention to this issue.

On the other hand, there is a future opportunity for ESG and impact, building on the data that companies publish. As regulations around ESG and impact emerge, again focused on comparable information for financial services, companies are mired in the push to disclose. Still, they may miss the opportunity to use that data collection effort to analyze the data and mainstream ESG across the business for their internal purposes, which is one area Technology can help. But this point is only a stop on the way to the real opportunity: to help manage ESG risk across value chains or drive systemic impact in preparation for future resilient business models.

The world is becoming more complex, and collaboration is needed to deal with pressing systemic and interconnected risks and crises. In the future, collaboration must move beyond current data-sharing methodologies across stakeholders and consortiums. To effectively collaborate at speed and drive insights and action at scale, companies need to securely break down data siloes across the value chain and share information between companies. Much of ESG sits in the data, but there is more to ESG than just data, and the difference comes through in the outcome and its interpretation, which will vary by stakeholders. In other words, an investor wants comparable data to make an investment or lending decision. A Procurement team may ask for value chain data for contract analysis and to report to the Chief Sustainability Officer. Regulators may ask for data to ensure the company delivers consistent and high-quality information to financial services firms and stakeholders. However, something new might happen if a company has an ESG mindset and receives value chain data and its context. If the company democratizes access to the data across key internal stakeholders and has mainstreamed ESG, it opens up the components that drive improvements and innovation at scale.

Even if a company did mainstream ESG and worked across its value chain to do the same, there is one considerable Governance risk in the way. Since ESG data represents core business data and the company's intellectual property, suppliers and their business customers are reluctant to move past calculated and aggregated ESG metrics, which is only partially helpful. For example, if a supplier shared too much of its logistical information around climate risk or forced labor analysis, it might reveal its IP. If too much of its IP is digitized, a cybersecurity risk may surface. This information could allow another business to create a similar model and displace the supplier. As a result, this information remains locked away, reducing collaboration.

While there are risks to oversharing proprietary company data, companies share opaque information already, as it is requested by financial services firms and across the value chain. Unfortunately, there is a Governance issue on the other end, with many financial services firms, companies, and ESG rating agencies attempting to own the value chain data due to its immense value, infinite reusability, and nonrivalry characteristics. Value chain players have little choice but to share ESG information and cast data ownership and control out since data sharing has become required to find financing and close new business. Complicating this concern is that the current methodologies to share ESG information are plentiful, proprietary, and painful, requiring responders to fill out an endless array of bespoke surveys depending on which system subscribers invest in and jurisdictions they operate in, each with individual nuance with little opportunity for automation or operationalization of the reporting. In the end, companies have well-founded fears for data sharing and are subject to complex systems that create pain around data collection.

Technology is already in the data collection mix, but it offers a new path forward to give control back to companies and streamline the process. Achieving these goals requires updated standards and regulations with global coordination. A flexible digital taxonomy based on broad ESG metrics that allow for material metrics and qualitative, nuanced descriptions would be a starting point. Taking this further by aligning to an open-source digital publishing standard, like an agreed-upon API format or XBRL, a digital business reporting format, could also help. Publishing companies could retain control of the information through digital watermarks or permission checks requiring unlocking the data, so only approved stakeholders could access it. This common digital taxonomy and the publishing capabilities would give companies direct ownership and control of the data, allowing them to automate its collection from business systems, saving them time in publishing to multiple formats.

The end state would be digital company feeds of ESG data and context closer to real-time across the value chain that could be supplemented by external datasets, allowing for more informed and complete decisions. Of course, to take advantage of this at scale would require all stakeholders in the value chain to have a consistent definition and to mainstream ESG. Overall, this path forward is a highly ambitious proposition that requires global coordination of regulators and Technology across a multi-year horizon and may be an unreasonable goal. Yet, if this doesn't happen, companies will continue reporting data for data's sake and releasing the value of their ESG data openly to others, which could introduce unintended risks.

Technology's impact on the future of ESG can go further into advanced analysis. To assist in understanding the mountain of value chain information that will result regardless if standards remain as-is or evolve, companies will need help as mainstreaming ESG is a circular effort that requires continual assessment and feedback. Business stakeholders may turn to existing technologies that are strong in processing quantitative data, like machine learning, to understand reported metrics. New technologies, like Generative AI, can play a role in understanding qualitative data and contextual nuance across descriptions of activities and progress. For example, financial services firms or companies can use Generative AI to summarize published supplier and investment information from CSR reports and news feeds, look for new insights and trends, and create unique, individualized reports for internal stakeholder groups looking to improve and innovate through engagement models with external stakeholders. There are even ways to combine machine learning models with Generative AI to leverage both capabilities through one interface. Through targeted summarization, stakeholders only get the material information for the decision or stakeholder need, not every irrelevant data point mined from the mountain of available materials.

As always, companies must layer on Governance principles to Technology's use and understand ESG across the company to use these potential new applications effectively. For example, any final AI design must afford enough understanding of these complex issues to give stakeholder groups a perspective beyond a single ESG pillar, even if the targeted audience is a climate scientist. Also, as companies and their value chain share more and more ESG data, the management team and IT must be the ethical custodians of its use to help alleviate fears from those sharing data. Otherwise, the company risks damaging trust and its business reputation.

The evolution of current ESG trends will determine its near future

Many of the trends covered in this book will continue for the foreseeable future, and new ones will most certainly emerge. Management teams must support the company to evaluate trends continually, consistently engage stakeholders, and review crises for materiality. For example, leading up to the Russian invasion of Ukraine, fears about fossil fuel prices in the UK and Europe were rampant.[2] Unfortunately, it was too late to make a hard pivot to renewables and prices increased after the invasion. Fossil fuel availability represented a geographical risk to these companies, and it wasn't until 2023 that the EU announced it would drive towards renewables in the next decade.[3] Looking at fossil fuels through this complex lens is an example of how management teams need to pivot to drive the adaptability and balance needed to weather disruption and anticipate challenges.

However, as found in Chapter 10, continual, complex, interconnected crises, especially war, can be challenging to predict and might push one of the pillars forward and refocus attention on ESG in new ways. The combined Social tipping points of 2020 and the resulting focus on DEI are also good examples. Even a singular crisis along any of the pillars, such as the fall of Silicon Valley Bank, can kickstart renewed ESG attention, regulations, and changes across industries. Each trend described next represents a reasonably linear path to an outcome. In reality, many movements will shape the future ESG of business in concert, obfuscating the final results.

The path of resistance leads to clarity

ESG is in trouble, as we saw with the controversies surrounding it in Chapter 9. However, between activists and conservative complaints, it is more likely the conservative backlash is the one that could end ESG entirely, or it could lead nowhere. The question is how far the battle will go.

While US state legislatures are examining their relationships with investment firms for what they can control—state contracts and pensions—they are escalating the talking points by placing a thumb on the scale of consumer sentiment in some cases and engaging in outright motions against companies. In March 2022, Florida Governor Ron DeSantis signed the "Parental Rights in Education" bill, which prevented teachers from instructing on gender identity from kindergarten to the third grade.[4] Disney's CEO at the time, Bob Chapek, came out against the bill after employee unrest and then re-evaluated the company's stance on political contributions.[5] This move sparked a back-and-forth fight between DeSantis and Disney, resulting in lawsuits from both sides. At its core, this appears to be a battle for conservative values on the side of DeSantis and a material Social and Governance issue for Disney.

Both sides have experienced losses. DeSantis attempted to take control of the special Reedy Creek district, which helps govern the land use and properties for Disney World in Orlando, Florida. The previous board voted to strip itself of its power the day before DeSantis's new district board was installed, except for basic road and infrastructure maintenance.[6] Meanwhile, Disney scrapped plans to relocate 2,000 employees from California to Florida, which would have added new facilities and taxpayers for the state at an estimated $1 billion.[7]

The anti-ESG talking points from US politicians are gaining global attention from worldwide financial services firms, companies, and politicians. In 2023, UK politician Nigel Farage, who at the time held no office, started to take on the financial system as banks closed down consumer accounts, including his, with the blame placed squarely at the feet of "wokeism."[8] The bank reportedly considered the commercial thresholds in place, but a source stated that having Farage as a client was at odds with being an inclusive organization.[9]

For ESG, a non-political concept, the artificially manufactured connection to politics is a dangerous trend that has caused some companies to back away from ESG entirely, ironically for Governance concerns, as new regulations and reputational risk emerge. Pursuing values, which have a complicated intersection with ESG, may put a target on the company's back resulting in boycotts, lost revenue, and more.

Still, there is a chance that more clarity will come out of the political pushback. The anti-ESG push allows financial services firms and companies to foster a common language around ESG, separate from values-based impact. Companies can still pursue both efforts, but differentiate. As in the previous chapter, the company that leads with an ESG mindset can better defend against pushback for impact projects. This clarity would enable stakeholders to align with companies in ways that make sense and provide defensibility for those that don't.

Companies must monitor this trend but remember that politicians have lifecycles. Some politicians might be long-lived, but many come and go with elections. Monitoring new generations and their shifting preferences can provide a more consistent guidepost for what's coming. After all, ESG builds resilience over the long term and therefore has a longer shelf life than a politician.

DEI offers lessons for the future

Even though many attribute the rise of ESG to Larry Fink's letters and the CEO Roundtable focus on stakeholders, it appears that perhaps the Social tipping points pushed ESG over. As a result of this connection, the timing between related efforts like DEI seems to be tied to ESG.

The period around the Social tipping points, from September 2019 through September 2020, saw job postings around DEI on Indeed.com increase 56.3 percent.[10] Unfortunately, this was a short-lived phenomenon. As economic pressures built through the summer of 2022 and the ESG push-back grew, DEI programs that were stood up, mainly in response to the social justice issues of 2020, began to decline disproportionately to the broader layoffs that were occurring at the time.[11] In Chapter 4, we covered how the attention to the crisis and not the material intersection with the company caused these programs to be transient.

DEI and ESG are on parallel tracks in this way. Attention for both rose around the same tipping points. Still, if companies don't take the opportunity to focus on the core and systemic issues at the intersection of their business and industry, they risk slipping backward. The attempt to build a long-term program around a crisis, not core challenges, is folly. Technology can provide us with an example of why this doesn't work. If a company is hacked via a vulnerability in its identity management system, such as a lack of multi-factor authentication, adding only that capability is unlikely to prevent the next attack. A company that takes a holistic cybersecurity approach to protect its material Technology portfolio and educate its people will be better placed.

Yet, as the Social tipping points fell and stakeholder focus grew, companies started DEI and ESG programs to address the one-off Social events and stakeholder pressures, ignoring the material intersection with the business. Both efforts now experience pushback in political circles and uncertain economic conditions. These pressures are a recipe for management teams to cull costly DEI and ESG programs.

DEI seems to be ahead of ESG in the pullback. This early retreat may be due to emerging ESG regulations, which the management team cannot ignore, and the confluence of ESG with climate-focused issues, which garner much public attention, but there could be another reason. While DEI and ESG have material implications, DEI directly connects to morality and ethics through systemic problems around diversity, walls that prevent equity, and systems that prevent inclusion. Companies that haven't led with materiality ESG concerns can barely defend against pursuing values, let alone create meaningful, long-term programs.

There are learnings between the similarities of successful DEI and ESG programs, which management teams can use to build future resilient programs:

- Act with intent. If the company must react to a crisis, address it, but explore the broader systemic implications and potential paths forward.

- Look to leaders with domain-specific expertise, but go further to integrate and mainstream that expertise across the business.

- Consider your entire universe of stakeholders, not just employees. Still, leverage employees and their sense of purpose to deliver meaningful work.

- Never lead long-term programmatic decisions with a crisis or transient trends, or with the metrics, but use them to inform the strategy.

- Manage expectations. Be consistent and communicate transparently with stakeholders, as not every purpose-filled project can be funded and pursued. Recognize that there will be trade-offs and determine what is acceptable and aligned with the company's purpose.

- Continuously operate within the legal boundaries of what is permissible.

- Learn from mistakes and grow. Don't be afraid to walk away from projects that aren't working, but don't use failure as an excuse to entirely shut down efforts.

Since DEI and ESG gained popular attention in parallel, declining DEI efforts may predict ESG's decline, but the compliance difference may keep ESG afloat. There is hope, however, because if ESG survives, DEI will likely return with more effective programs built on a more informed and material perspective.

Growing focus on Governance and accountability

The Environment and Social lead the acronym and the mindshare around ESG, even though the company cannot effectively execute ESG work without quality Governance. Companies scramble to prove their E and S efforts with quantitative and qualitative datasets and a good story, as both can represent competitive advantages. Governance, perhaps the least controversial of the three, is the one that may be the hardest to measure, toughest to see as a competitive advantage, and is also the one pillar that can take a company down.

Much of Governance and operating principles sit with the board of directors, meaning the influence sits with the people elected by shareholders to serve. A common complaint is that institutional investors often cast these votes on behalf of shareholders who invest in ETFs and other financial products, disaggregating the end investor from the voting process. The three largest asset managers worldwide, BlackRock, Vanguard, and State Street, have started experimenting in recent years with allowing individual shareholders to vote via their investment products.[12] Typically with proxy voting, the shareholder has three choices: vote directly, choose a voting policy to adhere to, or give voting control to the firm. To better support Governance, engaged shareholders opting to vote or pick a voting policy will now need to pay close attention to nominated candidates if they hope to elect new board members that will take a more active role around ESG issues.

While Governance is a set of operating principles around the company, real people with various expertise, experience, morality, and ethics must execute it. As accountability for selecting these leaders shifts from the financial services firm to individual shareholders in the coming years, there is a rich opportunity for shareholders to vote their preferences, but only if they are paying attention and engaged. In a 2020 review, Proxy Pulse reported that 92 percent of institutional investors vote their shares, but only 28 percent of retail (think individual) investors do the same.[13] As the status quo shifts and new voting methods open, the implications could range from accelerating transitions, focusing more on activist concerns, to addressing CEO pay issues and executive compensation models, but only if shareholders become more active.

Meanwhile, activists are adding new accountability pressures to the board and aren't sitting by patiently waiting for them to act. Two trends around board members are worth watching that could shape the influence of how Governance might develop in the future.

First, a well-executed and coordinated shareholder strategy, even with minority ownership, can move institutional investors and others to action. In 2021, an activist hedge fund, Engine No. 1, made headlines with its 0.02 percent ownership in Exxon, as it swayed the big institutional investors and pension funds to vote against the company's recommendation around three out of four board seats.[14] These were no simple activist candidates but qualified candidates with material energy industry experience. In its Vote Bulletin, BlackRock outlined that the three candidates that it supported from Engine No. 1's recommendations had expertise in energy, renewables, legislation, and the ability to bring fresh perspectives.[15] In this case, the alignment of activism and material expertise won out. How this will play out has yet to be seen as fossil fuels are one of the sectors hardest to abate, and material expertise can quickly give way to short-term thinking.

The second trend to watch is how activists influence board members directly and creatively. During the pandemic, Starbucks workers began exploring unionization. The reasons vary, including safety concerns, financial security, consistent working hours, fair treatment, and other benefits.[16] Starbucks CEO Howard Schulz believed that unions had no place at the company.[17] In early 2023, a judge stated that Starbucks had displayed "egregious misconduct" against some of the attempts of its stores to unionize.[18] Within a month of this ruling, union activists took a different tack and went after Starbucks board members in a coordinated campaign. The effort included a butter sculpture of Beth Ford, CEO of Land O'Lakes, sent to her; a LEGO Star Wars trailer plea posted online targeting Jørgen Vig Knudstorp, Executive Chairman at the Lego Group; and a brass band meant for Nike COO, Andrew Campion.[19] These efforts directly escalated the activists' issues to the board members through creativity to bring attention to an ESG issue with personal accountability at its core.

Activists now expect they can influence board members directly with their elections and through real-world and digital interactions, introducing new levels of accountability. The time of the passive board member may be coming to an end.

The Earth and its people as stakeholders

While public benefit corporations and B Corps were covered in the previous chapter, Patagonia has done something remarkable from a business perspective. It may have set an example for ambitious companies in the future, but it takes time and practice.

From its early days making mountain climbing pitons to the modern clothing company it has become, Patagonia has had a long history of environmental activism. Even before the pivot to clothing, the pitons it manufactured needed to be hammered into the rock, damaging it. The company replaced the piton design with aluminum chocks that climbers could use by hand in 1972 to lower the impact.[20] Over time, the company explored, studied, and witnessed environmental risks. In 2002, the company's founder, Yvon Chouinard, and the founder of Blue Ribbon Flies, Craig Mathews, created a new organization, 1% for the Planet, creating a path for other companies to take responsibility for their impact on the Earth.[21]

Patagonia and its founder continued to focus on the company's impact on the Environment. The company made a huge marketing splash with its efforts in a 2011 Black Friday ad proclaiming, "Don't Buy This Jacket." The campaign tackled consumerism head-on by educating customers on repairing their Patagonia clothing to extend its life.[22] The campaign was also financially successful, resulting in a 30 percent growth in sales by 2012.[23] That same year, Patagonia became California's first public benefit corporation and a certified B Corp.[24]

Patagonia has continued to evolve, with many impact decisions having a material intersection with the business. For example, in 2021, Patagonia announced it would stop adding non-removable corporate logos on its garments. It explained that the logo shortened the garment's lifespan, as an employee might leave the company or company names and logos change.[25] It later updated these Responsible Logo Guidelines to include flexibility for removable items, like lanyards, zipper pulls, and hem labels. Now, Patagonia even has a partner that can shave off embroidered logos, all to get the most use out of the garment as possible.[26] Over the years, Patagonia has put a lot of thoughtful work into its impact like this, too much to list here in a book about ESG. However, running its business has been tied to Environmental progress throughout its history.

As evidence of the company's commitment, Patagonia changed its mission in 2018 to "save our home planet."[27] In 2022, Patagonia built on decades of work to take this idea further. Chouinard worked with his family and a team of lawyers to create two new trusts to run the company while working to save the planet. The family transferred 2 percent of shares and all voting control to the Patagonia Purpose Trust to ensure the company continues to operate responsibly.[28] The other 98 percent of non-voting shares went to the Holdfast Collective, a non-profit that receives all profits and works towards combating climate change.[29] When the company's management changes like this, it sits squarely with Governance, yet observationally, this shift feels like the company's principles haven't changed because Patagonia has been at this for so long with consistency.

On the surface, this is an inspirational move towards a purpose. While aligned directly with impact on the world, there are also ESG intersections. This move shows that a company can evolve to break the chain of public or private ownership to pursue impact goals along its purpose. As we've seen throughout this book, there is a strong connection across purpose, impact, and ESG. In the case of Patagonia, it has long had a strong purpose, steeped in Environmental values and backed by mountains of education and work over decades. This consistent attention and execution allowed the values to lead a material transformation for the company, putting it on solid footing to kick off its next evolution.

Of course, Patagonia serves as a one-off example for future inspiration and perhaps a framework for other public benefit companies to consider. If a company can find ways to align ESG and values consistently in its business over time, it may be set up well for this kind of change.

Timing the end of ESG well

Many forces are conspiring to end the ESG acronym altogether. In talking with Chief Sustainability, Diversity, and Impact officers, there is a common refrain that they look forward to the day when their work integrates into the business. Some believe their job will go away, and others think they can continue as key advisors with domain expertise to the company. Activists want to end ESG so companies can focus on saving the world and its people. Yet, a counter-movement is growing as some conservative politicians seek to hasten its end before mainstreaming ESG can take root and systemic issues decline. Others believe ESG is nothing special and represents core business challenges that any responsible business leaders are already working on. However, ESG has a way to go before its usefulness runs out.

It matters more what companies do rather than what we call it, which seems a bit contradictory in a book meant to empower companies around the topic. Yet, ESG has immense value for a company, its management team, and stakeholders. The acronym provides a simple framework for considering material issues in pursuing long-term value, but companies haven't widely adopted ESG consistently. This challenge is apparent since the term has only been around for 20 years, and MBA interest started to peak around 2021.[30] The corporate world barely had time to integrate ESG-trained students into the business.

Companies stand to lose much if they back away from mainstreaming ESG and stop discussing it or the interconnected relationships between ESG issues. Many companies still don't understand this topic well enough and need help building effective programs to execute on. If ESG ends too early, those companies will never have the opportunity to transition responsibly and integrate ESG into their strategy, ultimately putting them at greater risk over the long term. Companies will lose the ability to address material issues or build defensibility across systemic pressures to deliver impact. The board and management teams may react hastily with poor execution to crises, as stakeholders saw arise from the Social tipping points and resulting transient DEI programs.

If ESG is poorly understood or incompletely mainstreamed, employees lose the ability to understand shifting stakeholder preferences that can inform the creation of new opportunities to capitalize on those changes. And, of course, there is no escaping the material impact of these issues on the company, putting it at a disadvantage. But perhaps the most damaging problem is the complex intersection of ESG with the world's most pressing challenges. Without this simple framework to understand why these issues matter to the company, collaboration may slow, shared learnings will be lost, and nothing will change, which is an unsustainable proposition for companies, the world, and its people.

Overall, ESG is a stop on the path to business resilience and sustainable growth. The companies that mainstream ESG and build new programs around their unique value proposition will find it easier to drive systemic change and align with concepts like double materiality. Companies have unique ways to save the world, but those paths lie through their intellectual capital and understanding of ESG issues. Through this ESG mindset, the company creates long-term resilience, allowing it to survive and potentially thrive long enough to see the world change and have the power to impact it however it chooses.

Notes

1   United Nations (2004). *Who Cares Wins*. p. ii. www.unepfi.org/fileadmin/
    events/2004/stocks/who_cares_wins_global_compact_2004.pdf (archived at
    https://perma.cc/3HPN-FHUW) .

2   Hume, N. and Wilson, T. (2021). UK and European gas prices rise on Russia-
    Ukraine concerns. *Financial Times*, December 14. www.ft.com/content/
    17b58434-be03-4cb8-b75a-456e49f3bc0b (archived at https://perma.cc/
    S2VG-NGXD).

3   Abnett, K. (2023). EU on pace to end Russian fossil fuel reliance within the
    decade. Global News. globalnews.ca/news/10045056/eu-russian-fossil-fuels/
    (archived at https://perma.cc/ECR4-S37C).

4   Diaz, J. (2022). Florida's governor signs controversial law opponents dubbed
    "Don't Say Gay". National Public Radio, March 28. www.npr.org/2022/03/
    28/1089221657/dont-say-gay-florida-desantis (archived at https://perma.cc/
    JP49-4FUX).

5   Atterbury, A. (2022). Disney pledges to stop Florida campaign donations over
    "Don't Say Gay" bill. Politico. www.politico.com/news/2022/03/11/disney-
    pledges-to-stop-florida-campaign-donations-dont-say-gay-00016705 (archived
    at https://perma.cc/2RRU-NH8L).

6   Swisher, S. (2023). Disney stripped power of board before DeSantis takeover,
    new board says. *Tampa Bay Times*, March 29. www.tampabay.com/news/
    florida-politics/2023/03/29/disney-desantis-board-reedy-creek-special-district/
    (archived at https://perma.cc/CS7H-586T).

7   Anderson, Z. (2023). Disney deals major blow to Florida, cancels $1 billion
    investment as DeSantis feud escalates. *USA Today*, May 18. www.usatoday.
    com/story/money/2023/05/18/desantis-disney-fight-dooms-florida-project/
    70233608007/ (archived at https://perma.cc/RGB8-SATD).

8   Pickard, J. and Morris, S. (2023). Nigel Farage, NatWest and the fight over
    "woke" capitalism. *Financial Times*, July 28. www.ft.com/content/f7c5300a-
    b92d-44dd-bc03-22cf4d840902 (archived at https://perma.cc/LN38-Y7CH).

9   Jack, S. and Thomas, D. (2023). Nigel Farage bank account shut for falling
    below wealth limit, source tells BBC. BBC News, July 4. www.bbc.com/news/
    business-66097039 (archived at https://perma.cc/U5ZW-N57C).

10 Kellogg Murray, J. (2022). Jobs in diversity, inclusion and belonging have risen
    123% since May—Here's how to get one. Indeed Career Guide. www.indeed.
    com/career-advice/finding-a-job/diversity-inclusion-and-belonging-jobs-rise
    (archived at https://perma.cc/6RLQ-LV8S).

11 Alfonseca, K. and Zahn, M. (2023). How corporate America is slashing DEI
    workers amid backlash to diversity programs. ABC News. abcnews.go.com/
    US/corporate-america-slashing-dei-workers-amid-backlash-diversity/story?
    id=100477952 (archived at https://perma.cc/FU3C-RKH3).

12 Andrew, T. (2022). State Street joins BlackRock and Vanguard in devolving proxy voting powers. ETF Stream. www.etfstream.com/articles/state-street-joins-blackrock-and-vanguard-in-devolving-proxy-voting-powers (archived at https://perma.cc/U4GY-UV3L).

13 Broadridge Investor Communication Solutions and PricewaterhouseCoopers LLP (2020). *2020 Proxy Season Review*. Broadridge Financial Solutions, Inc. www.broadridge.com/_assets/pdf/broadridge-proxypulse-2020-review.pdf (archived at https://perma.cc/NYU4-S995).

14 Phillips, M. (2021). Exxon's board defeat signals the rise of social-good activists. *The New York Times*, June 9. www.nytimes.com/2021/06/09/business/exxon-mobil-engine-no1-activist.html (archived at https://perma.cc/ZV9T-HGG6).

15 BlackRock (2021). Vote bulletin: ExxonMobil Corporation. BlackRock, p. 4. www.blackrock.com/corporate/literature/press-release/blk-vote-bulletin-exxon-may-2021.pdf (archived at https://perma.cc/YQ29-5NTL).

16 Higgins, A. (2022). More Starbucks stores want to unionize. These women and nonbinary workers are leading the push. *Washington Post*, March 4. www.washingtonpost.com/lifestyle/2022/03/04/starbucks-employees-unionizing/ (archived at https://perma.cc/U589-6ZQH).

17 Jaffe, G. (2022). Howard Schultz's fight to stop a Starbucks barista uprising. *Washington Post*, October 8. www.washingtonpost.com/business/2022/10/08/starbucks-union-ceo-howard-schultz/ (archived at https://perma.cc/E9FK-CWZ7).

18 Wiener-Bronner, D. (2023). Starbucks displayed 'egregious and widespread misconduct' in union fight, judge says. CNN Business. www.cnn.com/2023/03/01/business/starbucks-union-ruling/index.html (archived at https://perma.cc/RGL8-SMJE).

19 Reuter, D. (2023). Starbucks union is using billboards, a brass band, and a butter sculpture to pressure board members from Nike, Land O'Lakes and Lego. Business Insider. www.businessinsider.com/starbucks-union-using-brass-band-butter-sculpture-to-pressure-board-2023-4 (archived at https://perma.cc/8LLT-YJXG).

20 Patagonia (2022). Company history. Patagonia. www.patagonia.com/company-history/ (archived at https://perma.cc/Z94E-UCTL).

21 1% for the Planet (n.d.). The 1% for the Planet Story. 1% for the Planet. www.onepercentfortheplanet.org/about/story (archived at https://perma.cc/YM49-DXGC).

22 Patagonia (2011). Don't Buy This Jacket, Black Friday and the New York Times. Patagonia. www.patagonia.com/stories/dont-buy-this-jacket-black-friday-and-the-new-york-times/story-18615.html (archived at https://perma.cc/FX57-4375).

23   Stock, K. (2019). Patagonia's "buy less" plea spurs more buying. Bloomberg. www.bloomberg.com/news/articles/2013-08-28/patagonias-buy-less-plea-spurs-more-buying (archived at https://perma.cc/HQ5E-FQQW).

24   Patagonia (2022). Company history. Patagonia. https://www.patagonia.com/company-history/ (archived at https://perma.cc/Z94E-UCTL).

25   Gilbert, B. (2021). The finance bro uniform is officially dead as Patagonia stops adding corporate logos to its ubiquitous fleece vests. Business Insider. www.businessinsider.com/patagonia-no-longer-adding-corporate-logos-to-its-clothing-2021-4 (archived at https://perma.cc/9Q3Y-QE53).

26   Patagonia (n.d.). Group Sales & Logos. Patagonia. www.patagonia.com/transitioning-away-from-logos.html (archived at https://perma.cc/5MDN-XUX5).

27   Feloni, R. (2018). Patagonia's environmental mission hasn't just been good for the planet—it's also boosted the bottom line. Business Insider. www.businessinsider.com/patagonia-mission-environmentalism-good-for-business-2018-12 (archived at https://perma.cc/VH4C-D7PC).

28   Gelles, D. (2022). Billionaire no more: Patagonia founder gives away the company. *The New York Times*, September 14. www.nytimes.com/2022/09/14/climate/patagonia-climate-philanthropy-chouinard.html (archived at https://perma.cc/32VC-QBL7).

29   Gelles, D. (2022). Billionaire no more: Patagonia founder gives away the company. *The New York Times*, September 14. www.nytimes.com/2022/09/14/climate/patagonia-climate-philanthropy-chouinard.html (archived at https://perma.cc/6AMB-MNNC).

30   Gross, J. (2021). Business schools respond to a flood of interest in E.S.G. *The New York Times*, November 13. www.nytimes.com/2021/11/13/business/dealbook/business-schools-esg.html (archived at https://perma.cc/Z8HC-3LP4).

LIST OF ABBREVIATIONS
(OR ESG ALPHABET SOUP)

B2B	Business to business
CDP	Formerly the Carbon Disclosure Project, but now known as CDP
COP	Conference of the Parties
CSR	Corporate social responsibility
CSRD	Corporate Sustainability Reporting Directive (EU)
DEI	Diversity, equity, and inclusion
EFRAG	The European Financial Regulatory Advisory Group
EHS	Environmental, health, and safety
ERG	Employee Resource Group
ESG	Environmental, Social, and Corporate Governance (or Governance)
ESGT	ESG, plus Technology
GHG	Greenhouse gas
IFRS	International Financial Reporting Standards
IoT	Internet of Things
IP	Intellectual property
ISSB	International Sustainability Standards Board
NGO	Non-government organization
NIST	National Institute of Standards and Technology
PPA	Power purchase agreement
REC	Renewable energy credit
RFP	Request for proposal
SASB	Sustainability Accounting Standards Board
SBTi	Science Based Targets Initiative
SDGs	The United Nations' Sustainable Development Goals
SEC	The United States Securities and Exchange Commission
SRI	Socially responsible investing
TCFD	Task Force on Climate-related Financial Disclosures
TNFD	Taskforce on Nature-related Financial Disclosures
VRF	Value Reporting Foundation

INDEX

Note: Page numbers in *italics* refer to tables or figures.

Looking for another book?

Explore our award-winning books from global business experts in Responsible Business

Scan the code to browse

www.koganpage.com/responsible-business

More books from Kogan Page

ISBN: 9781398604049

ISBN: 9781398612242

ISBN: 9781398612280

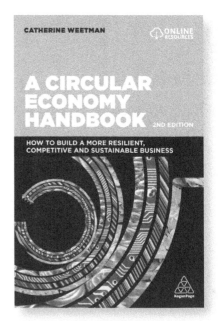

ISBN: 9781789665314

www.koganpage.com

Printed in the USA
CPSIA information can be obtained
at www.ICGtesting.com
LVHW050709060424
776442LV00020B/185